Ex Libris

To Howard,
Our good friend

Lots of Love & Prayers
" The Hiebnenki 's "

Gene, Louise
   Karla, Brenda
     Lorinda & Dana

Happy Easter 1978

The Guideposts Treasury of Love

Guideposts

Carmel, New York, 10512

CONTENTS

3.

LOVE FOR THOSE WHO NEED HEALING

4.

LOVE FOR THOSE WHO HAVE SUFFERED LOSSES

5.

LOVE FOR THOSE WHO NEED FORGIVENESS

6.

LOVE FOR THOSE WHO FEEL UNLOVED

7.

LOVE FOR THOSE WHO FEEL LONELY

8.

LOVE FOR THOSE WHOSE FAITH NEEDS STRENGTHENING

INTRODUCTION

*"Thou shalt love the Lord thy
God with all thy heart, and
with all thy soul, and with all
thy mind. This is the first and
great commandment. And the
second is like unto it, thou
shalt love thy neighbour as
thyself."*

Matthew 22:37-39

The word "love" courses throughout the New Testament, admonishing all who would follow Christ to love one another, even those who are unloving. "Love your enemies," Christ said, "Bless them that curse you, do good to them that hate you, and pray for them which despitefully use you, and persecute you." (Matthew 5:44)

In this volume we have gathered some of Guideposts' most helpful articles that witness to the power of love. We have divided the stories into eight chapters:

Love For Those Who Are Discouraged
Love For Those Who Are Fearful
Love For Those Who Need Healing
Love For Those Who Have Suffered Losses
Love For Those Who Need Forgiveness
Love For Those Who Feel Unloved
Love For Those Who Feel Lonely
Love For Those Whose Faith Needs Strengthening

We are confident that from each section you will derive personal counsel and direction, because the writers of these experiences—people from all walks of life—have found God more than capable of dealing with any problem. Intimately, they share with you what they have learned about God's grace and love.

Our hope is that you find *The Guideposts Treasury of Love* spiritually strengthening and inspiring. Our prayer is that as a result of reading these stories, you will rededicate yourself to loving God with all your heart, mind, soul, and your neighbor as yourself.

THE EDITORS

1.
Love for Those Who Are Discouraged

*Come unto me, all ye that labour and
are heavy laden, and I will give you rest.*
(Matthew 11:28)

My Two Built-In
Blessings

by TOM BRADLEY
Mayor of Los Angeles, California

One day in 1924 a Model T Ford rattled across the city limits
of Los Angeles, California. Inside that rickety old "lizzie,"
jammed to the roof with everything they owned, was a family of
seven sharecroppers from a little town in Texas called Calvert.
It had taken them over a year to get to California. They had
broken down along the way, their money had run out, they'd
gone into the fields to pick cotton so they could eke out enough
to push on.

These people thought that once they got to California their
lives would be easier, but they were wrong. In the city they
were worse off than before, and soon the father of the family
became disillusioned and left his wife and five children, the
eldest of whom was nine. After that, their hopes for a decent
future seemed to die.

That family was my family. And that is why, on the July day in
1973, when I was sworn in as mayor of the City of Los Angeles, I
think people forgave me a short personal reference. "It's been a
long, long way for Tom Bradley," I said in my speech that day.

Mine, of course, is a familiar American-dream story. Yet
when I look back, I can't help but wonder, why me? City Hall is
no more than a quarter of a mile from the Temple Street
community in which I grew up. I often think of the kids I used
to know there who were just as poor as we were, who had hopes
as high as mine, but who grew tired and frustrated and turned
to other things. Why was I the lucky one?

3

Some of the answers were obvious. Hard work, sure. A strong ambition, yes. A talent for sports that opened the way to college scholarships, certainly. But long before I had a dream or a part-time job or put my running shoe to a cinder track, I had two built-in blessings that made everything else in life possible.

The first of these blessings was my mother, Crenner Bradley. She was a loving woman and a strong woman; a practical, yet dreaming woman. After my father left, she found work as a maid, and she worked hard, getting up early and coming home late, staying up deep into the night washing our clothes, sewing, cooking the meals that we would eat while she was away cooking for some other family.

Mother taught us kids about pitching in, and as soon as we were old enough we all managed to get little jobs that funneled in much-needed extra pennies. I myself was a paper boy for the old *Daily News*, a swamper in a wholesale produce market, a gardener. Yet when I told Mother about the possibility of an athletic scholarship, she had me quit all work outside of school so I'd have time to practice. Though she'd never seen a track meet or a football game, though the loss of my extra income meant she'd have to work harder herself, she did not flinch.

Only somebody who has lived through hand-to-mouth poverty can know the insidious ways it destroys people: It shrivels the spirit. Poor we were, and sometimes hungry, but my mother saw to it that we were never in despair. She held her family together by sheer tenacious will, a will that came from a faith in God as solid as concrete. Every Sunday morning, no matter where we were living at the time—and we moved a lot, sometimes because we were forced to—Mother would martial us five kids into clean clothes and shining faces and off we'd go by streetcar to the New Hope Baptist Church at 16th and Paloma. This church, with the prophetic name, was our auxiliary home. But that was on Sundays.

For the rest of the week we were on our own, five kids at school or on the streets or in a house whose only parent did not come home until after supper. Those were the six days in which my mother put her faith to work; she turned us over to the

Lord. She made us feel that we had a Heavenly Father taking care of us, keeping us from harm, watching us when we did right, and when we did wrong. It was true that our father had left us, but, no sir, we Bradleys were not a father-less family!

That was my second built-in blessing. You see, my mother's God was a real God, and from the time we were tiny children she strove to make Him just as real to us. I remember the day when I was six years old and we were stalled in a town called Summerton, Arizona, near Yuma. For a long time I'd been fascinated by watching the adults picking cotton, and one morning I took a sack and went out into the fields with them. At first it seemed easy; at least I didn't have to bend over to reach the cotton the way my mother did. But gradually the bag on my shoulder got heavier and heavier, and my fingers got raw-red from the prick of the cotton bolls.

By nightfall I had only a paltry amount of cotton to show for my work, and I was dog-tired. That was the first day in my life that I understood the meaning of ambition, when I resolved that I was not going into the fields ever again. "I'm going to be somebody," I told my mother that night as she salved my sore hands.

"Son," she said, "the only way you can be somebody is if you *are* somebody."

That seemed to me a curious thing to say. "But how do you know if you are somebody?" I asked.

"You know it when you stand up before God and you say, 'Lord, You gave me life. You gave me this body and this brain. Now, Lord, how'm I doing with these things?' " As she told me this, I could picture God standing there, approving or disapproving. If you were living your life His way, then, to Crenner Bradley, you *were* somebody.

In just such ways as this, Mother made God a specific Someone I wanted to please. Which is not to say there weren't plenty of times when I did a pretty poor job of pleasing Him. When I was about 13 years old we lived across the street from the police station, and I became friendly with a number of the officers, especially with one tall, warm-hearted fellow whom I called by his first name, Bill. It also happened about that time that some of the neighborhood kids and I used to snitch things from the five-and-dime store.

On our way home one day one of my friends threw a big rock on the porch of the neighborhood "crab," a man who was always giving us a hard time. We didn't think anybody was at home, but The Crab was sitting in his living room, and without our knowing it, he followed us.

That night Bill came to our door. He wanted my mother and me to come across the street. The Crab was there complaining about the damage to his porch and, during the interrogation, someone noticed my pockets bulging with ten-cent-store loot. I was asked to display the suspicious contents. Never, ever, have I done anything more agonizing. Slowly I reached in and brought out a yellow pencil. Then a pencil sharpener in the form of a world globe. Then a candy bar. Some trinkets. Another candy bar. I put them on Bill's desk.

Those items sat starkly before us while Mother, Bill, The Crab and I stared at them. Every one of us knew they were stolen property.

I was scared to death I was going to be arrested, but that fear wasn't half as bad as the feeling of what I'd done to my mother and my trusting friend Bill. I was not arrested. Eventually we returned the stolen goods to the store and, with money we could ill-afford to spend, paid for a number of other objects I admitted having taken. That night Mother said only one thing to me, but it was enough to bring the point home one more time with profound effect: "It's not what *I* think, son, it's what *God* thinks that matters." Somehow Mother always managed to get across the idea that the Lord was the real disciplinarian in our family.

I am told that there are nine million single-parent households in America today. I realize that in society's arithmetic, two parents do not necessarily add up to family success, nor one parent to failure, but from my own experience a family without faith in God is struggling under a severe, and needless, minus sign.

"It's been a long, long way," I told the crowd that day I became mayor. My mother, who is dead now, lived to hear me say those words. I often wonder if she realized, as I do, that the most important part of the journey was the start, that the two basics of my life were her strength and the reality of her God. Knowing Mother, she would deny that it was *her* strength. "Why, son," she'd say, quoting her favorite line from Isaiah, " 'He giveth power to the faint.' " (Isaiah 40:29)

She'd be right, of course, Again.

WHAT DOES LOVE LOOK LIKE?
It has the hands to help others.
It has the feet to hasten to the poor and needy.
It has the eyes to see misery and want.
It has the ears to hear the sighs and sorrows of men.
That is what love looks like.
　　　St. Augustine (354-430)

My mother had lived on the river over a dozen years . . .
and she had never seen anything like this.

Miracle on the Homosassa

by NELSON HUTCHINSON

B ack in those days, our family was very poor. We lived in a small house on the Homosassa River, four miles upstream from the Gulf of Mexico. My father struggled to make ends meet as a commercial fisherman.

To help, my mother and I would gather oysters when they were in season. Other times, we went into the woods and chopped fallen trees into firewood, which we sold to the people in town. On good days, we could make a dollar or two.

This was 1939. It was a bad time. A lot of people were poor. The fortunate people who had jobs earned 30 cents an hour.

That year, my mother joined the Church of Jesus Christ in town. There was no road from our house into town. To get there, we had to go by boat three more miles upstream to the highway and the little village. Even so, my mother was at the church every time the doors opened. She loved the church. It gave her a certain strength that carried her through the ordeal of raising a family in such dark days.

We didn't have a Bible in our home. We couldn't afford one. This was a great sadness for my mother. Week after week, she tried to put a few coins aside, saving for enough to buy a Bible, but time and again some emergency would come up, and she had to use the money for food or clothes or medicine. She never complained, but her face showed her hunger for the word of God in our house.

One day my father came home from work with an empty boat. He had caught nothing. He went into the house discouraged, as though he never wanted to look at the river again.

I watched my mother. She got into the boat, arranged the nets, started the motor and headed downstream. As she later told me many times, she went about a mile toward those vast, shallow flats that reach as far as the eye can see at the mouth of the Homosassa. She cut off the motor. Then she knelt in the bow of the little boat, and she began talking to God.

"Father," she said, "I want a Bible for my home and my children. We don't have any money, and so I need Your help. Let me catch some fish today and I'll take them to the market and buy a Bible before nightfall. I have been working hard, trying to get enough ahead to buy a Bible, but I can't seem to make it. Anything I catch today will be Yours. Please help me."

She started the motor. Standing up, she threw into the water the staff that held one end of the net. Slowly she moved the boat in a circle to close off the net. Even before she had gone halfway, fat mullet began jumping into the net. And by the time she had completed the circle, the trapped area was alive with flouncing fish. My mother had lived on the river over a dozen years, ever since she had married my father at the age of 16, and she had never seen anything like this.

As fast as my mother could empty her catch into the boat, the net filled up again. In an hour, there was hardly enough room in the boat for herself and the net. She headed home.

I was on the dock as my mother arrived. The boat was riding so low in the water that I wondered if it had sprung a leak. Then I saw the cargo. I couldn't believe my eyes.

"Come on," Mother called to me. "We're going into town to get our Bible."

We went upstream to the highway, where we borrowed a cart from a farmer, transferred the catch into it, then hurried into town to a wholesaler who sold fish to stores and restaurants. The scales showed that my mother had brought in nearly 300 pounds of fish. The wholesaler paid three cents a pound for the catch—almost ten dollars, as well as my father could do during a good, seven-day week.

We went directly to a bookstore and bought the best Bible the money could buy. My mother let me carry the Bible as we went back to the river and returned the cart. She let me hold it on my lap as she maneuvered the boat back to our home. That evening, my mother read aloud to us from her own Bible for the very first time.

After nearly 40 years, the Bible is still in our family, a bit tattered now from so much use. Every morning, my mother would read the Bible to herself; every evening, she would read aloud to the family. We children studied the Bible as we prepared for our Sunday-school classes. And my mother never tired of telling people how she had acquired it.

In December of 1976, my parents celebrated their golden wedding anniversary. In the special ceremony at our church, my mother and my father held the family Bible between them—living proof that the miracles of the Bible can come alive today for those who have faith enough to believe in them.

---

*Verily I say unto you, If ye have faith
as a grain of mustard seed, ye shall say
unto this mountain remove hence to
yonder place; and it shall remove; and
nothing shall be impossible unto you.*

(Matthew 17:20)

When Someone
Believes in You

by DON SUTTON

"SUTTON'S CAREER FADING?" The question stared up at me from the headlines of the newspaper scattered on the breakfast table. I couldn't answer it myself.

The 1974 season had started well enough. I'd pitched my team, the Los Angeles Dodgers, to a few victories in April and May. But I'd gone into a slump as the weather grew warmer. Two weeks without a win at first, then three. *I'll shake it off*, I thought casually. But bad became worse, and the summer turned into one long frustration.

Now it was eight weeks since I'd won a ball game. Four days ago, I'd been hit hard. The opposition rocked a couple of long home runs as the Dodgers lost, and our fans had booed me as I left the field. Now, I was scheduled to start again tonight. I found myself dreading it.

I spilled some coffee on the table.

"I'll get it," my wife Patti said, grabbing a sponge. While sopping up the spill, she noticed the headline.

"Don't read those things!" she said, with a little flush of anger on her cheeks.

Thank God for Patti, I thought. Without her, I'd have been ready to give up, but she steadied me when things got rough.

Strange, but as I look back, the Lord always had provided someone with advice or encouragement when I didn't know which way to turn. And somehow I knew my Heavenly Father

11

would provide a solution for my pitching slump.

I suppose my optimistic attitude has been conditioned by my parents. What great models of faith they were during my growing-up years in the South!

My father was a sharecropper, earning $25 a week raising corn and peanuts. Yet he and my mom saw to it that my brother, my sister and I were never limited by that income. When we had an ambition in life, a dream, my folks did everything they could to help us realize it.

For example, my brother Ron and I had heard about the heroics of Mantle and Mays, and hoped one day to imitate them. Seemingly out of the blue, Dad produced a bat, a ball and gloves—for each of us.

My father did seasonal work as a construction worker, too. But unlike most of the men who walked through the woods to the job site, he carried no lunch bucket. It was only as I grew older that I realized the connection between my baseball glove and Dad's missing lunch bucket.

Yet, for all the sacrifices being made in the Sutton household, I don't remember anything gloomy about the place.

"Let's go fishing!" Dad would call in the evenings when he'd tramp in from work. "Something tells me they're bitin' now!" And off we'd go to the creek. My father would never say he was too tired for anything: home from work; he knew it was "time for my family."

Sundays were time for church. My parents were deeply religious, and their example strongly affected all of us. For my part, I discovered what a wonderful thing it was to find a fellowship of other young people at our Baptist church.

I still had a passionate interest in baseball. Maybe that disappointed my mother a bit at first; she wanted me to go to college, maybe become a teacher. But she didn't interfere when Henry Roper, a former Giant pitcher, took an interest in me while I was in sixth grade and drilled me in many baseball fundamentals, the same ones I practice even now.

I had a good athletic record during my school years, and was somewhat deflated by the reports on me that came back from major-league and college scouts.

"Too small. Can't throw the hard stuff ," they said.

Stubbornly, I decided I would take a shot at the minor leagues. I'll never forget Mom calling me aside before I left for Santa Barbara.

"Don, I guess you know I'd once hoped you'd be a professor of some sort. But I guess it was my own bookish way comin' through." She smiled. "Now, I want you to know—we're very proud of you, son, and we pray you succeed at baseball or whatever you want to do. Just keep living for God and you'll know I'm pleased."

It was what I needed to hear then, just as I needed encouragement from Norm Sherry, my first minor-league manager. He was an easygoing man who knew exactly how to relax a young pitcher.

"You can't do your best if you're nervous," he told me. "Relax. Have a good time. Baseball should be fun."

Under Norman's tutelage it *was* fun.

My next manager, Roy Hartsfield, at Albuquerque, was a stern tactician. But there again, I was coming to him as a brash youngster, and I needed his strong disciplinary influence.

I made it to the major leagues with the Dodgers in 1966 and earned a reputation as a steady, solid performer over the years. Each season I'd average about 250 innings pitched, 200 strikeouts and 17 or 18 wins. I realized my career was the result of some natural abilities God had given me, plus the help of other people who'd been there to help me along. Like the time in 1971 when I'd almost quit over an arm ailment—until a doctor's treatment and Dodger coach Red Adams got me back in pitching form.

But now it was 1974, and I hadn't won a game for eight weeks. And suddenly I was feeling very alone.

The Dodgers had a good lead over the Cincinnati Reds in the National League's western division, despite my poor performance, largely because my teammates had picked up the slack. Tommy John, in particular, had been doing an outstanding job. But on July 17, Tommy ruptured a ligament in his throwing arm and was knocked out for the season. A lot of people expected the Dodgers to fold then, and many fans and sportswriters believed our club needed new starters—one for Tommy John and one for me.

I felt terrible in the clubhouse that evening before the game. Even jokes from teammates about my long winless streak had become very self-conscious, and finally there weren't many more of them. I felt nervous. "God," I prayed silently, "I know that baseball isn't the most important thing in the world, so I can accept defeat, but show me how to use my skills properly."

Just before I started out onto the field, Dodger manager Walter Alston tapped me on the shoulder. "I'd like to speak with you, Don," he said.

Here it comes, I thought.

Managers read newspapers, too. I knew he'd been getting a lot of criticism from fans and the press about keeping me in the starting rotation. Maybe this would be the night he'd switch to another pitcher.

"Don," he began, "I know how the past couple months have been for you. Everyone's wondering whether we can make it to the play-offs without Tommy now. You know there's a lot of pressure." He stared at me. "I've had to make a decision about you.

"If the Dodgers are going to win this year," he said, "they're going to win with Don Sutton pitching. Come what will, you're staying in the starting job. That's all I wanted to say."

Words wouldn't come to me. Walter Alston has never been a fiery, speechmaking kind of manager. But this simple statement was exactly what I needed to hear. Once again God had sent someone to straighten me out, lift me up, give me strength. Suddenly I felt all my old confidence returning. As I strode down the long concrete tunnel to the playing field that evening, I knew the worst was over.

Not that I won that night. I went two weeks more without posting a victory. But it didn't hurt so much any more. I knew I had people behind me. It's the same no matter what our jobs. When we are sustained by our friends and God, we can endure a lot of pain and disappointment. Ultimately we know things will improve.

When I finally got turned around, I found myself pitching

the best ball of my career. In the pennant drive I won 13 of 14, plus a couple of play-off victories and my first World Series game.

The Dodgers didn't win the championship that year. That's a goal I've still to accomplish—to play on a World Series winning team—but I've got the feeling it'll happen.

The important thing I've learned is to do my best and to keep in mind Mother's advice: Keep living for God, and everything will turn out just fine.

GOD ANSWERS PRAYER
I know not when He sends the
word
That tells me fervent prayer is
heard;
I know it cometh soon or late,
My part is but to pray and wait.
I know not if the blessing sought
Will come in just the guise I
thought.
I leave all care with Him above,
Whose will is always one of love.
Source unknown

The Measles
Christmas

by LILLIAN CARTER

C hristmas was a time of enchantment for the Carter family
when our youngsters were growing up in our little farm
community in the pinewoods and red-clay country of western
Georgia. Everything had a breathless expectancy about it.

There was always the afternoon when everyone piled into
the old pickup truck with my husband Earl driving to go
Christmas-tree hunting. I remember how our breaths steamed
in the frosty air as we bounced along the red-rutted roads, and
the arguments about which tree looked most promising, and
the chorus of shouts when the right one was spotted. I remember how Earl and Jimmy would jump out with axes to cut
it while Ruth and Gloria and I gathered holly branches and pine
boughs to decorate our house.

I remember the solemn-eyed expeditions to the 5 & 10 gift
counters, with nickels and dimes clutched in small perspiring
palms. And visits to less fortunate families with baskets of food
and clothing. Oh, it was a magic time for all.

There was one year, though, that was different, a year when
gloom fell like a thick curtain over everyone—because just
before Christmas the children came down with old-fashioned
measles.

There were just three of them that year (Billy hadn't been
born yet) and all three were spotted and miserable. Instead of
baking cookies and preparing for our traditional Christmas
breakfast and dinner, I spent my time bathing feverish little

foreheads, easing sore throats and soothing pain-filled eyes.

To care for them better and give them companionship, Earl and I had moved their three beds into one big bedroom.

Now it was Christmas Eve. I leaned against their bedroom doorway as Earl read them the Bible story from Luke about the birth of Jesus. Normally they'd be fresh from their baths, lying like puppy dogs on the rug around their daddy's big old leather chair as he'd read the wonderful words. Now wan white faces looked bleakly up from their pillows.

I turned from the door, wiping my eyes. Why did sickness have to come now?

Earl and I had really looked forward to our children discovering what Santa had brought. This year we had bought them their first bicycles. Normally they would have been ecstatic. But they couldn't even think of riding a bicycle now.

Later, after the children were asleep, Earl opened the big cardboard cartons and started assembling the bikes anyway. He said it was something to do.

I looked at the tree and noticed one of the light strings was out. They were the old-fashioned kind where when one light burns out, the whole string goes dark. As I searched among the bulbs for the dead one, I thought back on the Christmas story Earl had been reading. The realization struck me that things had not worked out for that little family in Bethlehem either. I thought about how Mary must have felt, having her first-born under such awful conditions in a strange place. How she must have missed her mother's comfort, plus all the family festivities that go with the birth of a first-born child.

And yet, it was clear from the Bible that Mary did not complain but "kept all these things and pondered them in her heart" as she quietly accepted the visits of all sorts of strangers—from rough shepherds reeking of sheep to exotic, curious foreigners.

The string of lights flared to life as I found the burned-out bulb. I walked back into the children's room and touched their foreheads. Thank goodness, their fevers seemed almost gone. They were all asleep. As I stood listening to their soft breathing, I tried to think of some way in which they could enjoy

Christmas tomorrow. They couldn't enjoy the succulent turkey, and they could only stare forlornly at the bicycles they couldn't ride.

From the living room, where Earl was assembling the bikes, came the strains of Christmas music from our battery-powered RCA console radio. Then I heard the announcer tell about Little Jack Little, a nationally famous radio and vaudeville personality of that day, who was in Atlanta for the holidays and would be singing over radio station WSB tomorrow.

A thought struck me. Could it be? *No*, I thought. *It is too much to hope for*. But the idea persisted and I went to sleep that night with a prayer on my lips.

In the morning I called the radio station and hesitantly asked to speak to Little Jack Little.

Miraculously, his famous voice came on the phone and I explained my request. There was silence on the line for a moment. Then he said, "Let me see what we can do."

After hanging up the phone, I sank against the wall quietly praying. Then Earl and I moved the radio into the children's bedroom.

"Merry Christmas!" I greeted them as cheerfully as I could. Inside I wanted to cry; the three bicycles leaned against the wall, hardly noticed by their tired eyes. I switched on the radio and as we waited for the console to warm up, said, "I thought you might like to listen to some Christmas carols."

The old RCA hummed, and then came the sound of music. A spark of interest flickered across the speckled little faces as Little Jack Little came on singing Christmas tunes and thumping the piano. Inside I prayed. The program continued as Mr. Little played and talked, and my youngsters' heads settled back on their pillows. I glanced at my watch, my throat tight; it was almost time for the program to end.

And then his voice boomed out, "And now I'm going to sing a song especially for three little Carter children who are ill: Jimmy, Ruth and Gloria."

Their three little heads jerked up. Eyes wide in astonishment, they stared at the old console as if Santa himself was about to burst through the speaker.

"*Wooden Head, Puddin' Head Jones*," sang Little Jack Little.

The children looked at each other. Ruth giggled. Jimmy sat up, a big smile on his face. Gloria squealed in glee. An explosion of delight filled the room.

> *"He couldn't spell Con-stan-ti-nople,*
> *Didn't know beans from bones.*
> *Pencils and books were never made for*
> *Wooden Head, Puddin' Head Jones."*

Then three quavering little voices joined the rollicking one coming from the speaker and bedsprings squeaked as they bounced in rhythm to the tune.

I stood at the door, my throat tight and tears streaming down my face. Earl stepped up behind me and his arm stole around my waist.

It had promised to be a sad Christmas and I had thought no one could give the children anything that would make it otherwise.

But thanks to someone who had room in his heart to listen to a farm wife's plea, it turned out to be one of the most memorable Christmases we ever had. Jimmy, Ruth and Gloria still talk about it today.

I love to hear all the old Christmas carols. But right up among them is a song that to me is just as meaningful:

Wooden Head, Puddin' Head Jones.

> I'm convinced that everyone has some kind
> of hidden talent. God sees to it—it's as simple as that.

The Talent I Didn't
Know I Had

by MICHAEL LANDON
Star of TV's "Little House on the Prairie"

If there's one thing I can't stand people saying, it's, "I'm no good at anything. . . . I don't have any talent." I just don't buy that at all. To me, everyone has at least one talent, and while it sometimes takes you a lifetime to find, it *does* exist.

There was a time, of course, when I didn't believe that. What changed my mind was a seemingly small event that took place back in 1953.

At that time I was a skinny little high-school sophomore in Collingswood, New Jersey, a town just across the Delaware River from Philadelphia. At Collingswood High I was a good student, but as far as I was concerned, in just about every other department I was a loser. As a funny-looking pip-squeak named Eugene Orowitz, who weighed barely 100 pounds, I desperately wanted to fit in, to be something and do something well. But because I hadn't found anything I was good at, I looked upon myself as being a total flop.

One sunny afternoon during the spring of that year, our gym class went out to the school's running track. The teacher was going to acquaint us all with various track and field events. We were shown hurdles, the broad jump, the pole vault. I stumbled weakly through them all.

"Now we'll try the javelin," the teacher said.

I watched as he picked up a gleaming metal spear about six feet long and gave it a short toss. Suddenly I was captivated and

20

didn't know why. Something inside me began saying, "Try it! Try it!"

I had to wait my turn, though, because several others wanted a crack at the javelin too. Shy and scared, I watched them, trying not to look too eager. Finally, when everyone had had a chance to throw—the longest heave going about 30 yards—I looked at the teacher.

"Hey, Orowitz, you want to try?" he asked.

Embarrassed, I looked down, but managed to nod my head.

"Well, come on then," he said impatiently, and handed me the javelin. Behind me I could hear some of my classmates chuckling.

"Think you can lift it, Ugy?" one said.

"Don't stab yourself," another added, laughing.

As I grasped the javelin in my hand, I was seized with a strange feeling—a new-found excitement. Seeing myself as a Roman warrior about to do battle, my fears vanished. For some crazy reason, I was relaxed over what I was about to do, even though I'd never done it before.

I raised the javelin over my head, took six quick steps and let the thing go. The same voice that had urged me into throwing it, now told me it was a good throw. I watched as the spear took off. While other students' throws had wobbled or turned cock-eyed in the air, to my surprise, my throw was traveling straight and true.

My heart quickened as I saw it continue to sail, 30 yards out, then 40. As it went past the 50-yard mark, it was still going when it went crashing down beyond some empty bleachers.

For a minute nothing was said. Then someone whispered, "Holy cow!" and others began cheering and slapping me on the back. Nobody could believe what little Orowitz had just done. Neither could I, really. And when I think back on it, the whole scene must have resembled something out of a grade-B movie.

I ran to retrieve the javelin and when I found it, I saw the tip had been broken off in landing. Expecting a real bawling out, I took the javelin back to the gym teacher.

"Don't worry about it," he said, still shaking his head in wonder. "You keep the thing."

That night I took the javelin home with me and, much to my parents' astonishment, never let it out of my sight. The very next day I began practicing with it, and every day that summer—for six hours or more—I would throw it in a nearby schoolyard. The joy of finding something I could do made me determined to do as well in it as I could.

By the time I was a senior and a member of the track team, all my practice paid off. I threw the javelin 211 feet that year, the best throw by any high-school boy in the country.

That record gave me a track scholarship to the University of Southern California. With my eye on the Olympics, I continued to work out until one day in college, after not warming up properly, I tore some ligaments in my left shoulder. While I still could throw, I was never able to achieve the distance I once could, and so I gave up my track scholarship and my dream of the Olympics.

Though that was a terrible disappointment, I've learned since then that as we are developing one talent, others seem to spring from it without our realizing it. While the javelin gave me a chance to go to college, it also provided me with a new-found confidence and the ability to shed my inferiority complex. I was able to see the importance of that when later, after I dropped out of U.S.C., I took a job in a Los Angeles warehouse. There, a co-worker, an aspiring actor, asked my help in learning his part in a small playhouse production of *Home of the Brave*.

When I began reading the script, I became mesmerized. The same kind of fascination that took hold of me when I picked up the javelin now turned me on to dramatics. Immediately I enrolled in acting school. That led to small parts in movies, which in turn brought me the roll of Little Joe Cartwright in *Bonanza*. That TV series lasted 14 years and while it's no longer running, it led me to still another area—directing—which I'm now using in my *own* series, *Little House on the Prairie*.

I'm convinced that everyone has some kind of hidden talent. God sees to it—it's that simple. The difficult part for some of us is in finding the talent. That's why I feel strongly that we must keep our minds open; we can't let ourselves be discouraged or depressed when the talent doesn't readily appear. Yet when it does, we must be prepared to grab hold of it right away.

Whenever I think about what made that scrawny kid pick up that javelin, I know there was a reason. God was on that high-school field whispering to me, "Here's an opportunity. Take it." And am I glad I listened to Him—glad I trusted my enthusiasm—for I not only found my talent, but I truly found myself.

In all these things we are more than conquerors through Him that loved us. (Romans 8:37)

**Even in sports, there's something more
important than being No. 1.**

Ten Words That I
Never Forgot

by CATHY RIGBY
Champion Gymnast

T he woman was a famous movie star. She had come to visit
her daughter at the summer gymnastics camp for girls that
my husband and I run near Fresno, California. When the time
came for the daily workouts, the actress watched her daughter
from the sidelines. The girl was good, though not good enough
to ever compete at a championship level. And I noticed, today,
how nervous she was.

When the girl finished, her mother called out: "That was
awful. You looked like a sack of potatoes tumbling downhill."
The girl burst into tears. My heart went out to her.

I found myself remembering the day one of my own gymnas-
tic performances put me close to tears. I might have gone ahead
and shed them, except for something my mother said to me
then.

When my mother was carrying her first child, she was strick-
en with polio, and she has been confined to a wheelchair and
crutches ever since. But she never let that discourage her. She
managed to raise five children and have a career as well.

One day I decided to join a gymnastics program at a nearby
park. Before long, I was totally absorbed in it. By 1972, I was on
the U.S. Women's Gymnastics Team for the Olympic Games in
Munich. I couldn't think of anything else but winning a gold
medal.

It had become my habit, during practice sessions and the
warm-ups before a contest, to pray—asking God for the

24

strength and the control to get through the routine. That day in Munich, I was tense with the determination not to disgrace my country and myself. But, though I competed to the best of my ability, I didn't win a gold medal. I was crushed. After the winners were announced, I joined my parents in the stands, all set for a big cry. I managed a faltering, "I'm sorry. I did my best."

"You know that, and I know that," my mother said, "and I'm sure God knows that, too." She smiled and said ten words that I never forgot: "Doing your best is more important than being *the* best."

Suddenly I understood my mother better than ever before. She had never let her handicap prevent her from always doing her best.

Now I went over to the sobbing girl and put an arm around her. "Honey," I said, "I've been watching you improve all summer and I know you have done your best, and doing your best is more important than being *the* best. I'm proud of you."

She smiled at me through her tears. Maybe somewhere, someday, she'll pass those words along.

They Said I Didn't
Have a Prayer

by GEORGE SHINN

The five men seated at the conference table looked at one another. Then they looked at me. No one said a word, but I could read their minds, and what I read there made my heart sink.

I had used my last funds to hire these men, all experts in business management, to advise me on how to resolve the financial difficulties I was facing. For two hours we had been going over my books and records. They had asked searching questions, and I had attempted to answer them honestly.

Finally one of the lawyers—three of the men were lawyers and two were certified public accountants—cleared his throat. "George," he said, "would you mind stepping outside for a few minutes? We'd like to discuss all aspects of your situation frankly among ourselves."

Feeling like a condemned man, I waited outside. The minutes passed slowly. Finally the door opened and I was asked to rejoin the group. The lawyer spoke again. "I'm sorry to tell you this, George, but we can see only one solution for you. We feel you should give up and close your business schools." Give up! Here I was at age 28 with my own business—and now I was facing bankruptcy.

One of the lawyers accompanied me to the elevator. I guess he meant to be kind, but his parting words went through me like a knife. "George," he said, "why don't you go to work for someone else? You don't have a prayer, not a prayer!"

I went out of the building like a man in a daze. Give up. That

26

was all the experts could suggest. Well, I thought with sudden grim determination, I wasn't going to take that way out. There had to be a better way, there *had* to be. But still I could hear that lawyer's voice with its mocking echoes: "You haven't got a prayer, not a prayer!"

The whole thing had come as such a shock that it almost seemed unreal. In the first place, I never expected to have a business of my own. When I finished high school in Kannapolis, North Carolina, my goal was to make $100 a week and to buy a new car every three or four years.

My first full-time job was as an unskilled laborer in a factory. After a couple of years I developed trouble with my back. X rays showed an injury to my spine, probably from playing football in high school. The doctor told me I could do no more heavy work.

My mother recommended college.

I knew I needed more education, but there wasn't any money for it. My father had died when I was eight, leaving a lot of debts, and my mother had gone to work, sometimes holding down two jobs at once, to keep us going.

College seemed out of the question, but in nearby Concord was a small business college. I registered there for a two-year course.

Six months later, my savings ran out. I asked the school manager if there was any way I could earn my tuition, and he took me on as the school's janitor. For pocket money, I found a part-time job in a bakery.

One Saturday morning, I had just finished my janitorial chores and changed into my street clothes when two high-school girls came in. One of them asked, "Do you work here?"

"Yes," I said. But I didn't tell them the distinguished position that I held!

She said, "We're thinking of going to college after we finish high school. Can you tell us something about this school?"

That was easy. I liked the school. I felt I was learning important things about business administration, and I knew the school was providing a valuable community service in training young people who still were too inexperienced to get a good job in business. As I gave the girls a tour of the rooms I had just cleaned, I also told them what a great school it was. Before they left, they enrolled for the fall semester.

Monday morning, when I gave the applications to the school director, he was delighted. "George," he said, "in addition to your job as janitor, if you want to do some recruiting for the school, I'll pay you ten dollars for each student you bring in."

When you believe in something and are enthusiastic about it, you can't help but be successful. Eventually I was earning enough from recruiting to quit the bakery job. Then, when I finished the two-year course myself, the director hired me as a full-time recruiter.

I really enjoyed my work. I looked upon recruiting as more than a job. Not only was I helping the school, but I was also helping young people to improve themselves and their futures. Even so, I wasn't satisfied. I wanted to become more involved in the school and feel more like a part of it. I was looking for a future myself.

One day I asked one of the owners if there was any chance that I might buy into the school as a partner. To my surprise, he said yes. We agreed on the price and that he would make deductions in my salary each week until I paid him off.

They owned three other business colleges in the state. I visited those and met the staff members and liked them. Soon I heard that the owners were ready to get out of the school business and move into other fields. With an audacity that was beyond my years and experience, I offered to buy them out.

After I took over, I soon discovered I was facing trouble. There were unpaid bills totaling thousands of dollars. On the horizon were creditors with their lawyers. Some staff members hadn't been paid for weeks, some for months. Properties were mortgaged to the hilt. I tried to get a loan at practically every bank in North Carolina, but my applications were rejected. I didn't know any people I could borrow money from. That was when I decided to have a meeting with the lawyers and accountants.

For days the words I had heard there haunted me: *not a prayer, not a prayer, not a prayer*. Then late one day, as I was driving home, deep in despair, I suddenly realized, "But I *do* have a prayer! It's all I have left." As a small boy I had been active in the church, but when I became a little older I drifted away from it all. My faith had not diminished; I just hadn't called upon it lately.

I stopped the car along the road, and I let the words pour out of me: "Lord, You know what a mess I'm in. Everybody says I'm sunk. I don't believe You feel that way. Help me, Lord. I'm turning the company over to You. You do the guiding and I'll do the work. And anything that comes to me, Lord, I'll share with You."

A sense of great relief shot through me. I felt as though I had just been lifted out of a nightmare. I still had my problems and I still had no money. But even so, it seemed that a huge burden had been lifted.

That night I had my first good sleep in weeks. When I awoke in the morning, I felt so exhilarated that I bounded out of bed and said aloud, "Good morning, Lord!"

When I got to the office, the secretary was on the phone. She placed a hand over the mouthpiece and whispered, "It's that textbook publisher in New York. He's having a fit."

"I'll talk to him," I said. She was surprised. For weeks I had been dodging creditors on the phone and not even reading their threatening letters. I took the phone. "Good morning, Mr. Johnson," I said. "I hope you're in good health."

"Not financially," he said. "Mr. Shinn, what are you going to do about this bill of yours?"

"I'm going to pay it," I said. "In fact, I'll send you a check today. I don't know how much, but I'll send you something."

"Good," he said. "I look forward to it."

I didn't even have to open the checkbook to know that the most I could send him was one dollar, so I sent a check for that amount. A few days later, he called again and said, "Mr. Shinn, I got your check this morning. It's only for one dollar. Did you make a mistake?"

"No, I didn't," I said.

"Then are you trying to be cute?"

"I've never been more serious," I said. "I'm going to pay that bill, but you'll have to let me do it in weekly amounts I can afford. Will you go along with that?"

He thought about it, then said, "For the time being."

The next week, I was able to send him seven dollars. Gradually the bill was paid off. So were other bills, as creditors agreed to give us more time.

At first, I didn't want to tell others about my experience with the Lord on the highway, fearing that they would think I had gone off the deep end. But then I figured that if the Lord was guiding me He was probably guiding others on our team, and I decided it would be a good idea if they knew about it.

At a staff conference one morning, I said, "I think we ought to open this meeting with a prayer." Puzzled looks went around the table, followed by bowed heads. Knowing that I was going to have trouble with my first public prayer, I had written it out beforehand. And then I told them what had happened to me.

This was the turn in the road for us, as a company and as individuals, a turn to the Lord. And the answers started coming, sometimes even popping into my mind in the middle of the night. We began to reorganize the schools, expanding curriculums, increasing facilities and trying new ideas, such as offering valuable programs for veterans returning from Vietnam. We did our best to offer first-class training in many business skills at moderate tuition costs, preparing students for successful careers in the business world.

Enrollment grew to over 5000 students; new schools were added to our chain of colleges. As our expertise increased, other schools throughout the country started coming to us for consultation services. Today the once nearly bankrupt organization has a staff of over 800, and serves as a management consultant to colleges in over 28 states.

When I look back through the years, I'm amazed by the difference that simply turning to God and letting Him direct things has made for me. Every morning when I wake up and get out of bed, I still say, "Good morning, Lord!" because, thanks to Him, that's just what it is.

"Don't Waste a Single Day, David."

by DAVID HARTMAN
Star of ABC's "Good Morning, America" show

F ive days a week when I get up it's dark outside. It's always dark because it's always four a.m., the time my alarm clock has to ring if I'm to make it to the studio in time to prepare for our five-day-a-week *Good Morning, America* show. Driving through Manhattan's pre-dawn streets I think of a million different things, but I'm sure of this: Every year when Father's Day comes near, I think of my dad and the things he taught me, which have made my life so much more exciting and rewarding.

Dad was a Methodist minister who loved life and believed in squeezing the most out of every single minute of it. "God loves doers, not grumblers," he used to say. "Remember this, David: You're made in God's image, and so you have His power in you. Who's going to waste *that* kind of power?"

Dad thought that a day used to meet challenges or conquer disappointments was well-spent. When Dad was called to a church in Massachusetts, he thought that he was going to a lively, dynamic church. But on his very first day in the pulpit there were four people in the congregation—and one of them was my mother.

Dad could have gone around wrapped in gloom, but he didn't. He worked. He went out and met people and talked to them and all but dragged them bodily into the church. Before the year was out he had two Sunday services that were packed with people who came willingly. Dad refused to give in to discouragement. "God is a part of me," he'd say. "There's no separation from Him twenty-four hours a day, seven days a week."

Dad tried to teach me to handle discouragement the way he did—by facing facts and, if necessary, making a new start with a new set of facts. For example, throughout four years at Duke University, my big dream was one day to fly jets for the Air Force. I was the Air Force's biggest booster; senior year I was ROTC commander on campus. After I graduated Duke in 1956, I went immediately to pre-flight training in Arizona, but there were too many people in the class; somebody had to be dropped—and it was me.

Why? I was too tall—six-feet-five.

I was almost in tears when I called Dad. "Okay, David," he said gently, "it's not what you wanted to happen, but it's a fact. So face it and go on to the next thing. The world is packed with things to do."

Dad believed in the direct approach. Sometimes I remembered to follow his advice, sometimes I didn't. One time, when I was fresh out of drama school and struggling to get some acting parts, there was one casting director I particularly wanted to see. I made elaborate plots in my mind for getting through his barricade of secretaries. Then one day, riding a crosstown bus, I asked myself, "How would Dad handle this?" and the answer came right back: "Why not simply telephone the man?" I got off the bus, found a phone booth, put a dime in the box, rang his office and asked to speak to him. I got through. I told him I was an aspiring actor and I'd like to see him. He said, fine, let's make an appointment. It was as easy as that! Dad was tickled when I told him.

I'll never forget a conversation I had with Dad. It was on my birthday in 1968. He called a few minutes after midnight when my birthday was fresh and new, and the last thing he said in the conversation was that familiar and beautiful quotation: "It's better to light a candle than to curse the darkness." He died, unexpectedly, the following week, so those were the last words he spoke to me.

Sometimes when I'm making my morning drive to work

through the dark streets of New York, I think of that candle and the opportunities that God gives each of us, every single day, to light one. When I arrive at the studio, I look down 66th Street and see the darkness beginning to dissolve above the trees in Central Park. Then I go inside with a picture in my mind of dawn reaching across the Hudson River to New Jersey and on to Pennsylvania and Ohio and beyond. I see people stretching and yawning and blinking at the 16 hours or so of activity that lie ahead of them, and I, remembering my dad's positive philosophy, think of what he would have said: "Hey, you've got a gift of a thousand minutes waiting for you today. Don't waste one of them. Do something with them. Do something with your life, with yourself." In fact, at the end of the show everyday, I sign off by saying to millions of viewers the words my dad said to me so many times: "Make it a really good day!"

TODAY
Give me . . .
    ears that hear my brother's cry,
    eyes that see his need,
    feet that bear me to his side,
    hands that heal and feed,
And over and above—
    filled to overflowing—
    a heart that gives him love.
       Irene Sharp

A world-famous singer reveals what lies at
the heart of success.

Grace Before Greatness

by MARIAN ANDERSON

The faith my mother taught me is my foundation. Whatever is in my voice, my faith has put it there.

We were poor folk. But there was a wealth in our poverty, a wealth of music and love and faith. My two sisters, Alice and Ethel, and I were all in the church choir. There is still a vivid memory of our mother and father, their faces shining with pride, watching us from the front pews. And when I was six I was once fortunate enough to be selected to step out in front of the choir and sing *The Lord Is My Shepherd*.

It was a Baptist church we attended in Philadelphia. But my mother taught us early that the form of one's faith is less important than what's in one's heart.

"When you come to Him," she said, "He never asks what you are."

My father died when I was 12, and thus my mother's burden became heavier. Before she had become a housewife and the mother of three daughters, she was a schoolteacher. Now she became a father to us as well as a mother and she earned our whole livelihood by taking in washing. It was terribly difficult for her, I know, but she would not even hear of any of us children leaving school for work.

During those years I began to have my first opportunity to earn a little money by singing—almost entirely for Sunday evening concerts for the church or for the Y.W.C.A. and the Y.M.C.A. At those affairs I could sing, perhaps, two or three songs, and my fee was a very grand 50 cents or, once in a great while, one dollar. Sometimes I would dash to four or five of those concerts in one evening.

Many people were kind to me—teachers who took no fees, those who urged me forward when I was discouraged. Gradually I began to sing with glee clubs and churches in other cities. After one minor effort in Harlem, a group of well-meaning people hastily sponsored me for a concert in Town Hall in New York City.

It seemed at once incredible and wonderful. But I wasn't ready; indeed, I was far from it in both experience and maturity. On the exciting night of my first real concert I was told Town Hall was sold out. While waiting in dazed delight to go on, my sponsor said there would be a slight delay. I waited five, ten, 15 minutes, then peeked through the curtain.

The house was half-empty! I died inside. But when the curtain went up I sang my heart out. And when the concert was over, I knew I had failed. The critics next day agreed with me, but what they said was really not so important. I was shattered because within me I felt I had let down all those people who had had faith and confidence in me.

"I'd better forget all about singing and do something else," I told my mother.

"Why don't you think about it a little—and pray a lot—first?" she cautioned.

She had taught me to make my own decisions when I could, and pray for the right ones when I could not. But I did not heed her now. I refused a few offers to sing at other concerts. I avoided my music teacher. For a whole year I brooded in silence. My mother suffered, too, but she knew I had to find my own way back alone. From time to time she just prodded me gently. "Have you prayed, Marian? Have you prayed?"

No, I hadn't. Nothing would help. I embraced my grief. It was sufficient.

But in those tearful hours there slowly came the realization that there is a time when even the most self-sufficient person cannot find enough strength to stand alone. Then one prays with a fervor one never had before. From my torment I prayed with the sure knowledge there was Someone to Whom I could pour out the greatest need of my heart and soul. It did not matter if He answered. It was enough to pray.

Slowly I came out of my despair. My mind began to clear. No one was to blame for my failure. Self-pity left me. In a burst of exuberance I told my mother, "I want to study again. I want to be the best and be loved by everyone and be perfect in everything."

"That's a wonderful goal," she chided. "But our dear Lord walked this earth as the most perfect of all beings, yet not everybody loved Him."

Subdued, I decided to return to my music—to seek humbleness before perfection.

One day I came home from my lesson unaware that I was humming. It was the first music I had uttered at home in a whole year. My mother heard it and she rushed to meet me. She put her arms around me and kissed me. It was her way of saying, "Your prayers have been answered, and mine have, too."

For a brief moment we stood there silently. Then my mother spoke quietly. "Prayer begins where human capacity ends," she said.

The memory of that moment has always been with me through the years of struggle that followed. I have been blessed with an active career—and the worldly goods that come with it. If sometimes I forget and listen only to the applause, my mother reminds me quickly of what should come first.

"Grace must always come before greatness," she says.

2.
Love for Those Who Are Fearful

There is no fear in love; but perfect love casteth out fear . . .

(I John 4:18)

Desperately I continued to struggle with the hatch, not realizing the whole capsized rig now rested 50 feet below the surface of the Gulf.

Trapped at the Bottom of the Sea

by DERRELL JOHN DORÉ

Some people say we should be thankful that we can't see the future, and I agree. For if I had known what was going to happen out on our drilling rig that Sunday afternoon, I would have lost my mind.

Located five miles out in the Gulf of Mexico, our steel platform was as remote as an island. On it, our crew worked, ate and slept for days at a stretch while we drilled into the sea bottom for sulphur. A drilling rig can be a dangerous place even under normal circumstances. One must continually be wary of thrashing machinery, steel pipes winging past one's head and whipping snakelike cables. One misstep and a man can be crushed or hurtled to death.

On that Sunday afternoon, June 1, 1975, our platform was being towed to a new drilling location. Hydraulic jacks had hoisted our four thick column "legs" from the sea floor. As they rose into the air above us, our 60 by 120 foot watertight platform settled into the water and floated for towing. Ten feet thick, the platform had most of the crew's living quarters inside it.

It was a bright sunny day as our tugboat slowly pulled us along at three miles an hour. A sharp salt breeze ruffled my khaki work clothes as I stared unseeingly at the blue waters. I was thinking of home and my wife Dorothy. We had had five wonderful years together in the little French Cajun town where we lived.

39

Because Dorothy and I were a praying couple, we attended church together on Sundays and on holy days of obligation. But religion had not had as much reality for me as it had for my wife until I met and associated frequently with Father Bertrand, whose special talent for relaying God's word helped to increase my own faith.

A school of porpoises exploded from the waves, their glistening black bodies arching in graceful formation. I turned my back on them and strode to the stern of the rig to help the other men change a swab line. At this time there was only a skeleton crew of 12 aboard.

As we worked, other men who had labored hard the previous night were sleeping below within the platform. We stopped for a break, and as I leaned against the rail, I looked up.

Something was wrong! The support columns looming over us were angled crazily against the horizon! I gasped as they slowly leaned farther across the sky. My mind groped frantically for some explanation—too much towing speed, a freak wave, some deadly unforeseen wind pressure? But there was no time to think.

"We're going over!" I screamed. Then I remembered the men asleep below.

I leaped down the companionway and raced through the passage to the sleeping quarters. I threw open the door and yelled at the men, then I dashed farther up the passageway to start the pump. A powerful jet of sea water exploded through the wall. I ran back along the tilting passageway to the ladder leading to the deck. Green water roared down at me. I sprang back, hearing the crockery in the galley crash to the floor. We were going over—and I was trapped!

Heart pounding, I thought of an escape hatch in the laundry compartment. I fought my way down the hall; it was like being inside a revolving barrel. Reaching the laundry room, I leaped at the hatch in the ceiling. As I strained at the hand bolts, a man's cry down the passageway was smothered by a thundering roar. A wall of water exploded into the laundry compartment as I struggled with the hand bolts. They were rusted shut!

The lights flickered, then went out, and icy water surged up my body. In the blackness I fought to open the ceiling hatch, which was now on the "wall" before me. The water covered my shoulders, then swirled around my neck.

As I held my chin above water, words came from my past as I prayed for deliverance. And then, strangely, the water seemed to stop rising.

In the inky blackness and the terrible stillness I seemed to be suspended in time. Desperately I continued to struggle with the hatch, not realizing the whole capsized rig now rested on the sea bottom—some 50 feet below the surface of the Gulf.

I finally let go of the hatch. Treading water, I began to shiver violently in the bone-freezing cold. Feeling around in the dark, I touched a large water pump; its side seemed to be only inches below the water surface. Painfully I hoisted myself up and lay on it. Stretching out my arms, I felt cold steel about two feet on every side of me. I was in an air bubble, trapped in a corner of the compartment.

The pump's sharp pipes bit into my back as I balanced on it. Would anyone ever find me? Oh, God, would anyone come in time?

The minutes ticked away. I could see nothing. The silence screamed in my ears. *Buried at sea*. The phrase rang in my mind like the tolling of some great iron bell. Many men, I knew, had been buried at sea. But I was being buried *alive*.

Panic surged within me, but I fought it. With my pocketknife I began pounding on the steel side of my coffin. I knew it was futile, but I had to do something. The metallic sound seemed to echo the tolling of the great bell in my mind.

Hours seemed to go by as I clung there. Cramps wracked my body in the icy water. Out of the blackness Dorothy's face came to me as I had kissed her good-by on Wednesday. Would I ever see her again? The air was now growing hot and I knew I was gradually consuming its oxygen. I breathed as slowly as I could. I gave up pounding with my knife.

How much time had gone by? I could not tell. My chest began to burn. Hallucinations began to haunt me. At one moment I seemed to be back home in my skiff on the bayou. At another I was back in the service on the deck of a Navy assault ship in Vietnam. Guns roared over me and the explosions made my head hurt. At times I couldn't tell whether I was awake or dreaming. Either way, it was all one nightmare. I grew thirsty and my face perspired in the hot, fetid air. I splashed salt water on my face and tried to think clearly, but it was impossible. Grim questions flashed through my mind. What kind of casket would Dorothy get for me? Would Father Bertrand lead the services?

Suddenly I was aware of a searing pain in my scalp; my hands were clutching my hair, trying to tear it out! I screamed and forced them down. I remembered hearing about people who, when buried alive, had torn their hair out in their death agony.

Oh, God, why doesn't someone come?

Oh, my Jesus, forgive us our sins. Save us from the fires of hell and lead all souls to Heaven, especially those who are in most need of Thy mercy. . . .

In agony I prayed words I had learned as a youngster, words that until now had not had such intense meaning for me.

Oh my Jesus, forgive us . . . lead us to Heaven . . .

Again and again I said the words, but something strange was beginning to happen. No longer was I saying them to empty blackness; I found myself actually talking to Someone. Jesus was there with me. There was no illumination, nothing physical. But I sensed Him, a comforting Presence. He was *real*; He was *there*.

I relaxed in the blackness, fear and hysteria draining out of me. With my new-found calmness, I prayed for the other men who, I thought, died when the rig capsized. I found my knife and with a sudden surge of hope again began to tap it against the wall.

Suddenly there was a strange bubbling in the water. I froze. Escaping gas? I held my breath as long as I could, then surrendered, inhaling deeply. It had a strange coolness, a freshness. It was fresh air!

How long I lay there thanking God for this miracle, I don't really know. All I know is that finally I saw a light, a strange greenish illumination under the water. It moved upward. From it, incredibly, emerged a black, polka-dotted hand. I reached for it.

As if startled, the hand slipped back into the water and the light disappeared. I groaned. Now I realized it had been a skin diver searching the rig. He'd found my compartment seemingly empty and left.

I lay back in despair. But suddenly the strange green light returned. I sat up on the pump. A dark shape materialized under the water and a helmet broke the surface. I beat on it furiously with my knuckles.

Two polka-dotted gloves removed the helmet and a grinning, sweaty face said, "If you only knew how happy I am to see you!"

"Oh, God, thank You!" I prayed.

After the diver called on his radio for another helmet, I asked him the time. He checked his waterproof watch. "Noon, Monday," he said.

I had been down there 22 hours.

He explained they had strung air hoses to the submerged platform, hoping that the air would find its way to any trapped man.

Led by my rescuer and another diver, and wearing a helmet they gave me, I swam down the passageway and out into the dark gloom of the sea bottom. Slowly we floated upward, the water now paling to an iridescent emerald and getting brighter and brighter.

Finally we broke the surface and I was helped onto a rescue barge. Hands removed my helmet and I was blinded by the brightness of the sun. The first thing I did was fall to my knees on the deck and thank God. The next was to ask what had happened to my crew mates. My rescuers told me that four other crewmen, trapped together in another compartment, were also saved. Seven other men working above deck when the rig capsized were thrown into the water; one drowned and six were saved.

Later, when Dorothy kissed me at the hospital, she said people all over the country had been praying constantly for all of us.

Some weeks afterward Father Bertrand and I took my skiff up the bayou into the marshes. It was early morning. A great orange ball of sun burned away the mist hanging above the tall marsh grass. A snow-white crane stood poised against a green backdrop. An exultant bass shattered the mirror surface of the bayou into a shower of glassy fragments. It hung there for an instant, sparkling in the sun like a green jewel amidst diamond droplets, then plunged back into its own world. I looked up into the blue bowl of the sky, then glanced at Father Bertrand. He was smiling at me; he knew what had happened. A priest can always tell when a person has truly found God.

WHEN LOVE IS DEEPEST

I love you, not only for what you are, but for what I am when I am with you. I love you, not only for what you made of yourself, but for what you are making of me.

I love you for the part of me that you bring out.

I love you for putting your hand into my heaped-up heart, and passing over all the foolish, weak things that you can't help dimly seeing there, and for drawing out into the light all the beautiful belongings that no one else had looked quite far enough to find.

I love you because you are helping me to make of the lumber of my life not a tavern, but a temple; out of the works of my every day not a reproach, but a song. . . .

You have done it without a touch, without a word, without a sign. You have done it by being yourself.
        Roy Croft

To save himself and others he would need the
strength of Samson—and that's what he prayed for.

Last Flight
From Savoonga

by GILBERT PELOWOOK

A lmost, that day last summer, we didn't get on the plane at
Savoonga. Every one of the 28 seats was filled, but when
the airline agent explained why Abner Gologergen and I had to
get to Gambell, one couple agreed to give up their seats and
stay behind.

Abner is the magistrate at Savoonga, and I'm a state trooper.
Together we were due in court to process a case in Gambell, a
little seaside village at the northwestern end of St. Lawrence
Island, 160 miles off the Alaska coast from Nome and 41 miles
across the Bering Sea from Siberia. Savoonga is toward the
mid-northern end of the island, and once a week a Wien Air
Alaska airliner makes the three-stop round trip from Nome to
Savoonga to Gambell and back to Nome.

Taking a seat next to a young boy, I settled back with a
magazine. In a few minutes, we were airborne. The stewardess, a young black woman, moved up and down the aisle,
attending to requests of the passengers. All of them, like myself, were Eskimos from the island.

To outsiders, St. Lawrence can seem a remote and forbid-
ding land, rocky, windswept and stark, pocked with lakes and
ringed by gravel beaches that descend into the icy sea. To the
Eskimo, it is home, familiar. We know the brown, stony earth
and the blue waters that stretch endlessly from its shores. We
know Sevuokuk, the long, flat-topped mountain rising more
than 600 feet into the air, its craggy bulk a landmark.

45

For centuries, too, Sevuokuk has been the home of the village's dead. Villagers from Gambell carry the remains of their loved ones up the steep slope, place them among the rocks and leave them to time and nature. Over the centuries, to a people living close to nature, Sevuokuk became a symbol of the mysteries of life.

Many Eskimos are Christians now, and during the nearly 40 years of my life I went to church and believed in God. But He had never been very real to me, and from time to time I had the vague feeling that I was missing out on something important in life.

This missing element was one of the reasons I'd changed jobs three years earlier and joined the state patrol. All my life I'd wanted to help people, but along the way I had got sidetracked. Maybe working as a law officer I would have more opportunity to give of myself, I thought.

As we neared Gambell, I glanced out the window and noticed I could no longer see ground because of fog. Then, as if from nowhere, houses appeared right beneath us. We were very low. Much too low! Suddenly I knew with a heart-clutching surge of fear that our line of flight was toward Sevuokuk, hidden in the fog.

I grabbed my seat belt and jerked it tight, then covered my head with my arms. I felt the nose of the plane rise as the pilot frantically tried for more altitude. But it was too late. There was a terrible crash. Then everything went black.

When I came to, I was upside down, held to the seat by the belt. Everything was quiet. No sounds of life—no crying or moaning. I tried to determine if I had any bones broken. I seemed to be all right.

Others were not so fortunate. When the plane hit, the seats had torn loose from the cabin floor. Other passengers, still belted to their seats, were piled upside down, beneath me, behind me, on top of me. The boy who had been sitting next to me was now 15 feet away.

Now I could hear a noise—the sound of flames crackling. We were burning. I reached for my seat-belt fastener but couldn't find it. I couldn't get to it, there was so much twisted metal.

I pulled at the belt. Nothing happened. I strained and turned. I still couldn't reach the buckle.

The crackle was getting louder and I could feel the heat. Growing more desperate, I strained all my weight against the belt. Nothing worked.

When I knew there was no way out, I began to pray, "Lord, take me quickly!" While I was praying I asked for forgiveness, for things I'd done and things I'd failed to do, for the times I could have helped somebody and hadn't. As I prayed, a peace seemed to come over me.

Then a small voice spoke from the calm. I could hear it plainly. Was it real? I looked around.

The voice was Estelle Oozevaseuk's. I could see her. Her lips were moving; she was praying in our Eskimo dialect for God's mercy. *There are others alive!* I thought.

Now, instead of asking God to take me quickly, I prayed, like Samson, for strength. "Help me, God. Help me reach Estelle." I got a tight grip on a piece of metal that I thought might free me and pulled so hard that I could hear the joints of my arm crack. Strength seemed to flow into me and I kept pulling with all my might. All at once the belt flew loose. I pushed with my legs to get clear of the wreckage. I twisted and crawled free.

I moved to Estelle. Her legs seemed to be broken. I released her seat belt and began easing her out of the plane, through the torn metal. Out on the foggy mountaintop, I set her down a safe distance away from the burning plane.

Through the fog I could see that the airliner had slammed into the slope just below the mountain's crest, hitting with its nose up. Then it had ricocheted up through the rocks, turned up on its nose and fallen over backwards in a heap, with the tail broken off. Flames were bursting from the wings and cabin.

I knew the people in Gambell must have seen the plane and heard it crash. They would be coming to help. But it would take them at least half an hour to scale the mountain's 45-degree slope.

The fire was making little explosions and growing bigger. The whole plane could blow up any minute.

Estelle and I were the only ones out. If there were any other survivors, I knew they had to get out now. I couldn't wait for the villagers. Something in me was afraid, but there was also something stronger than fear, a feeling I had never before experienced, that gave me courage. "Lead me to those who can be helped," I prayed.

Back inside the wreckage, I shouted to the people in the cabin. "Is anybody alive?" "Where are you?" Whenever I saw someone move, I would free him from his seat belt and lead or drag him to the opening in the plane. I kept shouting, trying to rouse the unconscious ones. "Hey! Hey!" One passenger was held in by a tangle of metal. I pried it apart with my hands and pulled at his jacket with my teeth to move him from his seat.

A new explosion rocked the plane, and I ran frantically from the wreckage. Then I thought it must have only been an oxygen tank blowing up, and I went back in again.

The fire was very hot now, and the flames were getting closer to the people. I ripped a large piece of aluminum from the plane's wreckage and held it like a shield in front of me to keep the flames and heat away. Then I found Abner, who was badly injured, and placing the shield between him and the flames, I grabbed him and tugged. My hand stuck to his thick jacket as the melting nylon turned to sizzling jelly in my grasp. I freed him from his seat and flopped him onto my shield, then dragged him out among the rocks.

How many more can there be? I wondered. The fire was growing bigger and bigger. I could smell the fuel; it must have drenched the ground. My hands were hurting now, but I took my shield and went in again.

In the broken tail section I found the stewardess, screaming for help and hanging upside down, tangled in the metal of wire and cables. Close by, the left engine was burning, the magnesium fire giving off a greenish-blue light. I pulled at the metal; I couldn't move it enough. I stopped, rested and tried again. She twisted, then was able to slide free. I was afraid her back might be broken, and I tried to be careful when I moved her.

I knew I could not go on much longer. I was exhausted. My hand was burned and full of pain. And I had injured my leg on a jagged piece of metal. I sank to the ground. I had no idea how much time had passed since the crash, but I knew help would have to come soon if the other survivors were to get out. *The villagers,* I thought. *Where are they?*

At that very moment the first villager came scrambling over the crest. It was Leonard Apangalak; he and two other boys had run all the way from the village, then up the steep mountainside.

Now other village people were coming, too. I hollered to them. I was so glad to see them. Though they were completely out of breath, having run the whole way from the village, they went right to work. Many of them were National Guardsmen, trained in first aid, and they knew what to do with the injured. They moved into the burning plane and pulled out the remaining passengers, dead and alive.

By now the whole area was on fire, and the villagers moved the injured back from the flames. They put together makeshift splints and stretchers from the wreckage to help get the people down the mountain. I was the last to go. By then the plane was completely consumed by fire.

We were all taken to the schoolhouse in Gambell, given additional first-aid treatment, then flown to the hospital in Anchorage by a Coast Guard plane, which fortunately was near enough to reach Gambell shortly after the crash.

Of the 32 persons aboard the flight from Savoonga, 22 of us had survived. Diane Berger, the stewardess, was the only member of the crew to live. She and Abner Gologergen and several others would have to spend weeks in the hospital, but the doctors said they would recover.

Recently my job took me back to Gambell, and I paused for a long look at craggy Sevuokuk Mountain. No wonder generations of natives have thought of it as "the mountain of the dead." But now, for me, I realized it symbolizes life, for it was on that mountain that God became a reality to me, a personal, caring, loving God Who gave me a strength and courage beyond myself—supplying the power to minister to others when they needed my help.

We were far from all help—and our little
four-year-old was just a step away from death.

"Please, God, Save Our Amy!"

by LOIS OLSON

How many coincidences does it take to add up to a miracle? I never gave much thought to that question until one terrifying autumn day.

It was September, 1975, and the nights were already getting cold in the isolated valley of the North Cascade Mountains in Washington State where we lived. My husband Tom taught school in the little village of Stehekin, accessible to the outside world only by a four-hour ferryboat ride across Lake Chelan or a half-hour flight in a pontoon plane when the weather permits planes to fly. No roads over the rugged mountains. No telephones. Nothing.

Tom taught in a one-room schoolhouse built of logs where our eight-year-old Sally was the only third-grader in a total of 12 pupils. Having had some teaching experience back in Ohio, I often helped Tom around the school, and on this day I had brought along our four-year-old, Amy.

The older kids were playing baseball. Amy got excited and suddenly ran in front of the batter just as he swung. The bat struck her on the right side of the head. Numb with fright, I examined her. Blood was dripping from her ear.

As upset and concerned as two parents could be, Tom and I rushed Amy in our old car to a retired physician, the only doctor in the village, who cleaned and dressed the wound. "She should be all right," he said. I hoped with all my heart that this was true, because we had nowhere else to turn.

Tom went back to school, and the doctor's wife drove Amy and me back to our home, deep in the woods, five miles from the village. "Are you sure it's all right for me to leave you here?" she asked.

"I think so," I said. Amy appeared alert, her head was bandaged, and there seemed no reason for the doctor's wife to stay. But soon after she left, when I tried to change Amy's bloody shirt, she could not move her arms to help.

I was terrified. I knew that something was desperately wrong with my child. I had no telephone, no car. Even at the village there was no hospital, no medical facilities. It would be hours before Tom came home.

Holding Amy in my arms, I began to pray. I prayed because there was no other source of help or strength. I had always believed in God, but I was not certain of the extent to which He would go to help me. I had been told about His glory and power, but had not really felt them touch my life since my childhood, when I had had a siege with polio and recovered. Now I called on Him with every ounce of strength in me.

I knew that I had to get help for Amy somehow. So I began walking down the road. The boat landing was five miles away, and Amy weighed 40 pounds. My back had been damaged by the polio, and I didn't know how far I could go. As I walked, I kept praying.

Amy lay limp in my arms. Suddenly she looked up and said, in a strange, slurred voice, "Wha ah we ooing, Mama?" Amy had always expressed herself clearly for a four-year-old. Now her speech was so blurred that I could hardly understand her. I had worked with retarded children and I knew this might be a sign of brain damage. I tried to walk faster. I even tried to run, but my strength was ebbing. "*God, please!*" I cried over the pounding of my heart.

Exactly at that moment a car turned onto the road from a side road up ahead. But it was heading away from us, toward the village. I screamed, "Help! Help!" as loud as I could. But the car kept going and disappeared around a curve.

I was crying now, tears of hopelessness and despair. Then I heard the car stop. I began running and shouting again. I heard the car start up again; it then appeared around the curve, backing up.

It was my friend and distant neighbor, Rhoda Fellows. "Lois! What's happened?" she gasped.

"I've got to get Amy to a doctor." I cried. As we flew along the twisty road I told Rhoda what had happened. "It's strange," she said. "I wasn't sure I heard a call, and I almost never go into the village at this time." She drove us to the school because I knew Tom would want to be with us, and I needed him. Then she sped off to the boat landing to radio for a plane to come quickly.

As she left, another car pulled into the schoolyard. It was the ride home for the up-valley children. Somehow the man had come early, and was able to take charge of the other students so Tom could leave.

As we drove to the landing—Tom and our daughter Sally and I—Amy started trembling. Convulsive jerks contorted her left side and her tongue clacked against her mouth. I fought down panic as I realized that she was having a brain seizure. My only shred of hope lay in the fact that she was still conscious.

Tom and Sally and I began praying: "Our Father, Who art in Heaven . . . " As we prayed, I looked at Amy, lying in my lap—and I saw that she was praying, too—mouthing the words along with us in jerks and slurs and sounds ". . . Thy will be done, on earth as it is in Heaven . . . " Now Amy's lips barely moved, but I knew that her spirit was calling to God. I remembered how we had taught her the Lord's Prayer when she could barely talk, remembered how she would say it every night, and the thought came to me that if any prayer could be heard by a merciful God and answered, it was Amy's. I had to fight back tears as I looked at her. Then, suddenly, Amy lapsed into unconsciousness and slumped limply in my arms.

At this moment my panic should have been complete, but somehow in that moment of prayer, my daughter's prayer, my own faith in God had been heightened and strengthened as never before in my life. My heart was pounding, but deep inside there was a feeling of calm that can come only from God.

When we arrived at the landing, a gale was blowing. Tom

raced off to the radio to find out if the plane was coming and was told it was doubtful, the weather was so bad. We also found that the daily ferry had been delayed; it should have left long ago.

"There's a doctor on the ferry," someone said. "He stayed at the lodge last night."

"Oh, where is he? Where is he?" I begged. The gusts of wind were so strong I had to brace myself against them.

Tom came running up from the landing and took Amy from my sagging arms. "Ernie's going to try to make it," he said. Ernie was the airplane pilot, a brave and capable flier.

"There's a doctor on the ferry," I told Tom. "Let's try to find him."

Tom ran with Amy toward the boat and was met at the gangplank by a bearded, gray-haired man. We placed Amy on the back seat of a station wagon and the doctor climbed in and examined her. She was still unconscious and her breathing was now more labored and very rapid. The doctor turned to Tom. "I'll be right back," he said. He hurried back on the ferry and returned with another man.

"This is Doctor Dwiggens," he said. "We are colleagues at Stanford Medical Center, and I didn't know he was here until we met on the ferry a few moments ago. He's just the man you need."

I didn't understand why he was, but in the next half hour I found out. Doctor Dwiggens was a respiratory specialist who knew exactly what to do for Amy, and he worked frantically to keep her breathing.

I leaned over the seat and talked to Amy, hoping she could hear me. Tom put his arm around her and stroked her pale cheek, tears streaming down his face. The people from the village and the ferry passengers gathered around in uneasy little groups, many of them praying.

For half an hour we waited for the small seaplane, bucking its way against the wind to reach us. The ferry stayed at the landing, waiting to see if Ernie could make it. At last we heard the sound of the plane as it broke through the scudding clouds and swooped low over the choppy lake. We held our breaths as the crest of the waves tore at the pontoons. The plane bounced and tossed, but stayed upright and afloat. Ernie had made it! One of the old-timers shook his head. "Only a pilot with thirty years of experience could have done that," he said.

Suddenly Amy regained consciousness and began to cry. It was the most beautiful sound I've ever heard! All around me I could hear people saying, "Thank God."

Doctor Dwiggens, Amy, Tom and I squeezed into the little plane. After a perilous flight in high winds and a 35-mile ambulance ride to the Wenatchee Hospital, Amy underwent surgery. She had suffered a deep skull fracture. Five bone splinters were removed from her skull, but none had penetrated the delicate membrane protecting her brain.

Today, Amy has full use of all her limbs and faculties, and speaks as clearly as she did before the accident.

How many coincidences does it take to add up to a miracle? I still don't know. But I do know that Rhoda Fellows' car being in just the right place at the right time, the ferry being detained with just the doctor we needed, the courage of the only pilot who could have set that plane down on that storm-tossed lake and finally the miracle of Amy's undamaged brain—no one will ever be able to tell me that those things could have taken place without God's special intervention and guidance. He gave our little girl back to us. And we'll praise Him for it every day of our lives.

Fear thou not; for I am with thee: be not dismayed, for I am thy God: I will strengthen thee, yea, I will help thee; yea, I will uphold thee with the right hand of my righteousness. (Isaiah 41:10)

Never Listen to Your Fears

by HUBERT H. HUMPHREY

"Hubert," my father said, and I can still see the weary, defeated look in his blue eyes, "I've got to take your mother away for a while. The strain here is getting to be too much for her."

I stared at him in silence. It was a sultry August evening in the dusty little town of Doland, South Dakota. I was a young pharmacist trying to help my father make a go of a drugstore he had there. I knew what he meant about strain all right, but I hadn't expected this.

"It's everything," he said, and his big shoulders sagged. "The heat and the drought and the customers who can't pay their bills and the creditors who want payments from us. The last straw was having to sell our house to keep the store going. Your mother can't take it any more. I've got to get her away from all this. We're leaving tonight."

Times were hard, all right, back there in 1937. The dead hand of the Depression was heavy on the land. Three years of drought were forcing a lot of people to abandon their farms and ranches and move away. A lot of those who stayed on were being carried on our drugstore accounts because Dad was too big-hearted to refuse them credit.

For a long time Dad had clung to a kind of dogged optimism. "The whole country is in bad shape, son," he would say, "Still, we've been through tough times before. Things have got to get better." Muriel and I hadn't been married very long, and we wanted very much to believe him. But things just got worse. Ask anyone who lived through the Depression; those were grim days. A lot of strong men were driven to take their own lives.

Dad was watching me with those sad blue eyes. "Hubert, I want you to run the store while we're gone," he said. "Just do whatever you think needs to be done."

I felt a little quick clutch of fear. I'd practically grown up in the drugstore, which sold some general merchandise as well as all sorts of patent medicines, veterinarian supplies, and prescription drugs. But I'd always had Dad around to make the key decisions. "What about the bills?" I said apprehensively. "What about the creditors?"

"You'll have to do the best you can, son," he said. "I've reached the point where I can't even pray about them any more." He turned and walked out, and a little later, about ten o'clock that night, he and Mom got into the old Model A Ford and left town.

That night when I got home around midnight I told Muriel about my apprehensions.

"I don't blame Dad for wanting to get Mom away for a while," I said. "They need some relief from the strain of all this. But what if some crisis comes up? Business is so bad that one mistake can push the drugstore right over the edge."

But I had faith in the power of a loving God. I knew Him as the Heavenly Father Whose word we studied at our little Methodist church. He spoke to us from Scripture, from the prayers of His minister, from the music that filled the sanctuary when His people gathered to worship. But I wasn't altogether sure that He had His eye on the problems of a faltering drugstore in a small South Dakota town.

Two days after my folks left I was awakened around six one morning by an urgent rapping on my bedroom window of our little house on Idaho Avenue. It was a farmer who had been a customer of Dad's for many years.

I opened the window. "What can I do for you?"

"Where's your father?" he asked. "I went to his house and he's not there. He's not at the store, either."

"My parents are on a trip," I said. "Can I do anything for you?"

"It's my cattle," he said. "They're sick. They're all just lying around, and one of 'em's dead with black blood coming out of his nose. Can you do anything?"

I reached back into my memory, grasping for something I had seen when I had gone with Dad out into the countryside. This farmer seemed to be describing a deadly cattle disease that could go through a herd like lightening, spreading a poisonous contagion like a loathsome medieval plague. When it struck, preventive measures had to be taken at once, or it would wipe out cattle for miles around.

"Sounds like anthrax," I told the farmer. I quickly got dressed and took the farmer downtown with me and opened up the drugstore. I gave him enough anthrax serum to inoculate his whole herd, then got out a syringe and showed him how to use it. "And get rid of the carcass," I told him. "Burn it!"

He was no sooner out of the door than I began having some terrible qualms. If I was wrong about anthrax, if something else was killing the farmer's cattle, then I had only given him the wrong medicine. But if I was right, then the whole region was in trouble. If the drought and the Depression hadn't created enough economic havoc in the area, an epidemic of anthrax would wipe everybody out.

That meant I should order all the serum and syringes I could get, and order them fast. But if I ordered them and there *was* no epidemic, then Dad would be stuck with them and the bills from the suppliers would crush the remaining life out of our drugstore. And there were no veterinarians in the area I could consult.

I stood there for a long time in an agony of indecision. "Dear Lord," I prayed, "my dad's not here and I'm scared to death. Please show me what to do."

There was no answering roll of thunder, no change at all in the quiet drugstore. But I suddenly realized that I should not let my fears of what might happen freeze me into inertia. After all, which was more important, the future of one small drugstore or the future of the whole region we were living in? I knew how my Dad would answer that question, and I knew how he would want me to answer it, too. I reached for the phone.

As soon as I could get the serum suppliers in Minneapolis to answer their phones that morning, I started ordering anthrax serum—from Anchor Serum Company, from Sharp & Dohme, from Parke Davis, from everybody I knew I could get serum from. And I ordered it all on the drugstore's credit.

Well, the serum came, and so did the customers. Muriel and I kept the drugstore open day and night, selling to farmers and ranchers and to other druggists, too. There was suddenly so much activity that the news of it reached Dad, who was in Colorado and read about the outbreak in a newspaper. Within four days, he came charging up to the store in the Model A, wanting to know what was going on.

By then, it was obvious that we were facing a serious threat of an anthrax epidemic, and I was able to tell Dad the progress we had made to keep it in check.

In the next week or so we sold serum as fast as we could handle our customers. The cattle losses were held to a minimum, because the serum had been rushed in so quickly. And many farmers and ranchers whose businesses, like my Dad's, were teetering on the edge of ruin, were spared the fatal blow that an anthrax epidemic would have dealt them. And when the farmers and ranchers came in to pay for their serum, the drugstore's money problems were tremendously eased.

Well, Dad was just as pleased and proud of me as he could be. And I felt pretty good about it, too, once it was all over.

That happened in 1937, but it surely wasn't the last crisis I was to face in my life. Since then, I've gone through some things in politics and in my personal life that, when you think about them too long, could scare the socks off you. But in each tough situation, I have found myself drawing on the same power—the strength of a firm faith in God—that came to my aid that August morning in South Dakota.

The Battle of the Bulge. . . a desperate crisis. . . and a mysterious experience one young soldier will never forget.

Out of the Night

by JACK HARING

*Christmas Day
1944*

Dear Mom:
This is a very different Christmas Day than I have ever spent in my life. Right now I'm living in the hayloft of a farmer's barn, and I'm very glad to be here rather than out in a foxhole somewhere . . .

The Battle of the Bulge. The final desperate attempt of the Germans to break through Allied lines in Belgium and dash to Antwerp and the sea. For six days our 84th Infantry Division had been diverted from the Ninth Army in the north to the beleaguered First Army area in the Ardennes forest. The fiercest fighting of the war, and I, a 19-year-old private, was in the middle of it.

My letter home to Pennsylvania was written on a Christmas morning that was sunny and quiet—deceptively quiet. "The barn I slept in last night," I wrote, "made me think of the place where Jesus came into the world." Then I began reminiscing to Mom about the good Christmases we'd had as I was growing up—always starting with the traditional dawn service at St. John's Lutheran in Boyertown. Church had always been an important part of my life. I'd started college thinking I might go into the ministry.

The letter home was upbeat all the way. I didn't mention anything about the things that had been troubling me. How I had become disillusioned with organized religion because I saw so few Christians either at home or in the combat zone—

certainly not Christians trying to live the way Jesus had taught. Or how the weather had been so miserable and the fighting so blazing that I feared I'd never live to see Pennsylvania again.

The last straw was being sent to these snow-covered hills and woods where we might be attacked at any moment from out there, somewhere. I was beginning to think that God had forsaken me.

Still, even though we'd spent the last five days floundering around trying to stop the Germans, even though our supply trucks had been captured, at least we'd had a barn for shelter on Christmas Eve, and our cooks were promising us a hot meal for Christmas Day.

"Let's go, men," Sergeant Presto, our squad leader, shouted, "Collect your gear and fall out. We're going on a mission."

I groaned. We all groaned. There went our first hot meal in a week!

We drove for about ten miles and then the trucks dropped us and sped away. It was dusk. Troops were strung out all along a dirt road that circled through some hills. When Presto came back from a meeting with the platoon leader, he gathered the ten of us—we were one man short in the squad—around him.

"Okay, men, here's what we're going to do. This won't take long and we're going to travel light. Leave your packs and entrenching tools here." He made it sound so simple. Intelligence had said that some German infantry were dug into a nearby hill and were causing havoc by shooting down on the roads in the area. Our battalion's job was to go up and flush them out.

Single file on each side of the winding road, we moved up the hill. We moved quietly, warily. At the top, we were surprised to find, not Germans, but an abandoned chateau in the middle of a clearing. Our squad went into the building. We found a billiard table and the tension broke as we played an imaginary game of pool using our rifles as cues.

Then Presto came stalking in. The Germans, he said, were in the woods beyond the clearing. Our orders were to chase them out into the waiting arms of another battalion positioned at the other end of the woods.

"There'll be three companies in this deal," Presto said. "Two of us will stretch out along the edge of the forest while the other hangs back in reserve. Now, as soon as we push into the woods, everybody fires, got it?"

We spread out, walked through the darkness to the forest's edge, then, at a signal, we burst in, opening up with everything we had. We kept up a brisk pace, keeping contact with our buddies along the moving line, walking and firing for about a mile. But the forest was empty. There was no movement . . .

The trees in front of us exploded. Suddenly, the night went bright with every kind of firing I'd ever seen or heard of— rifles, rifle-launched grenades, mortars, machine guns, tracers over our heads, bullets at our thighs. But worst of all, Tiger tanks. At least six of them, opening up point-blank with 88-millimeter cannons. Their projectiles whined and crashed all up and down our line.

Our intelligence was wrong, I thought angrily, as I flung myself down on my stomach. *They told us there were no tanks up here. Now we're really in for it.*

Within seconds men were screaming in pain all around me. I saw a tree with a big trunk and made a sudden lunge to get behind it, but I wasn't quick enough. Something tore into my thigh. There was hot, searing pain.

We were completely pinned down. The Tiger tanks kept scanning their turrets and firing on every yard of our line. The German ground troops sent their small arms fire into anything that moved.

The minutes went by. Five. Ten. Fifteen. Then came a lull in the barrage. I called over to my best buddy, Kane. We called him "Killer." He was the gentlest guy in our platoon, but we'd nicknamed him that after the popular comic strip character, "Killer Kane."

"Are you hurt, Killer?"

"Naw. But I think everybody else over here is. Presto's hit bad."

I called to Cruz on my right. He was our squad's B.A.R. man. There was no answer. Then I barely heard him whispering, "I'm hurt. Real bad. Floyd's dead. Corporal John's hit bad."

Well, I thought, *if Presto's out and the Corporal, too, we don't have a leader.*

The pounding started again, this time with flares so they could spot us better. We did some firing back and then the action subsided into another lull.

Down along the rear of our line came a figure crawling. It was our platoon runner. "Captain says we're getting nowhere," he whispered to Killer and me. "We're pulling back in five minutes. Move out when you hear our covering fire."

I crawled over to Killer. "We've got to get our guys out of here," I said. "You go up your side and I'll go down mine, and we'll drag as many as possible to that big tree back there."

"How're we going to get them out of here, though?"

"I don't know," I said. "But we can't leave them lying here."

We were trapped. I lay there on the cold ground feeling helpless, that forsaken feeling again. Where was the God that I had prayed to during all those years of church and Sunday school back home in Pennsylvania? "And whatsoever ye shall ask in My name, that will I do," the Bible had said to me clearly. Was it necessary, when I needed help so badly, to ask?

"Oh, Lord," I mumbled, "help us. We're trying to get our wounded buddies out of here. Show us the way."

I had no sooner started dragging Corporal John toward our meeting tree when the firing started up in the center of our line. *There's the signal for pulling back*, I thought frantically, *but we can't do it. The Germans will sweep in on us; they'll mop us up before we can pull back.*

Just as I got to the tree, I saw that Killer had brought back three wounded squad members. So we had six in all to get back. I closed my eyes and in desperation said: "In Your name, Lord, help us."

I opened my eyes. In the black of night, moving mysteriously among the shattered trees, a giant hulk came toward us. *The Germans*, my heart thumped, *they've broken out of the brush. They're bearing down on us.* No, it was something else, something unbelievable. It now came into full view and stopped beside our tree.

A horse.

A big, docile, shaggy chestnut, standing there without a harness, as though awaiting our bidding.

Killer and I looked at each other in disbelief. We didn't question then where the horse came from, or how, or why; we just got to work. Moving swiftly, we draped Cruz and the Corporal on the chestnut's broad back, then Mike and Presto. Then, with Killer carrying one of our buddies and me carrying the other, we led the horse out of the woods. At the clearing the horse trotted on ahead of us, straight to the chateau, and by the time Killer and I got there, our wounded were already on medical stretchers. The two men we carried in were cared for; the medics gave a quick look at my shrapnel wound; and then, as fast as we could, Killer and I went to find the horse. We wanted to pat him, give him some sugar, anything to make him sense our gratitude.

But he wasn't there. We looked everywhere, asked everyone we saw, but no one could tell us anything about him. He had simply vanished—gone from us as mysteriously as he had come.

The next morning at the aid station the shrapnel was removed from my leg, and at noon Killer and I lined up for our belated Christmas dinner. The day before, 190 men in our company would have answered the chow call; today there were 35 of us. All the wounded men in our squad had survived, however, though some were never to see action again.

Killer and I looked at the turkey and sweet potatoes in our mess kits. Hot and savory and long-awaited as this food was, we had no appetite. We were still too full of our emotions: the sorrow for lost buddies; the shock of our own survival; the strange, deeply affecting arrival and departure of the horse. We could not get the horse out of our minds then, nor have I since, for that noble creature did more than just save our lives; he reaffirmed my faith. I have always believed that on that Christmas night 33 years ago, God sent that horse to reassure a doubting soldier of His presence, even as He had sent His Son for that purpose on a Christmas night twenty centuries ago.

One of America's favorite inspirational
authors remembers a bad Good Friday when
her heart was aching for . . .

A Runaway Son

by MARJORIE HOLMES

"Please pray for Ginny," the letter said. "She's 16 now—at least I hope she's 16. Today's her birthday. She ran away on her 15th birthday a year ago. We thought it was strange that she didn't get up in time to have her presents before leaving for school. When I went in to call her, I found her bed hadn't been slept in; she was gone! Her father and I have been in torment for a year. We've searched, prayed desperately, tried everything. Will you please pray she's safe and will call us or come home? I can hardly bear to pass that empty room."

That empty room . . . I thought a long time before answering that mother. I went to my files and read similar letters, searching out those that had happy outcomes. In my letter, I told her of cases I knew intimately—the daughter of our doctor, gone two years without a word, now in medical school. I told her about a neighbor's son . . . And my own.

Because now it can be told. I've been there. I know how it feels to call a child for breakfast, and getting no response, fling open the door—on an empty room. The bedclothes carefully arranged to look like a sleeping figure, but when you pull them back, no sign of the warm body that should be there. The closet mute. The room crammed with his things: books, records, tennis racket, fishing gear; things that should have made him happy, but didn't. All this paraphernalia curiously both a comfort (you tried), and an accusation (you didn't try hard enough).

In those shocked first hours, it isn't the sense of failure that is paramount. There is only this sickening chill in the pit of the stomach. This awful disbelief. He can't be *gone*; there's got to be some mistake! And you get on the phone and call his friends, call the school. And then as the frantic, incredible day drags on into the night, you call the police. *He's threatened, lost, in danger. Find him!*

The squad car stops at the curb; they come up the walk, two uniformed young officers, sympathetic but reassuring as they take down vital information. They say there are many runaway kids, but most of them aren't gone long. They tell you not to worry, but that's no help.

I put on the coffeepot and when it was hot, poured the first of many cups my husband and I would drink that marathon first night. There was no use trying to sleep. Like people at a wake, we had to keep vigil, as if staring out the kitchen window into the darkness would somehow produce him—that too-thin figure hunched into his plaid jacket, cowlicky head bent against the wind.

Soon our sense of guilt and failure took over, and the awful questioning began. *Why? Why?* Our discussion went on endlessly. Occasionally we'd disagree, quarrel, blame each other. But that was too devastating. No. No, we had to cling to each other, stick it out together.

I asked my husband if he'd ever run away.

"Sure; twice. Once when I was about ten—I got as far as the corner. Another time—I must have been about fourteen. A friend and I tied some clothes in a bundle and were going to hop a freight. But it got awfully cold that night and the train was late. When we finally heard it coming—saw that big headlight and heard that whistle—we got scared and raced home."

We talked about how it was when we were growing up. How mad we got at our parents, too, just as kids do today. "But almost nobody ever actually ran *away*. We didn't have the nerve!" Times are different now, we agreed. Youngsters have more freedom, more money.

"And we aren't as close as a family as we were with our folks. We can't be, there are too many distractions. . . ."

Yes, distractions—even the organizations in which we worked so frantically on behalf of them.

T he endless searching for where you've gone wrong. Times when you've been too strict or too lenient. Moments when you've been unfair, haven't really listened, mishandled situations about grades or a girlfriend or the car.

"Please God, bring us back together again. Protect Jimmy. Keep him warm and out of serious trouble. Help him to know we love him, want him back. . . ."

Those nightmare first hours ground into nightmare weeks. Our hearts pounded wildly every time the phone rang. We raced to it, praying for good news; weak with dread of bad.

The Lord led us to many fine people during this ordeal. Doctors, ministers, counselors, a chief of police with six boys of his own. They gave us insight and encouragement, if not answers. Out of these sessions came primarily the reassurance that although we had faults, we were not monsters. And we were not alone.

One night the doorbell rang and there stood a shy little Italian cobbler who fixed Jimmy's shoes. Excusing himself profusely for intruding, he sat down, nervously fumbling his hat. "He's a fine boy," he said. "And when you find him or if you hear from him, tell him he's forgiven. Please don't be too hard on him." Then he told us the story of his own boyhood with a feared stepfather. "It's why I came to America, to get away from him. But I knew he'd never forgive me for leaving; it's why I never went back." We learned there is a lot of the Good Shepherd in everyone.

We prayed, of course, day and night. Frantic prayers at first, frenzied prayers, for we knew that our fears had substance. A teen-ager alone and far from home without money or even a change of clothes can be prey to forces too terrible to contemplate. As St. Paul says, "We wrestle not against flesh and blood, but against principalities, against powers, against the rulers of darkness of this world." (Ephesians 6:12)

But ultimately we must let faith take over. I finally realized that during the Easter season. For the sake of the rest of the family, I was going through the motions of holiday preparation that spring—taking our little girl and her brother shopping for shoes and new outfits, watching the bunnies hopping about in a department-store window, buying bright-colored baskets to be filled.

Then suddenly we heard church bells, reminding us—Good Friday! We followed the sound of the ringing bells, and, trying not to rattle our packages, slipped inside, and knelt.

And there in that strange, hushed church, I felt unexpectedly very close to Mary. It was as if I stood with her on that hillside at Golgotha watching the unspeakable thing that was happening to her Son. And my heart broke for her, that courageous little peasant woman whose agony was so much greater than mine. But as I wept for her, it was as if my own soul was healed and cleansed. As if God had spoken to me clearly, quietly, saying, "Trust Me."

The children didn't understand. They reached out, one on each side of me, to pat and comfort me. And my little girl cuddled near to whisper, "Don't cry, Mommy. Jimmy'll be back." Her words were both an echo and a confirmation: "*Trust Me.*"

At that moment faith bloomed. *Hope. Trust.* That was really the message of the cross. The empty cross . . . and the empty tomb! When Mary was told on Sunday that the tomb was empty, she had to believe that God had other plans for her Son. Because He lived and would return!

I could hardly wait to get home to Jimmy's room. Even though he'd been gone for months now, I still had been avoiding it. Now I opened the door.

His things were still scattered about, just as he had left them. I began to pick them up and put them away. I dusted and cleaned, getting things ready, making it nice for his return. And as I worked I realized that the bitter and constant dirge of, "Why didn't we?" and "If only" and "Please, God" had stopped. As if the work itself was a kind of cleansing and purging of regrets that did no good. Making way for what God seemed to be telling me now: Life must go on. There will be other problems, but I will give you strength for them, too. Trust Me.

A lovely stillness came into my heart. I found myself releasing our son to his Creator, almost as Mary must have been

willing to release Jesus to His fate. Thanking God for sending
him to us in the first place, for watching over him now, and for
bringing him safely back . . . to a no longer empty room.

Jimmy was restored to us, unscathed. He'd washed dishes,
car-hopped, fought forest fires, seen a lot of the country.
Later, when he was old enough, he joined the Coast Guard,
distinguished himself, took courses and went on to college. The
family was ultimately able to laugh about some of his adventures.

But I knew how it feels to face an empty room. Easter has
special significance not only for me but for all parents alarmed
about their children—particularly those who have run away!
This is not the end. There *is* hope and life ahead—because
another mother long ago faced an empty tomb.

Lord, I do want to be Martha today.
Many guests are coming;
there's the house to clean,
flowers to arrange, food to prepare.
But, Lord,
in some other inner room of me,
sitting at Your feet,
let me be Mary, too,
choosing to hear, learning how
to love.
                    Emily Sargent Councilman

"We Are Going to Die, Aren't We?"

by MELVIN BITTER

The park rangers warned us that the lake was treacherous and that its winds changed suddenly. So when Gertrude and I pushed our nine-foot sailing dinghy across the sandy beach on that calm August morning, we fully intended to stay within a few hundred yards of the shore.

We were camping in Maine's Sebago Lake State Park, 88 square miles of beckoning water. As stronger air currents caught us and began to bear us along more swiftly, the sensation was so exhilarating that we forgot our caution and went with the wind, out toward the center of the lake.

Then we noticed that swells were coming up from behind and overtaking us. We must have covered about three miles when I decided we'd better turn around into the wind and head back. As the dinghy swung, the rudder pin snapped and the line holding up the sail broke.

I managed makeshift repairs and we began to tack toward the shelter of the shore. The lake was now being whipped by a stiff breeze. A sudden gust caught the boat broadside and we capsized. Gertrude and I found ourselves gasping in the chilly water.

Even then we had no feeling of panic, for we were both good swimmers. Each of us had a lifesaving seat cushion and we even managed to right the boat, but the waves, now about three feet high, just ran over it. There was no way of bailing it out and we decided there was a better chance of being spotted with the boat's white bottom uppermost—which also made it easier to hold onto.

We hung there in the heaving water and waited. After 15 minutes we were shaking from cold and knew we had to do something to generate heat. We started pulling the boat toward the nearest shore, about two-and-a-half miles away, struggling against the wind and the waves.

Occasionally other boats passed near us, but the waves hid us from them and the wind carried away our shouts. Several times we waved our cushions at small planes that flew over us, but they didn't notice us. After two hours of battling we realized that the shore was as far away as ever; wind pressure against the boat was canceling out every stroke we made. We decided to abandon the dinghy and swim with the seat cushions.

We realized that we were doing a dangerous thing—water-safety experts strongly recommend staying with a capsized boat—but we had tried that and it hadn't worked. Now we prayed that God would make someone concerned for us. We repeated together the Twenty-third Psalm. As we said, "Yea, though I walk through the valley of the shadow of death . . ." Gertrude suddenly felt the clutch of panic at her heart. "We are going to die, aren't we?" she asked.

"We've prayed for help," I answered. "Now we've got to believe that it's coming." But I, too, feared that we weren't going to make it.

Soon we could no longer see the boat. As we clutched our cushions and kicked and stroked with our free arms, we thought we were beginning to make progress. Then cramp pains, light at first, but quickly growing in intensity, began to cripple my legs and stomach. I had recently been in the hospital for treatment of ulcers.

We agreed that one of us had to try to reach the shore. Gertrude was in much better shape than I was, so with great reluctance she left me and swam on ahead. I watched her pink blouse crest one wave after another until I could see it no longer.

Now I felt a loneliness I had never experienced before. My whole body was wracked with spasms from the cold water.

Suddenly I heard what sounded like a cry of desperation from Gertrude. "Help! Help! Help me, Mel!"

I screamed into the wind, "Trust! Trust! Hold on!" My words were whipped away. I kept yelling, "Gertrude! Gertrude!", but there was no reply. I cried desperately to God to take care of her and somehow found the strength to begin swimming again toward the spot where I had last seen her. But I couldn't see her pink blouse, and now I was sure she had gone under. I thought of the agony of telling our six children and her parents that Gertrude was dead. The temptation came to let go of my cushion and sink.

But into my mind came the words, "Call upon Me in the day of trouble. I will deliver thee, and thou shalt glorify Me." (Psalm 50:15) So I began to call upon God, out there in the loneliness and the windfilled emptiness of the lake. I cried to God in my pain and suddenly my body flooded with waves of warmth. I realized that I was being warmed and encouraged by a power not my own. God came into my loneliness and filled it with Himself. No human help came, but the horror was taken away.

Then dimly through the fog of my mind I heard some voices. I had wanted to hear voices for so long that I was sure it was a delusion. Then a woman's voice said, "He doesn't see the rope—I'm going to help him." Suddenly she was beside me in the water, putting a rope under my arms. And strong hands were reaching out of a boat and pulling me over the gunwale.

"Is there anyone else?" one of the men asked me.

"My wife . . . if my wife is still alive, she's out there," I said and drifted into semi-consciousness.

Vaguely I heard the men talking of switching to the other gas tank. The woman who had jumped into the water now lay on top of me to try to warm my shivering body. The boat's engine was silent while the gas tanks were switched and then we were moving. It seemed only moments before the man said, "There she is!" and one of them called, "We've got your husband—he's alive!" Then Gertrude's head was next to mine. "Thank God, oh, thank God," I kept hearing her say.

Back at the shore, warm sand was heaped around me and

blankets were put on both of us. Gertrude asked the time. It was ten after five. "Seven hours," I heard myself say. "Seven hours in that water."

I heard Gertrude ask someone, "How did you know we were out there?"

"Your boat washed ashore on a beach where we were having a picnic," a man answered. "We weren't sure there'd been an accident, but we felt we'd better check. That's how we found your husband."

"And how did you find me?" Gertrude asked.

"We had to cut off the engine while we switched gas tanks," he answered. "The wind pushed us right to you. It's really amazing."

But I knew it was more than that. It was the answer to prayer.

For He hath said, I will never leave thee nor forsake thee. So that we may boldly say, The Lord is my helper, and I will not fear what man shall do unto me. (Hebrews 13:5,6)

When I Learned to Accept Myself

by CHARLES BULL

I've lived under a cloud nearly all my life. As an eight-year-old, I would suffer periods when I'd black out, losing control of the muscles in my arms and legs. "Petit mal psychomotor seizures," the doctors called it, using a terrifying language I was too young to understand.

My mother understood. It was epilepsy—but fortunately not the grand mal type that causes violent convulsions.

Neither she nor I, though, could understand neighbors who wouldn't let me play with their children because they considered me mentally ill and untrustworthy as a playmate for their youngsters. At school, while the other kids played softball or ran races during gym, I was restricted to solitary book study, because the gym teachers thought I was unfit to participate in athletics.

A person doesn't easily forget things like that. And as such experiences began to accumulate, they colored my attitudes and behavior. I became suspicious and distrustful of people.

Even as a grown man, with a lovely wife and wonderful young daughter, I still found myself sensitive to the way people reacted to me—especially to my bike riding. As an epileptic I am not allowed to drive a motor vehicle, something that makes me stand out in an area where everyone of age drives and can't imagine anyone not driving.

Despite my malady, I'd never been without a job since high school. The jobs may not have been all that great, but I managed to keep working.

Then a couple of years ago I found a new job, one that let me take advantage of my training as a computer operator, and my wife Carol and I moved away from New York City to settle down with our little girl in a comfortable old house outside New

73

Haven, Connecticut. It was like beginning a new life. The pleasant, tree-shaded neighborhood was close to the Long Island Sound beaches that Carol and I both loved. And I really enjoyed my job working as a data processor.

Things were going so well that I was totally unprepared for the shock one Monday morning in January several years ago when an office supervisor summoned me to his desk.

"Charles," he began slowly, "we've never had any complaints about your work. You're diligent and efficient." He paused significantly. "The problem is your personality." He paused again.

"Charles," he said. "I'm sorry, but I'm going to have to let you go."

My wary defensiveness probably *had* annoyed this man and caused our personality conflict. And now my worst fear had been realized.

When I got home that day and told Carol about getting fired, my heart sank as I saw how crestfallen she looked behind her wire-rim glasses. She tried to hide her disappointment. "Don't worry," she said, "I'm sure God will work things out."

I didn't feel as confident. Economic conditions in our area in early 1975 didn't favor a 32-year-old unemployed data processor.

After six weeks of search, though, I did finally land a job—as manager of a convenience food store. I thought I'd really found something. I liked the work, meeting customers and dealing with people. My boss seemed pleased with my efforts, too. I had deliberately neglected to reveal any health problem on my application and I did my best to avoid giving myself away. I didn't feel good about it, but I was terrified of losing another job because of my epilepsy.

One day, however, I suffered a brief seizure, and the boss must have heard about it. The next morning he told me that because of personnel shifts at the food chain's office, he would have to let me go. I didn't believe that excuse for a minute. I knew in my heart that he didn't want me in the store any longer simply because I was epileptic.

My ability to play the organ got me a part-time job in a

Protestant church for a short time. But one Sunday I blacked out in a seizure just before the doxology—and so I was found unsuitable for that job, too.

After that failure, opportunities simply dried up—and so did my spirits. My prayers for help were empty echoes now. I wondered if God would *ever* answer.

Carol worked occasionally when the local school district needed a substitute teacher, but there wasn't enough income to pay the bills. Each day I rose from bed, continuing the weary, futile search for a job. Meanwhile, our bank account was getting smaller and smaller.

Carol would hold long talks with me, trying to restore my self-confidence. She called those conversations our "pep-talk sessions," and until August they were the only thing that kept me going. That and our prayers together, for Carol's faith never wavered.

Finally we knew we were at the end of our rope. We'd been scraping together enough cash to feed ourselves, with enough left over to meet the minimum payments on our mortgage each month. But in September we'd have to pay our real-estate tax, which had gone up, and there just wasn't anything to pay it with. We'd depleted our savings. We were going to lose the battle to keep our home.

I found myself praying with a determination I'd never known before. "God, we've about had it," I said. "If You don't show us some way out soon, I don't know what's going to happen to us. I've tried everything I know. I've tried to hide my epilepsy, and I've tried to avoid situations where I knew it would hurt me. Nothing works. I'm tired of all the hiding, the deception and pretending there's nothing wrong. This is the way You made me, Lord, and I've got to live with it. Help me, Lord!" It was the strongest prayer I'd ever prayed, and I really meant it.

That was on Sunday night. On Monday morning, August 25, at exactly one minute past eleven—I remember it clearly because it really was the eleventh hour—the telephone rang.

The caller said he was Paul DeVoe, a supervisor in the services bureau of Accounting Systems Corporation in nearby Branford, Connecticut. I had had an interview at ASC several months before, but had almost forgotten about it because they hadn't been at all encouraging. DeVoe wanted to know if I'd be available for work the next day. I all but shouted my "yes."

Then I ran into a new problem. The only public transportation to Branford was a bus I could transfer to in New Haven. It would get me into Branford at 8:10—ten minutes late for work. Carol drove me to the office that first day, but I knew she couldn't do it every day, with our toddler to take care of.

Nervously I explained my predicament to Paul DeVoe. Since I couldn't drive, would he mind if I arrived on the bus ten minutes late every day?

He wouldn't hear of it. "You'd catch this bus at Temple Street in New Haven each morning?" he said. "How would it be if I drove over and picked you up there in my car instead?"

I was dumbfounded. Just like that, a near-stranger had volunteered an unbelievable kindness. When the other supervisors learned of my problem, each in turn volunteered to share the task of driving through New Haven to get me. Something was happening that I'd never experienced before.

I went home that evening eager to tell Carol about my extraordinary new employers. But in the midst of our elation, the old suspicions began nibbling at me. I began wondering if it was too good to last. In my eagerness to get the job, I had not told Paul DeVoe about my epilepsy. Eventually I'd have to own up to it. *What then?* I wondered. Would I have the courage to be honest?

Within a few days I got the answer to that question. The two of us were in his car, driving, talking, relaxed and easy.

"Charles, I don't mean to pry," he said, "and if you don't want to answer, don't bother. But is there a particular reason you don't drive a car?"

There it was. My mind began to boil as the horror of being jobless came screaming back at me. I looked across the front seat into Paul's face. Every fear I'd ever felt about myself seemed to bounce through my head.

Finally I got it out. "I have epilepsy."

He nodded, "I thought it might be something like that," he said.

I felt good that I had not lied or tried to cover up. I immediately knew I had done the right thing. But later, when the warm glow wore off, I started to worry about Floyd—or Woody, as he was called—Stem, the company's general manager and one of its owners. Sooner or later he would be told about me, and I had heard enough about him to know he could be very demanding. What would *he* think of having an epileptic in the office?

The confrontation came soon enough. Within a few weeks Woody offered to drive me home after we had both put in an unusually long day. I sensed that he had something to talk to me about.

As he drove, we talked about work, about my family, my house. Finally he arrived at the subject of epilepsy, and I braced myself for what might come next.

"I don't know if you've noticed," he told me, "but I'm handicapped myself." He motioned to his right arm. And for the first time I noticed how stiffly it hung at his side. "I suffered a paralysis when I was a kid," he explained. "I've never been able to raise my arm since.

"But I don't think it's made a difference in what I've been able to do," he went on. "It's affected the way I look at people, though. When I look at a man, I'm not looking for the things he *can't* do. I'm looking for what he *can* do." He turned toward me and grinned.

I'm not the type who is easily moved to tears, but I confess I was really touched, and not just by Woody. God had given me not simply a job, but exactly the right one, working with exactly the right people I needed, people who were not only willing to accept me, but also willing to go out of their way to help me deal with the transportation problems that have always made finding the right job even more difficult. And He had given me the courage to be honest. Yes, I decided, I could live with the way God had made me.

I can't describe the peace I felt as I came up the walk that evening, seeing my sandy-haired wife and daughter waiting for me at the window. They were never more beautiful. Even I felt beautiful.

**The old ice plant was a spooky place at night.
Yet even ghosts didn't match the terror of . . .**

Night Invaders

by ERWIN COLLINS

It was one o'clock in the morning, and I was at my summer job as nightwatchman at the Thomasville Ice Company. I was working there as a favor to the owner, Jimmy Keyton, a friend of my parents, until he could find an older man to take the job full-time.

Suddenly, from behind me, the door leading to the ice-making machinery swung open with a crash.

I spun around, startled. I saw that two men, one tall and one short, each with a crude ski mask pulled down over his face, had burst into the room. They wore old clothes, and their actions seemed nervous, jumpy. The tall fellow held a pistol in his hand, and the short one grasped a 16-gauge shotgun. I recognized the type, though I'd never seen one from this angle before—I was literally staring down its barrel.

Perspiration beaded my forehead.

"Hey, man, don't shoot," I said, surprised at how easily the words came. "There's no money here," I added.

"You're lying!" the tall man said coldly.

"No, I'm not!" I replied anxiously. "All our work is done on credit. There's no cash in the office."

I was relieved as they looked around at the few wooden chests and files in the office. They seemed to believe me.

"What's that?" the small gunman demanded, pointing at the money clip I'd left on the desk.

"My own money," I answered, reaching for the bills. "You can have it all."

"Give it to me," the man I thought of as "Shorty" snapped

78

impatiently. He tore the bills out, a five and a ten. "This all?" he muttered savagely. "Fifteen dollars?"

"It's all I ha—" I began, but the tall man stepped forward and, furious about the small "take" from the robbery, struck me on the head with his pistol butt. I didn't cry out, but the side of my face got sticky. I reached up to my throbbing head, and when I brought the hand down, it was stained with bright red blood.

"Now you shut up and do like I say," Shorty commanded. "You got a car?"

I nodded.

"Okay. Take us out there."

Blood trickled down my neck as I led them into the dark parking lot.

"Open up and get in," Shorty ordered. The words chilled me. These men had been short-tempered and unpredictable—as if they might be on drugs—and I knew I'd never survive an automobile ride with them.

My car didn't have much room in the back seat, but both men squeezed into it.

"Okay. There's a gun at your head," the short man said, jabbing its cold metal barrel behind my ear. "So don't try nothing. Now, move!"

Slowly we slipped through the dark, deserted streets of Thomasville. My eyes searched desperately for a police car, but we didn't pass a single one by the time we'd reached Route 84.

"Do you know the way to Miami?"

"Well, uh—" What should I answer?

The taller man started coughing just then. During this coughing fit, he couldn't seem to catch his breath. His desperate companion brandished his pistol near my ear.

"I oughta kill you," he said grimly. "Why didn't you answer him?"

"I'm sorry," I apologized, "I don't mean to excite anyone. I was just trying to think about the best way to go."

"All right," mumbled the taller man, who'd quit coughing at last. "That's real good. You just keep thinking that way."

After a while, the men told me to turn up the inside rear-view mirror, and not look back anymore, I guessed they must have taken off their masks.

"Are you worth anything?"

"No," I said. "If I were, would I be working in an icehouse?"

Shorty, soothed by my show of humor, asked some questions about the car and how to use the clutch. Next he ordered, "Stop here. I want to see if we can work this clutch business ourselves."

We pulled over. It was a dark, woodsy section of the highway. While Shorty held his gun on me, the tall man climbed behind the wheel. Suddenly I realized that the car was the only important thing to them now. Because they thought my family had no money, they would have no further use of me. The thought terrified me. Should I change my story? Run for it?

The decision was made for me—the car's stick shift was causing problems. After the car started, it moved forward in a series of violent jerks, and then the motor died.

"No good!" Shorty yelled in disgust. "We need a driver."

In several moments, I was back behind the driver's wheel. My head pounded, but it felt good to be alive.

We had been driving for half an hour or so, and we were in Florida now—a federal kidnaping case across state lines—but who would start looking? And where? No one would discover me missing until Mr. Keyton showed up at the ice factory later in the morning—around 7:30.

My thoughts switched to something more immediate. The car would run out of gas soon. What should I do? If I warned my kidnapers, I'd be sentencing myself to a longer drive in the car. If I said nothing and let the engine sputter out, they might become enraged.

"We'll have to gas up pretty soon," I mentioned cautiously.

The tall man peered at the gas gauge, where the needle dipped toward "E".

"It's okay," he said to Shorty. "It's still plenty dark."

We pulled up at an all-night service station. Shorty handed me the five-dollar bill—the one he'd stolen from me earlier— and said nothing as the sleepy attendant pumped gasoline. But a bundle of beach towels shifted at his side, and I knew a 16-gauge shotgun lay beneath it, aimed into my side.

We didn't get very far from the gas station before we came to the flashing lights of a half-dozen police cars.

"Looks like a roadblock!" the tall man shouted.

"Turn up the side road—quick!" Shorty yelled.

For a moment, I thought, *Now's the time! While the car is slowing up, I can jump out and hope my head doesn't hit something.* But even as I reached for the door handle, something told me, "Stay," I didn't make the leap.

As it was, I drove my car right through the glare of a parked police car's headlights, but nothing happened. The police, it turned out, had been crowded around an accident scene.

We headed east a while, on roads that got "country" quick. I pressed the accelerator a bit harder, remembering the dark woods before. If only we could make it to busy Route 1.

These hopes shattered when we reached I-95, the big interstate. Shorty noticed the signs indicating: "Miami—South."

"Turn here," he said. "This road looks good."

No, no, I sighed inwardly, even as I obeyed. No one would ever spot us on this high-speed thruway! Suddenly, releasing the fears that had mounted all night, I did something rare for me—I prayed. Until now, I had never put much stock in praying. My mother often said that I was always in her prayers, but I hadn't seen any evidence of answers, so I rarely tried it.

But now the urge to pray was so strong in me that I could almost see the words as they entered my mind: "Look, God, I'm scared. If these guys get me into Miami, they'll kill me and dump me in a swamp and nobody'll ever know what happened to me. Help me, God. Please be with me. Get me out of this."

I noticed that my wound was bleeding slightly again, and I asked Shorty to pass me one of the small beach towels so I could wrap it around my head. Then I tried to keep my mind on the driving.

Dawn had broken while we headed east, and now the pale light of morning grew on my left side. All the while the day came on, I shuddered at the thought that it might be my last.

We'd been driving for a long spell. Five dollars' worth of gasoline hadn't really filled up the tank enough to reach Miami, and I mentioned this as we neared the Titusville, Florida, area.

"Yeah, okay," agreed Shorty. "But remember—no funny stuff!"

A tall, curly-haired attendant came out and said good morning as we pulled in. All the while he was pumping our gasoline, though, I could feel his curious eyes surveying our car's peculiar riders. Two strange-looking men sat in the back seat, and a towel was wrapped around my head—we must have been quite a sight. When the attendant came for payment, though, he didn't say anything. I'd been hoping he'd noticed the dried blood on my jacket, but all he said was, "Thank you."

It took me a few moments to notice the state-patrol cars that started following us on the highway several miles later. There were two of them, I saw in the outside mirror. They were driving spread out across all the empty lanes behind me, and coming closer. But no one except me noticed until the police were right behind our car.

The tall man was startled, "Behind us—cops!" he burst out.

"What do I do?" I asked.

"Pull over," Shorty said. "Tell 'em we're going to Miami. If they notice your head, tell 'em you banged it on the door."

"And be convincing," the tall man said ominously.

I stopped the car on the shoulder of the highway. The state-patrol cars pulled off the shoulder of the road about 30 feet behind us. The next thing I heard was a patrolman's voice through a bullhorn. "Will the driver of that car step out with his hands up?"

"Go ahead," Shorty whispered.

After I climbed from the seat, the police told me to walk over to their vehicles. With every step, I thought I could feel a pair of guns aimed into my back, and the sweat ran down inside my shirt. Ten steps, 11, 12, and I was among the patrolmen. "My name is Erwin Collins," I exclaimed breathlessly. "I've been kidnaped."

"We figured as much, son," an officer in a state trooper's uniform said. "You're lucky that service-station attendant followed through on his hunch."

As soon as I could, I called home, and I was puzzled when I got no answer. I called the ice factory, and Mr. Keyton answered. I told him briefly what happened, then said, "Mr. Keyton, I just called home and there's no one there."

"Your mother just left here," he said. "We called the police right away this morning, of course, and then we started praying for you."

"That's amazing," I said. "That's just about the time the police here rescued me.

"The Lord works fast, doesn't He?" he said.

"Yes," I said. "But maybe that's because my mother had a backlog of prayers waiting for me when I really needed them."

3.
Love for Those Who Need Healing

Jesus turned him about, and when he saw her, he said, Daughter, be of good comfort; thy faith hath made thee whole. And the woman was made whole from that hour.
(Matthew 9:22)

"Your daughter Betty expired a few moments ago," the nurse said. The extraordinary story of what happened next is told by one of the distinguished spiritual writers of our time.

A Glimpse of Eternity

by CATHERINE MARSHALL

"Facts are often stranger than fiction," people say. True. Still, many are going to find the facts of Betty Malz's story difficult to believe.

It's a story I can vouch for. One October, in the living room of our Virginia farm, I heard this extraordinary adventure from Betty's own lips. Through subsequent weeks I investigated the details in depth. But that day at the farm I knew that the best and final proof was Betty Malz herself, along with her nine-year-old daughter, April Dawn, (born after her mother's "death")—both so vibrantly alive.

The adventure began one June night in 1959. Betty, 29, her husband John, a salesman for the Sun Oil Company in Indiana, their daughter Brenda, Betty's parents, the Glenn Perkins', and her little brother had just arrived for a two-week family vacation at Gulf Vista Retreat, Florida. They spent that first day swimming, water-skiing, surfing, shell-hunting. Exhausted, Betty and her husband went to bed early.

Then the pain began. Hand pressed on her stomach, Betty Malz first wondered, *What did I eat for dinner?* Then as the pain increased, she thought, *What a way to start our vacation!* Finally Betty turned on the light and woke her husband. When the pain became excruciating, he drove her to the hospital.

Betty lay in the hospital several days while the doctors made dozens of tests and debated her situation. Finally she was sent by plane to a hospital in her home town of Terre Haute, Indiana, where on the eleventh day of her illness, she was operated on by a gynecologist-surgeon. He found an appendix long-ruptured, with a huge mass of gangrene in her abdomen. Every organ was coated.

"I can give you no hope," the surgeon told her husband and her parents. "I've lost two-hundred-pound men in forty-eight hours with a fraction of the gangrene we have here. She can live only a few hours."

But Betty did not die that night, nor the next. In fact, on the fourth day she lapsed into a coma. She was to be in that coma for most of the next month.

The days passed. Ten. Twenty. Betty was given multiple blood transfusions (she had B-negative blood) and intravenous feedings. Not a mouthful of food passed her lips. Meanwhile, two more operations followed.

Betty's husband took time off from his business to maintain a constant vigil in her room—checking reports, seeking every possible avenue of hope. Her father, a clergyman, stood by her bed every day, his voice raised in praise and worship of the Lord.

More days passed—25, 30. The doctors were certain that the comatose patient could see or hear nothing.

"That was not the case," Betty Malz told me during our interview. "All that time that I was a prisoner of my own body, when I couldn't speak, see or smell, or control the movement of a muscle, I could hear everything the doctors, nurses and visitors said. It was as though when my physical senses went, all spiritual senses were sharpened. If people came into my room feeling hopeless about me, I knew it. When they had faith that I would get well, I knew that, and it helped me." "If only people could realize," Betty said with great emphasis, "that in any form of unconsciousness or coma—even under anesthetics, I do believe—unerringly the spirit picks up those attitudes."

Betty described how one day she heard footsteps coming into her room, followed by the pages of a book being turned. When the person quietly began to read a psalm, she recognized the voice of Art, a man she had never liked.

"In those days," Betty told me, "I was a thoroughgoing snob, and God chose this man as His instrument to correct that."

As Art read on—Psalm 107, all of it, and then Psalm 108—the words seemed to the helpless woman on the bed to be the most beautiful words she had ever heard: "Their soul abhorreth all manner of meat; and they draw near unto the gates of death. Then they cry unto the Lord in their trouble, and He saveth them out of their distresses. He sent His word and healed them, and delivered them from their destructions. . . ." (Psalm 107:18-20)

"He sent His word and healed them." To the desperately ill Betty the words seemed written in fire. She had been handed her lifeline. Betty silently blessed the man whom she had despised.

Then came a new crisis. All supplies of B-negative blood in Terre Haute, Indianapolis and St. Louis had been used. The doctor warned that unless they could find blood plasma for her immediately, Betty would be gone in a few hours.

Was it a coincidence that that very morning Betty's Uncle Jesse, a freight conductor-dispatcher for the Pennsylvania Railroad, felt a strange inner prompting that he should leave his job and go immediately to offer his blood? Unacquainted with this kind of guidance, the man argued with the inner Voice. "This doesn't make sense. I'm at the end of a run, still miles from home. I don't want to go in my work clothes. I'll wait until late this afternoon after I'm cleaned up. Why, I don't even know if my blood is the right type."

But finding no inner peace, the conductor finally dropped what he was doing and headed for the hospital. They discovered that Uncle Jesse had B-negative blood. Once again the blood transfusion helped Betty rally.

On July 31, Betty's fever shot still higher as pneumonia set in. Then her veins collapsed completely; no more transfusions or intravenous feedings were possible.

"The battle is lost," the exhausted family was told. "You'd better get some rest. We'll call you if there's any change."

Sadly Betty's husband drove home and her parents drove the 31 miles to their home in Clay City.

At 2:30 the next morning, Betty's father was sharply awakened—he did not know how. He had a strong compulsion to get to the hospital immediately. He resisted at first. Finally he gave in, dressed and was on his way shortly after four a.m.

Some time after he had left the house, the telephone rang. It was a nurse calling. "Mrs. Perkins, I'm so sorry to have to give you this message. Your daughter Betty expired a few minutes ago." There was a pause. " I've already called her husband, of course. He will be coming over as soon as possible this morning."

Concern for her own husband temporarily overcame Mrs. Perkins' anguished grief. "But *my* husband is already on his way there. *Please* have someone watch for him and intercept him. It would be a dreadful shock for him to walk into Betty's room and find her."

The nurse promised—and hung up.

But Betty's father parked at the side of the hospital and slipped in through a nurses' exit door. This next part of the story I heard from Betty's father himself.

"I walked down the hospital corridor. Everything seemed too quiet, too deserted," he told me. "I remember how my heart skipped a beat as I rounded the corner . . . stood in the doorway . . . saw the still form on the bed. Betty was covered with a sheet. Every bit of apparatus had been removed, all instruments; even the chart was gone.

"I was stunned and despairing. I couldn't even pray, I could only stand by the bed softly crying, 'Jesus! Jesus!'."

How could the sorrowing man possibly have known the extraordinary adventure his daughter was experiencing at that moment? Let Betty tell it:

"I was walking up a steep hill. Yet there was no muscular exertion. It was more like a light skipping or floating movement, without effort. I thought, *Why, steep hills have always affected the muscles in the calves of my legs.* There was none of that—all movement was a delight. The grass under my feet was a vivid green and of a velvety texture, yet every blade seemed alive.

"To my right was a high silvery marble wall. To the left, slightly behind me, was a tall angel. I could see only his feet as he walked, and the bottom of his garment swaying as in a gentle breeze. In the near distance were the echoes of multitudes of voices singing, worshiping Jesus.

"As the angel and I reached the top of the hill, I saw tall ornate gates, the tops of a scroll-like Gothic design. The gates had a translucent quality like pearl. There were no handles, no way I could have opened them. The angel stepped forward and pressed his palms against the gate.

"I stood there for what seemed like a long time, reveling in the wonderful music. The feel of beauty was everywhere. From time to time I would sing along with the voices in the distance. I remember two of the songs—old, old hymns: *For I Have Been Born Again* and *The Old Account Was Settled Long Ago*. Finally the angel spoke. 'Would you like to enter and sing with them?'

"I answered, 'No, I would like to stand here and sing awhile, then go back to my family.'

"The angel nodded. I sensed that the choice was mine. Then I was coming back down the grassy slope, and the sun was on my left coming up over the wall. I remember noticing details like the sharp shadow of the beautiful gates on the wall."

It was at that moment that the world of spirit and this world of time and space fused back together for Betty. In her room the sun was also coming up. Under the sheet Betty began to feel the rising sun warming her cold body.

Despite the sheet over her head, Betty saw moving, wavy letters about two inches high go before her like a ticker-tape message on the sunbeams. She has no idea whether she was "seeing" with her spirtual eyes or with her physical eyes. After what she had experienced on the grassy slope, she knew that the one is as real as the other.

"The letters," Betty told me, "seemed composed of translucent ivory, only fluid—moving through the rays of the sun. They stretched all the way from the window, past my bed, on into the room, and read, 'I am the resurrection and the life; he that believeth in Me, *though he were dead*, yet shall he live.' (John 11:25)

"The words were so alive that they pulsated. I knew that I had to touch those living words. When I, by faith, reached up to grasp the words, I pushed the sheet off my face. At that instant the Word literally became life to me; the warmth in the moving letters flowed into my fingers and up my arm. I sat up in bed. I was *alive!*"

At first Betty did not notice her father standing beside her; she had eyes only for the unearthly light in the room and she began to search for its source. Her first awareness was of the vivid greenness of the grass on the hospital lawn—*So beautiful!* she thought—and of a black man carrying on his shoulder a case of 7-Up into the building. Into Betty's heart welled a great love for that man. Then, at last, she noticed her father by her bed.

He was standing there stunned, too stunned to cry out or to hug her ecstatically or to shed tears of joy. Rather, he was rooted to the spot, struck dumb with awe before the majesty of the working of God Himself.

His second reaction was a consuming curiousity to know what Betty had seen. For most of the experience taking place before his eyes had been veiled from him. "Betty, Betty, tell me. What's been going on? *Describe it*," he ordered, completely forgetting that his daughter had not spoken in weeks.

Nurses and doctors streamed in and out, asking questions. There had been no breathing, no heartbeat, no blood pressure. Between 20 and 30 minutes had elapsed between the telephone call to Mrs. Perkins and the moment Betty had sat up in bed. Now everybody wanted to see Betty, wanted to hear the story from her own lips. When Betty's own doctor kept shaking his head in disbelief, she would look at him in astonishment. "But I'm *alive*. I can talk and see and smell and feel. I feel *fine*. And when do I eat?"

Betty had eaten nothing in almost six weeks. Her digestive organs had already started to disintegrate. Hesitantly the doctor authorized giving her an experimental four ounces of 7-Up over crushed ice.

Betty waited eagerly for the drink. Instead, around noon, a tray was set before her—two pork chops, applesauce, cottage cheese, a square of lemon cake with warm sauce, a pot of tea. Hungrily she ate every morsel, thinking it the most delicious food she had ever tasted.

Shortly after that, a flustered nurse rushed in a mobile unit. "I'm going to have to pump out your stomach. You got the wrong tray."

"Oh, *please* . . . " Betty protested as the nurse began uncoiling the tubing. "The food tasted so good. It's staying down fine—just *fine*." After the nurse left, Betty lay there speculating on God's sense of humor. (Pork chops for the doctor's first experiment?)

The next day the doctor closed Betty's door, pulled up a chair and sat by the bed holding her hand. He spoke softly, his voice kind. "There are some medical facts I must help you face," he began gravely. "You may have a hard life ahead of you. Peritonitis and gangrene have caused a disintegration of the organs of your body. You may have to wear a bag on your side for elimination. In my opinion, you must never try to have another child."

The doctor went on to warn Betty that she had been blind for weeks and should be ready for this to recur. Further, so many heavy narcotics had been administered that there was every likelihood of a severe withdrawal problem.

Betty lay there letting the grim words pour over her, but somehow they didn't penetrate. "I certainly want to be realistic," she told the kind doctor. She had always prided herself on being a down-to-earth person, but now, the knowledge of that other world—so beautiful, so solid, where everything is right, so close at hand—lingered and would not be denied. Deep within her was the assurance that God "doeth all things well." (Mark 7:37)

Many years have gone by. Betty never had to wear a bag. Her eyesight has been better than ever.

"And any other baby you have might well be deformed," the doctor had said. Sitting there in the living room at our farm, instinctively Betty's eyes, and mine, went to her delightful daughter April, who was romping in the yard outside. Nothing ethereal or other-worldly about this healthy little girl. Her mother's joy in life is clearly reflected in her.

Great as the physical miracle for Betty Malz is, much greater still are the gifts and graces that have accompanied it. Among them, a new appreciation for life itself, a new love for people. "I had to 'die' to learn how to live," she told me. "God had to take my life away long enough to teach me how to use it. Best of all, now I know there's nothing at all to fear in death. It's simply changing locations.

"Every morning is like Easter. I wake up to the light of day so grateful. Unfailingly the dawn breaks, part of the Light of the world. Just as unfailing is His love and care for each one of us. Now I know—we can trust Him utterly."

Verily, verily, I say unto you, he that heareth my word, and believeth on him that sent me, hath everlasting life, and shall not come into condemnation; but is passed from death unto life. (John 5:24)

The Nine-Hour
Prayer

by MAY SHERIDAN GOLD

He was only six years old when the accident happened. I don't know how I knew it was really serious, for he complained of no pain, but I knew—I was positive.

Andy had been out in the front yard helping his dad get rid of some tall weeds in the vacant lot adjoining our property. Suddenly he came in the front door wiping moisture from his left cheek and said, "My eye is watering, Mommy."

I'll never know how or why I was so certain, but I felt a reaction like a blow in the pit of my stomach, and words formed in my mind, "His eye is hurt badly." After trying to say some calming words to him, I went straight to the phone to call the pediatrician. It was 11:30 a.m. on a sunny Saturday morning. I told Doctor Wiedman that Andy's eye was hurt and that I needed for him to see Andy right away.

My husband Dan came in, and was surprised to find me calling the doctor since Andy was not even crying or saying that his eye hurt. But perhaps he thought my anxiety was due to the fact that I was expecting a baby, our third child, in two months.

While driving the two miles, I looked over at Andy, and with a sense of shock noted that his left eye was no longer shiny and blue. It looked dull, gray and almost flat. When we stopped at a light, I asked him to cover his right eye with his hand and tell me if he could see me. "No! That's funny," he said, "I can't see."

When we entered Doctor Wiedman's office, he greeted us, and after one hard look at Andy across the room, he left to bring back the eye specialist near his office. The eye doctor was very kind, but after a quick look and a few questions, he left. He returned quickly to say, "Mrs. Gold, there is one eye surgeon in this town who I feel might be able to help. I've called him at the Episcopal Eye, Ear, Nose and Throat Hospital, and he will meet you there." Noting my condition, both doctors suggested that my husband come and drive us there, which he did.

When the three of us reached the hospital, Dr. John Harry King greeted us in the gentlest way. He examined Andy deftly, talking to him reassuringly as he did so. He spoke to us privately. "Mr. and Mrs. Gold, the cornea of Andy's eye has somehow been pierced, perhaps by a thorn. The reason it looks dull is that all of the fluid has gone out through the hole. Unfortunately there is no surgery that we can perform."

"Is there any chance the eye can be saved?" I asked, desperately.

He paused, carefully choosing his words. "Yes, Mrs. Gold, a faint chance. The hole could heal and some of the fluid re-form. But, I must warn you it is a very, very slim chance and a medical rarity." He agreed that we should give the eye every chance for any possible healing, and as this meant both eyes must be bandaged, we felt I should stay with Andy in the hospital.

It was a very old hospital, and they led us to a long, narrow room where they put Andy in a bed with sides to be sure he didn't fall. A cot was brought in for me, and our vigil of keeping a healthy, active, six-year-old boy with bandaged eyes completely still and quiet began. When I quickly went home for a suitcase and some books to read to him, I made several calls, asking for prayers for our Andy.

Back at the hospital, the long evening finally drew to a close, and as things quieted down, I hoped Andy would sleep. Before he did, I asked him to pray with me. I'd found a special prayer at home, one I'd had but never used, except to read it casually. It was called a Nine-Hour Novena, and I had always liked its wording. "Ask and ye shall receive; seek and ye shall find; knock and it shall be opened to you. Dear Lord, I ask, I seek, I knock, and request that my petition be granted."

Andy repeated each phrase after me. I intended to make the prayer for him at hourly intervals all night long. He asked me to wake him so he could pray, too.

Though there was no air conditioning and the room was stifling hot, Andy quickly fell asleep. When I was sure he wouldn't hear me, I knelt beside the cot and wept. But then, prayer came, "Dear Lord, please heal Andy's eye . . . he wasn't

doing anything wrong or being silly . . . he was helping his dad.
You know how he always notices everything in the house with
his bright eyes; how he can find things for us all; how he tries to
help watch his little brother. Oh, please, please don't let that
eye be blinded." Then I added a special request, "Help me to
wake each hour, on the hour, to say the novena." As tired as I
was, this was asking a great deal.

I seemed to fall asleep quickly, as Andy had. I woke up later
and looked at my watch. It was exactly 11 p.m. I knelt again,
and read the prayer from a light in the hall. I whispered,
"Andy?" He, too, was awake and joined me in the prayer, then
seemed to go right back to sleep. I drowsed off too, but at
midnight some inner alarm clock sounded and I prayed again.
After the third time this happened, exactly this way, I was no
longer surprised. It seemed natural and right and I somehow
felt sure it was God's way of letting us know we were in His care.

When I read the prayer for the sixth time—at three a.m.—I
felt the greatest warmth and sense of comfort I can recall. The
words came alive, bringing tears of gratitude to my eyes.
Though I didn't hear an audible voice inside, I felt God speaking to me, reassuring me, inviting me to let go, to relinquish
Andy's problem to Him.

"Thank You, Lord," I murmured, "for caring, for staying so
close at this time. Yes, I trust You to deal with Andy's eye." I had
no way of knowing if my child would indeed see again, but
whatever happened I knew God would help us through the
ordeal. I felt so very loved, somehow, in that dismal little room.

At 6 a.m., as we said the prayer for the last time, we heard
activities beginning in the hallways. Doctor King had agreed to
come in very early, around 8:30, I think, and my husband and I
met him when he arrived. The doctor talked with Andy a bit
before beginning to remove the bandage to check for possible
infection.

As he took the bandage off, I saw the incredulous look on
Doctor King's face. Then I looked at Andy.

The eye was round again! It was bright blue, and shining,
exactly like the other eye.

"Mrs. Gold, what have you done?" the doctor exclaimed,

which, in retrospect, was an odd question. When I told him quickly and briefly of our "nine-hour prayer," the doctor himself had tears in his eyes. Gently he covered Andy's "good" eye, held up two fingers and asked, "How many?" Andy said, "Two," then replied correctly to other tests Doctor King tried.

"This is most gratifying," Doctor King said. "I've never seen anything like it."

Along with our joy and gratitude, he had to caution us, however. Now proper care was more important than ever. Andy must not risk bumping his head, which might collapse his eye. He must remain still, with both eyes bandaged. Infection could occur, so he must take antibiotics. A few days later, Doctor King soberly told me that I must realize that though his eye might be saved cosmetically, must not expect his vision to be normal. But, whenever I prayed, I seemed to remember that the whole thing had been handed over to God, and surely that must include Andy's vision.

Our next weeks were difficult ones, with five more days in the hospital and strict bed care at home to follow. Our second son, Skip, had to be sent to his grandparents, to help keep things calm for Andy. We visited Doctor King's office every third day, which meant a trip all the way to town, with Andy, by then, wearing a patch over one eye. When the day finally came to conduct a vision test, we discovered, joyfully, that the vision in that eye was almost normal and in later years it became perfect. The last time Doctor King saw Andy, he could not even find the scar where the hole was until he consulted his chart, the scar was so tiny.

In looking back, I know it was not just the novena that brought healing. It was prayer, repeated prayer, ceaseless prayer, unrelenting prayer—our own, plus the prayers of others —that brought us to the point where we relinquished the problem to God. To this day, if you ask him, Doctor King, the very famous eye surgeon whose cornea-preservation technique led to the beginning of the International Eye Foundation, will tell you that it was prayer that brought about one of the most remarkable occurrences he has ever witnessed—the restoration of a small boy's eye.

**Her husband was dying of cancer and it
would take a miracle to save him.**

Until Tomorrow
Comes

by WANDA KELLY

The spring day that was to change our lives so drastically
started like any other—in a humdrum way. The alarm
clock rang, I dressed quickly and headed downstairs to make
breakfast for my husband Orville and our four children.

In the kitchen I set the table, put the coffeepot on the stove
to perk and started preparing oatmeal. The sun was just coming
up, and it was probably a glorious sight rising over the Mississippi (we can see the river from our house), but I was too
preoccupied to notice. I was still trying to figure out the math
problem that had stumped my 13-year-old son Mark and me the
night before.

Before I could get the problem solved, Orville interrupted
my thoughts by slumping into his chair at the table. "Honey,"
he said with a sigh, "I discovered something just now as I was
washing under my arm—I felt a lump there."

Even though our kitchen was toasty warm, a chill of fear
swept through my body as I recalled how Orville had been
coming home from work for months complaining of being so
tired. But I didn't want anything serious to touch this husky
man I loved so much, so I said, "Now, don't worry so much.
You're probably still feeling the effects of that flu you've had.
But if the lump doesn't go away in a few days, you should have it
checked."

By the time he went to the doctor several days later there
were three lumps. Orville told him about the nagging tired
feeling and his lack of energy.

"Well, we'll remove one of the lumps," the doctor said

99

matter-of-factly, "and have it checked."

When the day came for the biopsy, we took my mother and Mark with us to the hospital. I didn't say anything to Tammy, 11, Lori, 8, or Britt, 4, about their father's problem. While waiting in the hospital lounge, my mother and I passed the time by recounting events of the 14 years since Orville and I had married. There was our first meeting one morning in the little restaurant where I worked—Orville's big brown eyes were heart-melters—marriage, children, chicken pox, drafty farmhouses, overdue fuel bills, Orville's struggle to find his calling. He had made a lot of job changes before he began writing for newspapers—and then his search was over. He loved newspaper work . . .

Mark interrupted us. I looked up to see a nurse beckoning; she escorted me into an office. The doctor was mercifully quick. "Mrs. Kelly, your husband has lymphoma."

"Can-cer?" I stammered. I could hardly bring myself to say the word. Numbly I stumbled out of the doctor's office. My eyes began to burn and I knew I was about to cry, but I bit my lip and drove a fingernail into my palm. "Not here, Wanda, not here," I told myself.

Straightening, I marched down the hall to the office to see about Blue Cross and hospital papers, then to the lobby and outside. The cold air had barely hit my face when the first tear ran down my cheek. By the time I got to the parking lot I was sobbing uncontrollably. "Mom, I'm going to lose him," I wailed. "Why, God? He's only forty-two."

After a couple of minutes I pulled myself together, dried my eyes, powdered my face and pasted on a smile. By the time we had driven around to the hospital entrance to pick up Orville, I thought I looked okay, but he knew I'd been crying. "Don't worry, honey," he said as he stepped into the car. "I'll be all right." But his voice was listless, and I had to clench my teeth to keep from crying again.

After dropping off Orville, Mark and Mother at the house, I took the baby-sitter home. Hurrying back home, I passed a church and suddenly decided to go in. I was grateful there was no one there because I ran down the aisle and threw myself on the floor in front of the altar.

"God, dear God," I sobbed, "please give us a miracle. Heal Orville. I beg You." I don't know how long I lay there pleading, weeping, but after awhile I got up, left the church and went on home.

Orville was lying on the davenport, staring at the ceiling. We exchanged some meaningless conversation and I went to the kitchen to fix dinner. At the table the kids were as noisy as ever, but Orville ate in silence and left as soon as he was finished. Not once did he say anything about the doctor's report and not once did the word cancer come up in our conversation.

After further hospital tests, the doctors told Orville he might have as little as six months or as long as three years to live.

From then on, Orville and I talked very little to each other. And a tension began to build up in our home. Gone was the gaiety that had always been a part of our marriage and our household. No longer were there picnics or barbecues or rides for an evening ice-cream cone as had been so common in the past.

Although the children didn't know what was wrong, they became edgy and upset. I became sharp sometimes with Mother, and she began crying over the slightest thing. When I tried to talk to friends about our situation, they said, "Don't think about it," and tried to change the subject. Gradually, perhaps out of fear and not knowing what to say, our friends stopped seeing us. There was no one to talk to, nothing to say. I've never felt so alone or lonely in my life. And I knew it was even worse for Orville.

He spent most of his time in the study lying down. In fact, that is where he slept at night. Coming to bed with me would have meant that we would be forced to talk to each other, something neither of us could bear. Though I wanted to say something loving, positive, hopeful, and I was sure he wanted to reassure me, we couldn't find any honest words, so we remained silent.

Meanwhile, I'd spend hours pleading with God. And every night before going to bed I prayed the same prayer. "God, heal Orville, please. . . ."

Then Orville was placed on chemotherapy. For his treatments we'd have to drive to a hospital in Iowa City. I'll never forget that first return trip. We had taken Britt along and he was asleep in the back seat. Inside the car there was complete silence except for the purr of the engine and the humming of the tires.

Suddenly Orville spoke, clearly and distinctly, in a tone I hadn't heard for weeks. "Wanda," he said, "you know, I'm not dead yet." Abruptly he pulled the car off the highway and parked. "Honey, I've got cancer. Cancer. And I'll probably die of it. But I'm not dead yet. We've got to talk about it."

I reached over and touched his hand. "Are you sure you want to?" I asked.

"Yes, I'm sure," he continued. "We've got to face it together. I know you haven't told me the way you really feel. I don't know how we can help each other if we don't talk about it. I've just been moping around the house making everyone miserable." He took a deep breath. "Let's go home and have a barbecue tonight," he said. "And tell the kids. I don't want to waste any more time living like we have."

Pulling me to him, Orville threw his arms around me and gave me a long kiss. For the first time in weeks I felt a flicker of our old happiness. The sun was shining brilliantly on the rich fields and bright fall leaves. Part of a great burden had been lifted off my shoulders and I felt alive again.

I bought spareribs on the way home and that evening we cooked out just like old times. After dinner I put little Britt to bed and we called Mark, Tammy and Lori to join us on the back porch.

It was a lovely starlit night. In the distance the moom shimmered on the Mississippi. As the children gathered around, Orville said, "I think it's time you knew what's wrong with me." Then he explained that he had cancer—a disease that destroys parts of the body—and the doctors said he would probably die of it. Tammy's eyes began to fill with tears and Orville drew her to him.

"But I'm not dead yet, honey. I've started treatments and I'm going to stay alive just as long as I possibly can. Sometimes things may get bad, but I want you all to help me to live with this. We don't have to like death, but we don't have to be terrified by it either."

Orville hugged and kissed each child and saw them off to bed. As he did, a dark cloud seemed to lift from our house. After the children left, Orville and I sat together on the porch for a long time.

"Wanda," he finally said, taking my hand, "when this happened, I cursed God. Why did He do this to me? Why not somebody like that drunk down the street who has no family?

"Well, driving home from the hospital today in our deathly silent car, I felt so bad I finally turned to God for an answer. And do you know what my answer was? To go home and barbecue. To start living again. *Why not?* I thought. I can still move about. The very idea that almost-normal life could go on, if I'd allow it, really charged me up."

Orville turned and put his arm around me. "You know, honey, it's like being on a train, and far ahead of you down the track you see your final destination. But there are many station stops in-between. Well, instead of concentrating on that final destination, I decided to take advantage of each stop along the way and make the most of the remainder of the journey.

"Wanda, I don't really know how many days I have left. For that matter, none of us knows how much time we have left on this earth. So why not grab each day as it comes, make the most of it, explore it to the fullest, enjoy all its delights and treasures. God wants us to, I'm sure."

With his new attitude, new energy seemed to flow into Orville. A few days later he sat down at his typewriter and wrote an article for the Burlington newspaper telling how it feels to be a person with a terminal illness. After the story appeared, we were deluged with letters from all kinds of patients and their families. It gave Orville the idea of starting some kind of club. Maybe people in life-threatening situations could help one another. The first meeting was held on January 25, 1974, in the Burlington Elks lodge. The 18 people who attended decided to call their group Make Today Count (MTC). Others heard of MTC and formed chapters around the country.

Soon Orville was traveling all over the country, to speak and to be interviewed.

And my life began to change, too. Becoming more aware of the potential of each and every day gave me the incentive to finish high school. Realizing that I might someday be shouldering responsibility for our family's welfare, I completed my high-school credits. Later on I hope to go to college.

Even more importantly, as I've watched Orville renew himself, my own faith in God has blossomed. God had always been real to me, but now, being involved in something so positive and fulfilling as MTC, I'm discovering new strength in God and feel that His word comforts me more than ever.

The other day Orville drew my attention to the lilacs outside our door. They were full-budded, waiting to break forth once

---

ORVILLE KELLY'S TEN SUGGESTIONS
TO HELP LIVE WITH A TERMINAL ILLNESS

1. Talk about the illness. If it is cancer, call it cancer. You can't make life normal again by trying to hide what is wrong.
2. Accept death as a part of life. It is.
3. Consider each day as another day of life, a gift from God to be enjoyed as fully as possible.
4. Realize that life is never going to be perfect. It wasn't before and it won't be now.
5. Pray. It isn't a sign of weakness; it is your strength.
6. Learn to live with your illness instead of considering yourself dying from it. We are all dying in some manner.
7. Put your friends and relatives at ease yourself. If you don't want pity, don't ask for it.
8. Make all practical arrangements for funerals, wills, etc. and make certain your family understands them.
9. Set new goals; realize your limitations. Sometimes the simple things of life become the most enjoyable.
10. Discuss your problems with your family as they occur. Include the children if possible. After all, your problem is not an individual one.

more. They reminded me so much of Orville's own renewal.

Today, Orville is busier than ever with his work. How many more spings God will give him is anybody's guess. What Orville does know is that in trying to help others he has found the life more abundant that Christ talks about. (John 10:10) And having learned what that means, he is living his life—and I am as well—one grateful day at a time. That's the only way each of us can make every day of our lives count.

As I leaned close to Orville, I remembered my plea asking God for a miracle.

God had answered. When Orville's physical body will die is no longer important. God has already healed him. In fact, He has healed us both.

EDITOR'S NOTE: In his book, *Make Today Count* (Delacorte Press), Orville Kelly tells how the organization that bears the same name helps terminally ill people cope with their problems. Says Kelly of MTC meetings, "They give cancer patients an opportunity to talk honestly about their feelings and to discuss their anxieties and fears with others whose circumstances are similar." In addition to informal discussions, ministers, psychiatrists, physicians and lawyers are often asked to speak at meetings. There are now over 100 MTC chapters around the country.

If you would like to know how you can help or if you want additional information about Make Today Count, please write to: Make Today Count, c/o Guideposts, Carmel, New York 10512

At age 17, Joni Eareckson suffered a broken
neck in a diving accident and was paralyzed
from the shoulders down. What has
happened since is a testimony to her
indestructible spirit and indomitable faith.

There's Only One
Handicap in Life

by JONI EARECKSON

It happened on a steamy, hot July day in 1967. The afternoon
was fast dying, and my sister Kathy and I were hurrying
toward Chesapeake Bay for a swim. It was exhilarating, zipping
down the road in her yellow VW. Dressed in our bathing suits,
we felt free as the wind that cooled our bodies and tousled our
hair.

At age 17, I had just graduated from Woodland High School
near Baltimore, where I'd been voted class athlete. Confident
and assured, I had everything anyone needs—loving parents,
three supportive sisters, a steady boyfriend and an acceptance
from the college of my choice. I was on top of the world.

Finally we arrived at our favorite swimming spot and in a
flash we were out of the car, running for the shore. I got to the
beach first and threw myself into the surf. I swam out to a raft
not too far off shore.

I knifed into the refreshing water in near-perfect form. The
water was much too shallow, and as my body broke the surface
my head was snapped back. "Diving into shallow water! How
stupid can you get!" I chided myself.

That thought was interrupted by a hot electrical current that
jolted my body. The next thing I knew, I was face down on the
bottom of the bay, immobile, unable to raise myself to the
surface. Finally my head was lifted out of the water by Kathy,
and I gasped for breath.

Kathy dragged my limp body to the shore. Then an ambulance came and took me to University Hospital, where doctors bustled around me and whispered to each other about dislocations and broken vertebrae. Over and over I told myself that my numbness would wear off, until someone plunged a needle into my arm, and I blacked out.

When I awoke I found myself sandwiched between a two-sided canvas frame called a Stryker bed. My head was held taut by some sort of tongs. I tried to move. I couldn't.

I soon learned that I had severed my spinal cord between the fourth and fifth cervical levels. That meant that I had broken my neck, and I was paralyzed from my shoulders down.

It took a while for the severity of my injury to take on meaning, but when it did I was filled with the fear of death.

"The Lord is my Shepherd," I said over and over through those interminable early hours and days. "God, don't let me die," I pleaded. "I'm too young, I have so much to live for. Help me."

As a teen-ager I had been active in my church and in an organization called Young Life. I was a Christian in a comfortable sort of way. It fit my purposes.

But now, suddenly, I found myself in a different position. No longer on top of the world, I was on the bottom looking up, praying for God to answer my prayers.

When it became apparent that I wasn't going to die, I realized that I might not get well either. That possibility was almost as scary as death.

"God, You wouldn't let me live in this shell of a body, would You?" I cried out in despair. "You wouldn't be so cruel as to let me spend the rest of my life like this?"

"Of course not," I told myself. "God isn't like that. He's going to heal me, and I'm going to run and swim and dance and ride Tumbleweed again." Tumbleweed was my jumper—a beautiful bay mare. We'd done well together in horse show competition, and I missed working out with her. But as time went by I knew I might never ride again.

For a while I held out hope that an operation would make me well. In fact, when the doctors said that I was to undergo a spinal fusion, we all took that to mean that the operation would enable me to walk again. But, after the surgery, the doctor's words were bluntly final.

"You're going to have to face facts," he said, after Mom had asked him when I could start getting ready for college. "Joni will be totally paralyzed below her shoulders for the rest of her life."

My parents, sisters and friends came to the hospital regularly to try to cheer me up, but it was mostly in vain. It was tough to hear of my friends' exciting plans without feeling depressed.

At some of our Young Life meetings, we would read Bible passages and try to apply the teachings to our lives. I was always an outspoken participant.

"Show me," I would challenge my friends, "how God is really working in our lives." Now, kids would bring their Bibles to the hospital and read me passages that they hoped would make sense of my situation. They likened me to New Testament characters who had suffered. "The key to their peace," offered my girl friend, Jackie, "was that they knew that life was just a fleeting moment compared with eternity." I turned my head and sighed.

"There's just no purpose to all this," I cried in frustration. "Please help me end it. Just give me some pills, *anything*." And I think I would have tried to commit suicide if I had had a way.

After nearly one year on the Stryker Frame bed I was able to sit up, and before long doctors were talking about therapy. One day a young woman named Chris, a therapist, suggested that I might be able to write or draw with my mouth. I refused.

"That's disgusting, degrading!" I growled.

After she left the room I prayed, "Please, God, I can accept the fact that I'll never be able to walk, but please give me back my hands. Let me have some semblance of normal life again."

Soon, thanks to the patience and understanding of my family, friends and therapist. I lost my stubbornness and took the pencil in my teeth. At first it was hard, but soon I was able to do some sketching.

My art helped me relax, and my new mental state apparently helped me physically. I'd had a problem with skin ulcers. Now, because I had gained weight, they started healing. Also, I was able to spend more time in a wheelchair. The doctors decided I could go home. Home! After nearly two years in the hospital, I was overjoyed at seeing, smelling and hearing the pleasures of my home again.

In the days ahead I read a lot, wrote many letters and drew some pictures. I went back to Young Life meetings. Sure, my old friends were in college and into different things, but I made new friends. Faith was still a challenging discussion at our meetings, and as I talked about my faith and my experience, I seemed to grow spiritually. "All things work together for good to those who love God," I began telling myself. Maybe He had some purpose in all this.

Then I met Donald—tall, ruggedly handsome—a guy from Young Life who seemed to look at me and forget all about my handicap. My sister Jay worried and kept cautioning me about getting too involved. But, I countered, Donald was 27 and I was now 22. Weren't we old enough to know what we were doing? I had prayed that God would bless our relationship and help it grow. Yes, I even dreamed of marriage.

In my blissful selfishness, I guess I didn't listen too closely for God's answer. Donald and I spent a year together, bound in professed love. Donald took me for walks on the beach, to the movies, on picnics—he made me feel like a woman.

Then the bubble burst. I had felt it coming for weeks, but refused to acknowledge it.

Donald was scheduled to be a counselor at a Young Life camp in New York that summer. But the day he was to leave he stopped at my house to say more than a temporary good-by. There was a finality in his voice.

"What do you mean, 'good-by'?" I said. "You'll be gone for several weeks, but then . . . "

"No, Joni, this is it. I'm sorry. We should never have talked and dreamed of marriage. It was a mistake."

"A mistake! What do you mean?" I said, my temper rising. "I went from fear to hope because you told me you loved me and wanted us to build a life together. Now you say it was a mistake. Were you just leading me along . . . ?" My voice faltered from the hurt I felt inside.

Tears streamed down my face. I was going to lose him!

I tried to get control of myself. "Maybe you need time to reconsider . . . "

"No, Joni," Donald said. "It's over. I'm sorry." Then he turned and walked toward the door. I wanted to run after him. "Wait!" I sobbed, but he went out the door and out of my life.

"Oh, God, why have You let this happen?" I screamed. "Why are You hurting me like this?"

For a while I sank into a depression as deep as the one I felt after I learned I would never walk again. I was full of rage at Donald and self-pity for myself. But this time, instead of turning away from God, I turned toward Him. Somehow I knew only God could make sense out of my confusion. I read the Bible. I prayed, "It is hard for me to accept the fact that marrying Donald was not Your will for me, God, but if You have something better, show me."

I recalled hearing a preacher say one time that God never closes a door but what He opens a window. I took the promise at face value and waited. And as I waited I began to come to grips with myself. There were some things that were not going to happen. I would never walk. I probably would never marry, but there were some other things I could do. Some options were left. I began to lay out my future, lining up the positive things I had on my side of the ledger. Slowly, like piling bricks one on top of the other, I felt God leading me toward a solution.

One day while sitting outside in my wheelchair, enjoying a warm, summer sun, some thoughts took shape and became unbelievably clear. I came to understand why Donald had been sent into my life. I had needed his love and support to satisfy my emotional vacuum. Now, though it had been painful, I realized I was free. I had finally gained emotional independence. My only real need now was complete dependence on God.

"Lord," I said. "I wish I could have seen this earlier. I could have, if I'd remembered Your grace is always sufficient."

As I sat there an inner joy flooded my soul. Then I looked up and saw something coming toward me from high among the trees. It was a beautiful butterfly, which flew mystically closer until it was only inches away. I am sure it was God's way of assuring me of His love.

"Lord, thank You for Your goodness," I said.

From that time forward I quit questioning God about the whys in my life and began asking Him how. And He has shown me in ways I would never have felt possible.

New understanding flooded my soul, and for the first time I could truly thank God for sending Donald into my life. The animosity I felt vanished, and in its place came deep insight about real love. I came to see how self-serving, enveloping, possessing and smothering I had been. My "love" for Donald had little resemblance to the generous, tolerant, giving kind of love Paul describes in 1 Corinthians 13.

Eventually, Donald and I sat down and discussed what God had taught us from our relationship. These conversations re-established a friendship which has continued to this day.

I began to spend more time at my drawing board, working with a new intensity, and the results were better than ever. Soon my art was opening new channels of fulfillment. The minister who had said that God never closes a door but what He opens a window, was wrong. He opens dozens of windows!

Whereas I once thought my handicap had robbed me forever of a full life, I discovered that I had everything I needed to serve God. A sound mind, an ability to write and draw, and opportunities to speak and tell others of His love and power. There is only one handicap in life, I have discovered. That is living without the knowledge of God. With Him, we have everything we need.

I was losing my hearing. I was deeply worried.
Then by chance—or was it chance?—I met . . .

The Remarkable
Doctor Rosen

by RUTH STAFFORD PEALE

The first time I realized I had a hearing problem was when I tried to listen to my watch tick and found I couldn't. With my left ear I could still hear it, but not with my right. When I consulted a doctor, he confirmed that I had a serious hearing loss. At that point, he wasn't sure why.

Months of tests and examinations followed. Fortunately, the hearing in my "good" ear remained normal. But if a person sat on my "deaf" side, I had to twist my head awkwardly to hear. It was troublesome and a bit frightening at times.

It was during this time that I learned to have a feeling of compassion for people with hearing problems, which has never left me. A blind person or any disabled person arouses sympathy immediately. But many people are insensitive about deafness or partial deafness in others. They can't "see" the affliction, and so they tend to be impatient with it. This causes a lot of unhappiness, because there are 14.5 million people in the United States alone who are hard-of-hearing or deaf.

My doctors finally came to the conclusion that my problem was otosclerosis, an overgrowth on a tiny bone called the stapes inside my right ear. This bone is the smallest in the human body; ten of them would just about cover the small fingernail. It's shaped like a stirrup, and is the closest bone to the auditory nerve. Sound makes the stapes vibrate. This stimulates the nerve, which in turn sends the sound-message to the brain where its meaning is deciphered. But in my case the stapes had

112

become rigid, unable to vibrate or react to sound.

Time went by. More treatments and one operation didn't seem to help. Then one day by chance (or was it chance?) I happened to mention to Dr. Louis Bishop, our personal physician, that I had this problem. Louis' wife Kitty, who had a similar problem with both ears, had just been greatly helped by an operation performed by a Dr. Samuel Rosen. A new technique, they told me. A real breakthrough. They urged me to go and see Doctor Rosen in New York. I did, and met a most remarkable physician.

Doctor Rosen was in his 70s, gentle, reassuring—fatherly was the word that described him best. I told him about my problem and asked if he could help me. He smiled. "If God is willing," he said.

He used the same phrase from time to time during subsequent visits when I came in for testing. One day I ventured to ask him why. "When my parents prayed," he said, "whether it was a prayer of supplication or of thanks, they always ended it with, 'If God is willing.' That's a cornerstone of my faith and work."

Doctor Rosen told me that his parents were immigrants. His father had peddled crockery, and his mother had suffered from severe asthma. He recalled that one morning, when he was six years old and preparing to go off to school, his mother had such a severe attack that she could not catch her breath.

"To a child that meant that she would suffocate," Doctor Rosen said. "A doctor came and gave her some medicine, which relieved her, but I would not go to school. I sat by her bedside all day. When I told her that one day I would be a doctor and cure her, she took my hand in hers and said only, 'If God is willing.' "

Doctor Rosen's mother died when she was quite young. His older brothers pooled their labor, their savings and love to send him through medical school. For over 40 years Doctor Rosen has been an ear surgeon at Mt. Sinai Hospital in New York City and has taught ear surgery in its medical school. In his early days he was baffled by otosclerosis, as were all ear specialists. They knew what it is, but not what causes it. The standard surgery, called fenestration, took over four hours, and required the removal of the second of three bones in the middle ear. Sometimes it helped; mostly, it didn't. It usually left the patient dizzy for weeks, even months, and often totally deaf.

Like so many dramatic discoveries in medicine, Doctor Rosen's was an accident. Or was it?

One day, in 1952, while operating on a woman who had had a hearing loss for over 20 years, he was startled to find that her stapes was not entirely rigid, even though otosclerosis had been diagnosed.

"I wondered how many times fenestration was performed on patients like her," Doctor Rosen told me. "I decided that from then on I would first try to test the stapes with a long, thin needle to see if it was rigid before I operated."

In the next five operations the stapes were rigid. So was the sixth, in the case of a 42-year-old engineer, who had been almost deaf for 15 years. But when Doctor Rosen inserted the long needle to make the test, the engineer suddenly shouted, "Doctor, I can hear you!"

"I knew something remarkable had happened," he recalled. "But what?"

He did not remove the bone from the ear; the engineer recovered his hearing. Afterward, Doctor Rosen tried desperately to recall every detail of what he had done. His nights became sleepless, as he tried to find the answer to the question: "How can I do deliberately what I did accidentally?"

For the next 18 months, after his day's work was done, he performed autopsies, studying the tiny stapes. What was its structure? How much pressure could it take? How could he get through the complex labyrinth of the ear to try to move the stapes without damaging it or the other fragile bones?

He designed and made at least three-dozen special instruments. None worked. When he finally made one that promised to work, it broke the arms of the stapes. The search seemed endless, the frustration was deep. I asked him what had kept him going.

"Only the Lord knows how the human mind works," Doctor Rosen said. "But there was something that filled me with hope.

How do you reinforce hope? You pray. I did, every day."

One night, he twisted the delicate sides of one instrument in the hope that it would grasp the neck of the stapes, its strongest part, without damaging it. He wiggled the instrument, and gasped when it moved the base of the stapes—without breaking it. He tried it again and again, and finally murmured, "God is willing!" He labeled the instrument "The Mobilizer," and used it 400 times before he ventured to try it on a living patient.

"Until then I don't think I really understood what my parents meant when they ended their prayers with 'If God is willing,' " he said. "I do now. It could not have happened without His help."

After a series of successful operations, (each takes 30 minutes and requires only a local anesthetic), Doctor Rosen published his findings in medical journals. He was invited to demonstrate and teach the procedure all over the United States and the world. He has done so in 45 countries including Arab and Iron Curtain nations. He always leaves the special set of surgical instruments behind when he departs. He has trained over 1000 doctors to perform the operation, and they in turn have trained others. Doctor Rosen charges no fees for such teaching. Over 750,000 people have been spared possible deafness in this chain of unquestioning love.

On the morning that I arrived for my operation in 1969, I prayed that God would guide Doctor Rosen's gentle hands, and prayed for the strength to accept the outcome, no matter what it was. Doctor Rosen began his work. There was complete silence. About 25 minutes later I thought I heard someone speaking. Was it a fantasy? No. The voice was whispering, "I love you." I looked up in amazement. Doctor Rosen was bending over me, smiling, his lips close to the ear that had been deaf. Now the sound was coming through in the form of the three most beautiful words in any language. "Oh, Doctor Rosen," I said, "I love you, too!"

Since then, my hearing has been perfect. My husband Norman wrote a grateful note to the surgeon. "Only God," he wrote, "could create a Doctor Rosen." I agreed with all my heart.

Doctor Rosen continues to be an active and sought-after consultant. At 80, he feels spiritually and physically ready for any challenge.

Doctor Rosen's latest challenge is to find a cure for nerve deafness, a problem that has baffled medical science for generations. When I asked him if he thought one day he might find the answer, he smiled. "If God is willing," he said.

A TOUCH OF LOVE. "Nice you've come," my grandmother whispered weakly from the bed. Just the night before we had brought her to this nursing home because it now took several people to move her large-boned, crippled body. Her complexion looked pasty in the morning light and her colorless hair was wispy against her pillow. Grandma, always so active, always doing for others. Now her hands lay limp on the sheets—hands which once served heaps of potatoes and fried chicken on blue willow plates, kneaded bread, patched overalls, gathered eggs, churned butter.

I shoved my hands into the pockets of my coat. I felt helpless and awkward, not knowing what to do or say.

Several days later I went to the doctor for a routine treatment. My three-year-old son stood wide-mouthed with fear and concern as we waited.

"Don't worry," I reassured him. "I'm all right."

Then he took my hand and held it quietly in his two small ones. My heart flooded with warmth and thankfulness. And suddenly, with my little boy still holding my hand, I knew what I would do the very next time I visited my grandmother.

Marcia Schwartz

A top country-music singer and television star
tells how God became a reality in his life.

That Long, Long
Night in Arkansas

by ROY CLARK

P eople are always saying how important it is to believe in
yourself if you're going to get anywhere or accomplish
anything. And maybe they're right. But I've learned one more
thing: Before you can really believe in yourself, you have to
believe in Something much bigger than yourself. I found that
out one terrifying but wonderful night in a town in Arkansas
named Conway. My life hasn't been the same since.

To get the story straight, I have to go back about 16 years to
the time when my wife Barbara and I were living in Maryland. I
was playing small local clubs there, struggling along, yet refus-
ing to give up on a boyhood dream to make it as a singer. Ever
since I was 16 and won a national banjo-playing contest, which
included a trip to the Grand Ole Opry in Nashville, being a
successful country-music performer was my one goal. But in
1960, at nearly 30 years of age, it really began to bother me that
nobody had the foggiest idea who Roy Clark was.

One Sunday during this time Barbara and I visited a nearby
church. We felt very much at home there, so much so that we
filled out a card expressing interest in joining. We'd both been
brought up in churches. Now that we'd been married a couple
of years, we wanted to get back to hearing God's word.

A few days after our church visit, a minister came to our
home and talked with Barbara. I was out at the time.

"And what does your husband do?" the preacher asked.

"Roy sings," Barbara said.

"Where does he sing?" he asked.

"Wherever he can," Barbara told him. "Sometimes on radio programs. Sometimes in supper clubs."

A long silence followed. "Well," the preacher said finally, "that's just not right, you know. I'm afraid your husband will have to change jobs if you plan on joining our church."

Barbara was speechless. Nothing more was said, and finally the minister left.

When I got home later, I found Barbara really torn up. She was crying and all confused.

"Oh, Roy," she sobbed, after explaining what happened. "I just don't understand it. We both try to live right. I know how much you want to be a singer. I can't see anything wrong with that."

I put my arms around her and smoothed her hair. "I don't understand either, honey," I said angrily.

God had always been a part of my life, starting back when my father held me on his knee and read me Bible stories. But if this was what religion required . . . *I'll forget about the church and everything connected with it*, I thought. *I've got everything I need to make it on my own.*

That scene provided the final push needed to drive Barbara and me from the East Coast. I was sure a change of place would bring me closer to my dream.

But out West, more disappointment awaited. In Las Vegas, where we stayed for several months, nobody seemed to notice that I was even alive. I played some small clubs, as I had back East, but I was always turned down for bigger things.

Los Angeles would be better, I thought. I was now thinking of recording, maybe even doing some television work.

A friend and his wife invited us to move in with them in their L.A. apartment. But even that turned sour. The landlady, who had rented the apartment to two people, didn't cotton to the idea of twice that number staying there. And my late hours, spent unsuccessfully trying to get record-industry people to listen to me, didn't suit her either. One morning she spotted me coming home as the milkman was making his rounds. Soon after that she served notice; Barbara and I were to be out the following day.

By this time we barely had a nickel to our name. Fortunately Barbara's mother came through and wired us some money. Just enough, we decided, to make it back to Maryland.

After piling all our belongings into a battered old Chevy, we went to a grocery store around the corner to do some last-minute shopping for the trip. Just as I reached into my pocket to pay for our supplies, Barbara slumped to the floor in front of the cash register.

I bent over her, terribly alarmed. "What's the matter, honey?" I asked.

"I've got this pain," Barbara said, holding her side. "The pain's been coming and going the last few days," she said.

We went quickly to a neighborhood clinic. The doctor there said it definitely was not appendicitis. He wanted to see Barbara again in the morning. In the meantime, he gave her a bottle of pills for the pain.

Later, Barbara insisted we keep to our schedule and take off immediately for the East. Pretty discouraged about everything by now, I didn't put up too big an argument. "But what about the doctor?" I said. "He wants to see you again."

"I'm fine," Barbara assured me, swallowing a pain pill. "Really, I am."

So, climbing into the Chevy, we began our 3000-mile trip back home. The more we drove, the more depressed I became. It was quite plain no one wanted me. Brooding as the miles went by, I told myself that I just wasn't cut out to be a singer. Once home, I would give up my dream and look for something else to do. For the first time in my life, I had completely lost faith in myself.

Since our funds were so low, we couldn't afford to stop anywhere. Late one night, after driving across Texas and part of Arkansas, I suddenly jerked my head up. Dog-tired, I had nearly fallen asleep. I knew I couldn't go another mile without some rest.

"Barbara," I said, "do you think you can take the wheel for a spell?" I looked over at her. I'd been so wrapped up in thoughts of my dead-end career that I hadn't taken much notice of Barbara during the trip. Glancing down, I saw the bottle of pain pills lying on the seat beside her, nearly empty. But still Barbara refused to say anything was the matter.

"I'll try to drive," she said finally.

As soon as we swapped seats, I was out like a light. Ten minutes later, however, Barbara nudged me awake. It was nearly two a.m.

"I can't go on," she cried out in agony. "Something's terribly wrong!"

Leaping out of the car, I ran around to the driver's side. I floored the old Chevy and searched for a light—any light— along the deserted highway. *Would anything be open at this hour?* I had no idea. My heart raced wildly; I didn't even know where we were.

Finally I spotted an all-night gas station and there was directed to the nearest hospital, 20 miles away in Conway, Arkansas. Incredibly, when we arrived at the hospital, a surgeon was still on duty. Dr. Fred Gordy was his name. After examining Barbara, he told me that she was bleeding internally. "It looks very serious," he said. "I'll need your permission to operate."

I stared at Doctor Gordy. Middle-aged, he had kind, compassionate eyes and an unmistakable air of competence.

"Whatever you say, Doc," I said.

Everything was happening so fast it all seemed like a nightmare. I went to an empty waiting room and slumped down in a chair, exhausted, confused and terribly frightened. Here I was in a strange town, far from home. I had hardly any money, didn't know anyone, couldn't call anyone. The person I loved more than anyone in the world was desperately ill, maybe dying. Never in all my days had I felt so alone, so afraid, so helpless. So crazily did my mind begin to spin that before I knew it I found myself praying.

"Lord," I said, "being a successful entertainer doesn't seem so important to me now. I love Barbara . . . she means more to me than anything. She's all I really care about. Please help her."

The prayer sounded so peculiar coming from me, the big, thick-headed, obstinate guy who thought he had left God back there in Maryland.

Then a strange thing happened in that little Arkansas hospital's waiting room. On the heels of my desperate prayer, a surge of warmth flooded my body, a feeling I'd never experienced before. It was like warm hands on cold flesh. No longer did I feel alone in the room. Someone was there with me—a caring Presence.

Then came a Voice, a comforting Voice, and to this day I swear it was God's, "Barbara's going to be all right," the Voice said, "Just wait and see. Trust . . . believe . . . "

And with that I knew she *was* going to be okay.

Just as the sun came peeping through the waiting room window, Doctor Gordy came back from the operating room.

"Mr. Clark," he said, "your wife had a tubular pregnancy. We almost lost her in there. I don't know how she made it, but she did."

Tears tumbled down my face, tears of relief and gratitude.

Looking at Doctor Gordy, I saw that he appeared almost as tired as I felt. I wanted to hug the guy.

"Thanks, Doc," I said, pumping his hand. "Thanks a lot."

A nurse found me a motel room where I slept till noon. Barbara remained in intensive care for a couple more days, but the worst was over. Soon she was transferred to another room with, of all people, a preacher's wife. Because of what had happened in Maryland, Barbara was a little doubtful about this. But I'd experienced so many fantastic things in the past few days that to me it seemed just another one of God's wonderful workings.

And I was right. When the woman's husband visited, and met us, we all got to talking about what the Maryland preacher had told Barbara. The Arkansas man said that he wouldn't say anything against another minister. However, he did tell us something that was the freshest breath of air I'd felt in a long time. "It's God's church, not any one person's," he said. "Only He can say what is right and what is wrong."

When he said that, Barbara looked over at me, smiled and squeezed my hand.

Later, on the road once again, heading for Maryland with a beautiful, healthy, Barbara beside me, I thought about those words—*what is right and what is wrong*. Doing right, I realized now, was following God and really listening to Him—not to one's own blind ambition. That was the way to make it as a singer or as anything else—to put Him first.

I had turned my back on God temporarily, but God had never turned His back on me. Not in Maryland, not in Vegas, not in L.A., not in that hospital waiting room. It had taken a life-and-death situation to show me how very real and how very caring He is. But that happens sometimes. It's when we're down at our lowest, I've found, that He makes Himself so known.

Through the years I've come to understand that whatever talent I have—to sing, to entertain—is God-given. I have faith in myself as a performer, sure. But only because I have faith in Someone Whose performance is always far greater than the human mind can even begin to comprehend—God Himself.

---

*For I will restore health unto thee, and
I will heal thee of thy wounds, saith
the Lord. (Jeremiah 30:17)*

A story for mothers and daughters everywhere.

"Mother, Something Wonderful Has Happened!"

by NANCY MARSH GRIFFIN

In the spring of 1974, my daughter Susan phoned from Boston to announce that she was coming home during her school's mid-semester break. Dread seeped through me as she spoke. I pictured another tense confrontation.

That was the way it always was when she was home, bossing her younger sisters, criticizing, venting her hostility. On one recent visit, she had come into a living room full of guests and gone around the room making caustic remarks to each one there. Her last visit, at Christmas, had ended in another argument between us.

The only way we could get along was for her to be away from home. Despite her outrageous behavior, though, I felt the fault was not hers alone. I couldn't help believing that *I* was responsible. I seemed to carry a jinx that caused people around me to suffer.

My mother, confined to her bed following a stroke when I was 14, had died during the night after she and I had had a quarrel. My husband Peter, a pilot, had been killed in a plane crash three days after a fierce argument that ended when he stormed out of our house, never to return. And for the past two years I had watched helplessly while John, my second husband, drank himself to death in a house filled with strife.

My four other girls had certainly been scarred by an alcoholic stepfather who shouted and railed at them, by the loud arguments and continuous turmoil. But Susan, the eldest, had suffered most.

In my frantic efforts to escape the torment of guilt after Peter's death, I had set a furious pace of social activity, all but abandoning six-year-old Susan to paid housekeepers. The other girls were too young to wonder why I was gone so much, but Susan was bewildered by it.

At one point I had had to place her temporarily in a school for emotionally disturbed children. Later, when she was a teen-ager, unable to handle the confusion in our home, she stayed with a former neighbor of ours.

In the past weeks, following John's death, my sea of guilt was deepened by the neglect I felt Susan had suffered. Morbid thoughts obsessed me. Every horrible scene I could remember flashed repeatedly through my mind. Surely, I thought, God would punish me for the tragedies I had brought into the lives of those dearest to me. I was so stricken with guilt I could not even pray; God would certainly turn a deaf ear to anything I had to say, I reasoned.

And now, into a home shadowed by my dark mood, Susan, rebellious and condemning, would be coming to visit. I knew I could not get through it.

When she arrived, though, the pretty, blond young woman who stood in the doorway as I hugged her was not the stony daughter I had known. She smiled, and her eyes brightened, and I knew there was something different about her.

"Mom," she said, "something wonderful has happened! I'm a Christian."

I laughed, thinking she was joking. "Of course you're a Christian, Susan," I said. Hadn't I made certain my girls were baptized and got a Christian education?

"Sure, Mom," Susan persisted, "but this is different." She then told me how some friends at school had told her that Jesus Christ could make a difference in her life. At first, she said, she wasn't interested, but the thought of a new life remained with her. Then one day in the dorm she decided to go along with them when they went to their room to pray.

"It was beautiful, Mom," she said. "I just asked Christ to

come into my life and straighten things out. And He did."

I was happy that Susan had found peace and that we could now talk without my feeling that she was condemning me. But I didn't understand it and didn't see how my own anguished life could be affected by such an experience. I felt I had damaged too many lives for God to forgive. I was stuck with the past, and it would haunt me as long as I lived.

When Susan returned to school, she began to phone me regularly, just to chat and try to cheer me. She would read passages from her Bible to me. She seemed to think I would eventually discover an answer if she could just penetrate my heart with something from her Bible.

Finally, in desperation, one day I blurted out to her, "How can I understand what you're saying if I don't even have a Bible to read?" Actually I had a Bible in the house, but I had never used it. I had had to say something, to make an excuse for the confusion in my heart.

A few days later a package arrived in the mail. It was from Susan. As I tore the wrapping open, I saw the cover of an American Standard Bible. I was touched, for I knew Susan had probably spent most of her weekly allowance to buy it for me.

As I was about to flip through the pages, I noticed that the first leaf was inscribed. I stopped to read what Susan had painstakingly lettered. It was a quotation from the fourteenth chapter of John's Gospel. As I read the words Susan wanted me to hear, something stirred inside me.

"And I will pray the Father, and He will give you another Counselor, to be with you forever . . . I will not leave you desolate; I will come to you . . . but you will see Me; because I live, you will live also. In that day you will know that I am in My Father and you in Me, and I in you." (John 14:16, 18-20, RSV)

At the end of the quote, Susan had also penned, "I thank God for giving me such a wonderful mother, one who cared for me and loved me. May we always be together in Christ."

Tears were now flowing from my eyes as I held the open Bible. "What sort of wonder is this that my daughter could write so lovingly to a mother who has so neglected her?" I asked myself. Her love and forgiveness simply overflowed the page, spilled into my heart and filled me with a warm and happy calm.

I clutched the Bible, and my eyes lingered over Susan's words. Suddenly I opened my mouth and whispered, "Forgive me, Lord."

It was as if a gash had been sliced into my wall of fear and guilt, and I felt my spirit lift. *Someone* was taking the burden out of my heart. I was being forgiven—I could feel the peace.

I ran to the phone and dialed Susan's number at school. My head said she probably would not be there to answer, but my heart said call anyway.

"Mom!" she shouted when I spoke into the phone. We laughed and cried as I thanked her for the Bible and tried to explain my feelings. "I know, Mom. I know," she said.

Now I knew, too. I knew just exactly what Susan had meant when she said, "I'm a Christian." And I knew just what a difference it makes.

TRUE LOVE
Love delights in giving attention rather
*   than in attracting it.*
Love finds the element of good and
*   builds on it.*
Love does not magnify defects.
Love is a flame that warms but never
*   burns.*
Love knows how to disagree without
*   becoming disagreeable.*
Love rejoices at the success of others
*   instead of being envious.*
*   Father James Keller*

Doctors had pronounced this woman
beyond medical help. Skeptically she
attended a service conducted by the late
Kathryn Kuhlman. What happened to her
there is almost beyond belief.

To God Be the Glory

by MARION BURGIO

It was in my fortieth year that I began to die. Not rapidly or all at once, but bit by bit. Slowly, across the next 17 years, my body stopped living—each section dying with agonizing pain.

I first noticed it one afternoon at the Boysen Paint Company in Emeryville, across the bay from San Francisco.

I had worked at Boysen as a printer and typesetter for many years. This particular afternoon I picked up my tweezers and reached into the tray for some extra-fine type. But something was wrong. It was almost imperceptible, yet my eyes were blurred and my hand was shaking. At the same time, I noticed a strange numbness in my hands and legs. Little did I know that at that moment death had tapped me on the shoulder.

A year passed. Then two. I had been to half a dozen doctors in the Bay area. One said I had hepatitis. Another said I suffered from spasms of the esophagus. A third doctor recommended gall-bladder surgery, which I had.

My husband Angelo, I call him "Ang," was a supervisor at the Alameda Naval Air Base. Every few weeks he would come home and say, "I heard about a new doctor. Let's try him."

One doctor prescribed glasses for my double vision. Another said the numbness in my hands was caused by poor circulation. My condition grew worse. One day I fainted at work. That night I told Ang I was going to leave my job. Actually I had been looking for an excuse to quit anyway. Rosemary, our daughter, was married and our twin sons, Arthur and Don, were both working. Besides, Ang and I had long wanted another child. We agreed this would be a good time for me to quit work and adopt a baby boy. If, as one of the doctors had suggested, all I had was frayed nerves, then the change of pace might be just what I needed.

It turned out I needed far more. Several weeks after little Eugene arrived, Ang went with me to the grocery store. Waiting in the check-out line, I suddenly grew dizzy, slumping against Ang for support. As the line inched forward, I found I could not pick up my feet. I had to force them to slide across the floor. I was scared!

A top neurologist in San Francisco recommended hospitalization and I spent a month in Presbyterian Hospital. Part of that time I was under the care of a psychiatrist. Still no diagnosis. I finally called Ang to come and take me home

Three weeks later I noticed the middle finger on my right hand infected. Ang took me to a new doctor on MacArthur Boulevard. He lanced the finger and then, after finishing with the bandage, turned to me.

"Is there something else wrong, Mrs. Burgio?" he asked.

I was hostile. "No, why?"

"Well, if I had treated a normal patient the way I treated you, she would have been screaming in pain. You didn't seem to feel the pain at all." He hesitated. "Could I give you a physical?" I sighed. "Okay. I guess one more examination won't hurt."

The finger healed slowly and I had to return twice before my scheduled appointment. Each time the doctor asked questions, and I knew he suspected more than he was saying. Then the day before I was scheduled for the physical, the bottom fell out of my life.

Ang went to work early as usual. Little Eugene, who was about two years old, came running into the bedroom and began pulling on the covers. I yawned, put my feet over the side of the bed and tried to stand up. Instead my legs gave way under me and I fell heavily to the floor. The carpet cushioned my fall, but when I tried to stand up, nothing worked. My legs were useless—paralyzed. My arms were almost as bad. I was helpless.

I finally managed to turn over on my stomach and wriggle out into the middle of the bedroom. Eugene was standing beside the dresser, staring. "Mommy's just playing a game," I whispered, not wanting to alarm him. Then I began the slow, laborious crawl down the hall and into the family room. My hands would not work, so I had to move painfully along using my elbows and hips.

It took ten minutes to make the trip to the family room. By then I was totally exhausted. I tried once again to get to my feet, but my muscles were useless. I couldn't even reach up for the phone.

Then, to my horror, I saw Eugene open the sliding glass doors and toddle out onto the patio. He was heading toward the wrought-iron gate that led to the busy street. I cried out, but my voice broke and faded. I started to crawl after him.

The wrought-iron gate was open. By the time I reached the patio, Eugene had disappeared. I kept crawling, pushing myself across the rough concrete on my elbows and hips. Panic swept over me as I heard the cars on the busy boulevard.

"Dear God, please help me. Help me!"

But the words were lost in my sobs. I could go no farther. I collapsed.

The clock inside was striking 11 when I looked up and saw Eugene coming back through the gate. "Up, Mama, up," he said.

I tried to move, but it was impossible. I tried to talk, but only hoarse tremors came out. Then I felt it. The muscles in my upper back trembled as they began to pull my shoulder blades together. "Dear God, what is this?" I cried. Then in my sudden flash of pain, I felt my neck snap back. My shoulders wrenched as though caught in a devilish vise. I began to gag as my head was forced backward.

Finally the spasms ceased. Mercifully, Eugene had disappeared into the house. For five long hours I lay on the patio, helpless in the blazing sun. "Please, God," I begged through my desperate tears, "let somebody come to help me."

It was around four o'clock when, as though in answer to my prayer, my friend, Anne Kennedy, appeared at the gate. "Marion, what are you doing there on the ground?" she cried. As she took a closer look and saw my distorted face, she gasped and ran into the house to call Ang.

Later, in the examining room, I could hear the doctor's voice, "I suspected it. Now I'm sure. Multiple sclerosis."

The nurse gave me a shot for pain and treated the raw, skinned places on my body. Later, at home, Ang took down the dictionary and read to me the definition of multiple sclerosis. "A diseased condition marked by patches of hardened tissue in the brain or the spinal cord and associated especially with partial or complete paralysis, jerking muscle tremors and sometimes intense pain."

As the months slipped into years, I lost track of the number of trips to the hospital. Over those years I was to learn that multiple sclerosis is a strange disease. It will take you right to the brink of death, back off and allow you, its victim, a partial remission, and then, without warning, send your body into horrible spasms.

Ang employed a full-time housekeeper and eventually a daytime nurse. We moved from our home in San Leandro to nearby Walnut Creek so I could be near our daughter Rosemary.

In the months that followed, I slipped deeper and deeper into the dark pit of despair. I knew the disease was incurable. Ang was having to spend every cent he made just to keep me alive. My old friends who used to visit me slowly drifted away. Who could possibly enjoy visiting someone so twisted and distorted, now unable to see or talk clearly, who at best could only drag herself around on crutches and utter slurred words?

One day in the doctor's office, I broke down. I was losing my hearing. I couldn't even comb my hair or feed myself. I was totally dependent upon others.

The doctor said, "Mrs. Burgio, there is nothing more that I can do for you. You are beyond medical help."

"I wish I were dead," I wept.

In June our family received an invitation to attend the golden wedding anniversary celebration of Fred and Helen Smith, former neighbors in Oakland whom we had not seen in 11 years. My enthusiasm for going anywhere was at an all-time low, but Rosemary convinced me I should go. "We'll make it a family affair," she said, "and it will please Daddy."

Helen, a striking woman with friendly blue eyes, was at the door with a warm welcome for all of us as Ang rolled me up the sidewalk in my wheelchair.

"Oh, Marion," she said as she bent over to kiss me, "I'm so happy you came. I just know you are going to be healed."

Puzzled, I looked up at Ang. Neither of us understood what she could possibly be talking about. However, during the evening Helen told us all about the miracle services held by Kathryn Kuhlman and introduced us to several priests and nuns from Holy Names College who told us about the prayer meetings they were having at the college, which was in Oakland.

Helen was very enthusiastic about this new dimension she had found in her religious life, but Ang and I just couldn't take it all in—prayer meetings, healing services, and what she called "the power of the Holy Spirit." Who was this Kathryn Kuhlman they were talking about? "What is a miracle service?" we asked ourselves.

A few weeks after the party, my disease exploded with all the fury of a hurricane and it was back to the hospital for me. But now my will to go on was all but gone. My vision was badly impaired, my hearing almost gone, and the muscles in my throat had deteriorated to the point where I could not swallow food. The sad look on my husband's face was becoming too much to bear.

It was during this time of deep depression that Helen Smith and another friend came to visit me at the hospital. While there, Helen asked, "Do you mind if I say a prayer over you?" I looked at Ang in puzzlement. He just shrugged as Helen placed her hands on my stomach and began to pray softly. Her eyes were closed, her face tilted up, her lips moving, quietly expressing words I was unable to understand.

As she was praying, from far off I heard the sound of music. Everything had been distorted for so long, yet this music was beautifully clear. It was the sound of a choir accompanied by stringed instruments.

I exclaimed, "Oh, Ang, I hear music! I don't know the song, but it's beautiful."

Ang thought I was having hallucinations. But Helen's face was radiant as she said, "Oh, honey, you are going to be healed. I just know you are."

I was released from the hospital two weeks later. The doctor told Ang there was nothing more that could be done and it would be better for me to spend my last days at home. Three days after I got home, I received a card from Helen. Ang read it to me.

"Dear Marion:

Glad you are home again. Hope you are feeling better. You are going to be well again. Praise the Lord. Both of you will enjoy the tape I am sending you today. You will find great help and inspiration from it. Hold on to your faith and believe. In case you go to Kathryn Kuhlman's meeting at the coliseum, I'll be there in the choir praying for you. Accept your healing when the time comes. God bless you, dear. Remember, you are being healed. Get there early, about 3:30 p.m. Wheelchairs go in first.

Helen"

"Do you understand her?" I said to Ang when he finished reading.

"Not really," Ang replied.

He examined the small cassette tape that had arrived in the same mail. "It's by Kathryn Kuhlman," he said. My hearing ability was so distorted at this stage that I could not get very interested in listening to a tape by Kathryn Kuhlman.

"I don't want to hear it," I said. "I don't know what's the matter with Helen. I just don't understand all this stuff."

Five days later, on July 28, we received another card from Helen urging me to go to the meeting. Shaking my head, I put it on the table. "I'm not going," I said to Ang.

The next evening the phone rang. I heard Ang say, "Yes, Helen, I'm taking the day off and I'm going to take Marion to the meeting."

When he hung up, I began to cry. "Please, Ang, I don't feel like going. We've never been in a Protestant service before. I don't want to go."

The next day was the worst day of my life. I was twisted far more severely than ever before. My hands looked like claws and I was shaking like a vibrator. Even before I got out of bed, I took three pain killers, but they had no effect.

"I'm not going!" I cried.

Ang was firm. "We have nothing to lose, honey; let's go see what it's all about."

The trip to the coliseum was horrible. I cried all the way, begging Ang to take me back home. When we arrived at the coliseum, one of the ushers tried to help Ang with my wheel-chair and I went all to pieces. "Oh, don't touch me . . . please don't touch me! I just want my husband to take care of me."

She moved back and stood by helplessly while Ang tried to calm me down.

Finally, we were settled in the huge coliseum, which was filling rapidly as the choir was rehearsing on the platform. Soon, every available seat was taken.

All around us were people in wheelchairs and on stretchers. I could not comprehend the amount of human suffering that had come together in that one place. Yet there was something else present—something intangible—*hope*. Everyone, or at least nearly everyone, seemed to have it on his or her face. It was as though each person was straining for some unseen hand to reach down and touch him or her. My heart ached for everyone and I began to pray, asking the Lord to help them.

Suddenly the choir began to sing again. This time the great crowd joined them. That song! "Ang!" I cried out. "It's the same song and the same choir I've been hearing ever since Helen's prayer."

To appease me, Ang turned and asked the woman next to him, "What's the name of that song?"

"*How Great Thou Art,*" she answered.

All the people around me seemed to have their arms raised as they sang. I asked myself, "What kind of meeting is this anyway?" I looked over at Ang and even with my double vision, I could see he had his arms up also.

"What are you doing?" I asked.

Ang smiled. "Well, everybody else has their hands up, so I put mine up, too. It feels good to sing this way. I like it."

I wanted to scream. Everyone seemed so happy—even those in wheelchairs—yet I remained miserable and confused.

I felt Ang's hand on my arm. "Here she comes. This must be Kathryn Kuhlman."

I strained to see, but my eyes simply would not focus on the platform, which was at least some 70 yards away. All I could see was a bright glow—like an aura. I knew it must be Kathryn Kuhlman.

"What's she doing?" I kept asking Ang.

He tried to describe what was happening. She introduced certain guests. She told a few stories. There was more singing and then she began to speak. To me the sounds were all jumbled. The only word I heard plainly was "Bible."

"Ang," I whispered, "I think we better get out of here . . . I feel funny."

He ignored me. His eyes were riveted on the platform.

Just then a woman dressed in red moved slowly down the aisle beside us. Her daughter was in front of her and her husband was walking behind her. As she got opposite our row, she fell to the floor.

"Oh, dear God," I moaned, "help her." Her family was bending over her, crying and trying to help her to her feet. I began crying also as I realized what my own family must have been going through as they had tried to help me.

When I looked up, I noticed another girl, a young woman, lying on a wheelchair stretcher farther down the aisle. She was dressed in a plaid suit, but it was obvious her body, like mine, was the twisted victim of multiple sclerosis.

"Dear Lord, help her, too," I prayed.

Later the woman in red passed by my wheelchair. She was transformed.

"Ang!" I cried out. "She's been healed!"

I could not tell all that was happening or even understand what was being said, but I knew it was the same woman. No longer was she hobbling and falling—she was almost running. Her face was radiant!

It was then that the struggle within my own body began. Suddenly my knees began to shake. I tried to hold them with my hands but things were happening too quickly. My feet were being pulled out of the foot rests of the wheelchair and pressed against the floor. It seemed as though two great forces were at work within my body—one pushing me down and another pulling me up. I felt myself being lifted up, but the downward force was too great and I fell back into the chair.

Ang was alarmed at my movements and said, "Marion, what's wrong? What is happening to you?"

I couldn't answer, for I was literally being pushed right up and out of my wheelchair. It was as though the chains that had bound me had suddenly broken. I was on my feet! Standing! And as I stood up, my twisted hand just stretched right out. I couldn't believe my eyes—my hand was straight and normal!

Just as quickly as I had stood up, I began to walk, I didn't know where I was going or why—but I was on my way. Past Ang. Past the place where Eugene was sitting. Down the aisle and toward the platform. Ang, in a state of shock, was close behind me.

The next thing I remember was Kathryn Kuhlman's voice. "You're healed, honey! Just walk across the stage."

And then it dawned on me that I was walking, sometimes half-running, in front of thousands of people. I felt bathed in God's love! He was real! He had come to me! He loved me enough to minister to me personally and, glory of all glories, to fill me with His beautiful Holy Spirit!

"Thank you! Thank you!" I exclaimed to Miss Kuhlman.

Her face was smiling. "Don't thank me," she said. "I'm just as surprised and happy as you. Thank Jesus. He's the One Who healed you."

"I thought you were a farce," I said, crying with joy." "I came only to please my family and my friends, Helen and Fred, who sing in your choir."

Amazed at myself, I realized I could talk! My speech was normal! My eyes, too. I could see clearly! My legs were working! The pain was gone! I could breathe! Just as Helen had said it would happen, I had been healed!

I came off the platform unaware that the Lord had yet another joy in store for me. I looked up and there was the girl in the plaid suit. Walking! She had been healed also! The tears started all over again. What joy to know that the two people I had prayed for—the woman in red and the girl with MS—had both been touched by God. And so had I.

The trip home was far different from the trip to the coliseum. We sang all the way. The first thing I did was call Rosemary. "I'm healed!" I shouted.

"Oh, Mama, you've gone bananas," Rosemary chuckled.

"No, I'm healed. Listen to me talk. I can walk and I can see! I hear you perfectly. No more pain!"

"Listen, Mama, just go to bed and wait until I get there tomorrow."

I passed the phone to Ang, but even he could not convince Rosemary of the miracle. She would just have to wait and see for herself.

The next morning, for the first time in ten years, I jumped out of bed and pulled open the window blinds so the summer sun could come streaming into the bedroom. I headed for the kitchen to fix Ang some coffee while he dressed.

Half an hour after Ang left for work, Rosemary came rushing through the door. I was in the kitchen drinking coffee. She stood there with her mouth open. "Mother! Mother! What's happened to you?" she cried in disbelief.

She was like that for the next two hours as I told her everything. All she could do was weep and shake her head. Everyone who came wept unashamedly in the presence of the miracle our Lord had wrought.

M onday morning I went to Doctors' Hospital for my regular X-ray appointment. The technician who had taken my X rays for the last two years looked at me strangely.

"You must be Marion Burgio's twin sister," she said.

I laughed. "No, Betty. I'm not Marion's twin. I'm Marion."

She grabbed me and pulled me into a side room. "What happened to you? Last week you were dying. Now look at you!"

After I told her about my healing, she gasped. "Twelve days ago I had to put the straw in your mouth when I gave you the milk shake for the X ray. Now you're fine!"

Just at that moment the door swung open and the doctor walked in. He stared at me but said nothing—just motioned me to get ready for my X rays. I undressed and leaned up against the slanted X-ray table. The doctor stood watching.

"Don't you have any pain?" he asked.

"No," I said evenly.

"Haven't you had pain?"

"Oh, yes, constantly. But not any more."

"When did the pain go away?"

"Last Tuesday night."

He asked no more questions, just kept turning me and snapping X-ray pictures. Through the thick glass window I could see Betty watching.

Finally she could take no more. She called out from behind the lead shield. "You remember Mrs. Burgio, don't you, doctor? She was here twelve days ago with multiple sclerosis."

The doctor's expression never changed. "You had an ulcer, too, didn't you?"

"I did, but I don't have it any more."

"H'm, how do you know?"

"I don't have any more pain. I eat anything I want. I don't have to take medicine any more."

He cleared his throat as if he wanted to ask more, but had decided to keep silent.

It was sheer joy to be able to dress myself without assistance. I was so wrapped up in the realization of what I was doing for myself that I did not hear the receptionist when she returned. "You may go home now, Mrs. Burgio, I don't think we'll have to see you again."

More than anything, I wanted to tell the doctor about the miracle service. But he was gone. I walked out into the hot August sun. A fresh breeze was blowing off the bay; the sky was so clear I could almost see into tomorrow. During my illness I had allowed myself to become bitter and seldom saw the day-to-day blessings the Lord heaps upon us all, but now everything was beautiful!

As I walked to my personal physician's office, I was wondering how he would react. After all, he had treated me for almost 13 years and the last time he saw me, I was completely helpless.

He was standing in the hall talking to the receptionist when I entered the waiting room. I rang the buzzer on the desk and stepped back. He glanced up at me and started to turn away. My heart went out to him as he turned and looked again.

"Mrs. Burgio?" he asked timidly.

I just grinned.

"Where's your wheelchair?"

"I don't need it any more."

"But your canes . . . "

"I've put them aside also."

He looked at this nurse "The hospital just called about her X rays. I told them they had made a mistake . . . that they had the wrong person. Now I'm not sure." He was silent for a moment. "Get all of Mrs. Burgio's files and bring them to my office."

I sat in the examining room waiting for the doctor to finish looking at my files. Finally he came through the door and closed it behind him.

"I suppose you're going to tell me your MS is healed."

"Right!" I grinned.

He had me sit on the side of the table while he tapped my knee with his little rubber hammer. For more than ten years there had been little or no knee reflexes. Now my leg jerked at the slightest touch of the hammer.

"I just don't understand," he admitted.

"Do you believe in miracles?"

He looked at me blankly. "No, I don't."

Once again he checked my reflexes, twisted my arms and legs and listened for long moments with his stethoscope.

"I'm completely baffled," he admitted. "It's as if you had been born again."

"That's exactly, doctor," I laughed. "I *have* been born again."

And then I told him the full story of my beautiful miracle healing. He listened patiently, then spoke.

"You've been my patient for thirteen years," he said quietely, "I am so glad for you."

My heart felt a deep twinge of sadness for him as I said, "Doctor, you cared for me all those years—that is true. I could not have asked for better medical care. I will always be grateful to you for that. But the Lord healed me. And the glory for that goes to God."

His eyes were serious as he studied my face. I knew that he was a learned medical doctor and that my knowledge was limited, but I also knew I had something he didn't have. He knew it also.

"While I don't understand it, I wish I had a little of whatever it is that you have, to give to my other patients," he said thoughtfully.

"All you have to do is reach out, doctor," I said, "and God will touch you, too."

His eyes were moist as he took me by the elbow and helped me to the floor from the table. He walked to the door of the examining room with me and lingered for a moment.

"Doctor," I said, "is it true that multiple sclerosis is uncurable?"

He paused, then answered, "Medically speaking, there is no known cure."

"Is it true that I am healed?"

He nodded his head and gently bit his lower lip. "You are not only healed, Mrs. Burgio; you are a new person!"

"Then to God be the glory," I said. I gave him a little hug, opened the door and walked out into the bright day.

4.
Love for Those Who Have Suffered Losses

For I am persuaded that neither death, nor life, nor angels, nor principalities, nor powers, nor things present, nor things to come, nor height, nor depth, nor any other creature, shall be able to separate us from the love of God, which is in Christ Jesus our Lord.
(Romans 8:38,39)

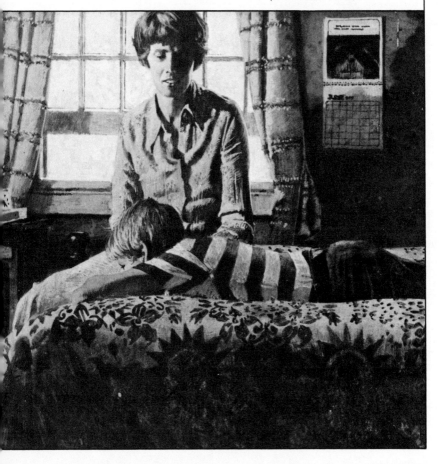

Farewell on The Mountainside

by BETTY BANNER

Snow had fallen all night and the mountain was a fairyland of whiteness. I was 21 years old and expecting my first baby in the spring. All my life until the past ten months had been spent in a fairly good-sized town, and the deep, narrow valley between the tall mountain and ridge where I was living with my husband and his mother, was a constant source of interest and new experiences for me. The mountain folks I had come to know and the many customs of the "old folks" that they still cherished had formed a new world for me.

During the previous summer I had insisted that we attend the little white Methodist church about two miles down the valley, and even though the circuit-rider preacher only came once a month, I had helped organize a Sunday school for the in-between time.

This particular morning was Monday and "washday" by an infallible rule of the mountain community. Snow or no snow, we washed, and I hummed a gay little tune as I helped my mother-in-law fill the zinc tubs on the glowing kitchen range and sorted the clothes for washing. My thoughts were of the coming baby, and the warm, steamy kitchen, accentuated by the white coldness seen through the windows, gave me a feeling of security and snugness. In thinking of my own happiness, I talked with my mother-in-law about the pity we felt for a young couple, who, we had been told, had lost their three-week-old baby during the night just the day before. We were still speculating as to what might have caused such a death

143

when a knock at the back door gave us both a start.

Opening the door we were even more startled to see the very same father of the dead child we had just been discussing standing there. His name was John and he seemed hesitant to come into the kitchen and stood twirling his cap in his hands and staring at his feet. All of a sudden he took a deep breath and blurted out, "Betty, we was aimin' to bury our baby today, and now this snow an' all, and the preacher can't get acrost the ridge, and from the way hit's snowin' can't reckon when he could get here." Then, as we started to sympathize, he said, "My Maude . . . she's right smart tore up, and ain't able to git outta bed this mornin', but she says we just can't put our baby away 'lessen we have a service over her, and you're the only one I knowed round here I thought could do it."

It was a moment before my stunned brain could take it in that he was talking to and about me, I couldn't believe he was asking me to do the service. I started to stammer that I couldn't possibly preach a funeral, and besides we couldn't get two miles down the valley. I might have saved my breath, for he stood there with such grief and stubborn determination in his eyes that I felt like I was butting my head against a brick wall for all the progress I was making.

Then he said quietly, "How'd you feel if it was your young 'un?" That did it. I had no answer for that, so I dumbly wiped my still wet hands on my apron and began to untie it. I don't remember another word spoken as I pulled on high rubber boots and coat and muffler. All I could do was pray frantically over and over, "Dear God, help me, give me words to help. Help me to say what will comfort them, Lord. . . ."

Leaving word about where I was going for my husband who was feeding cattle, I set out with John for the long cold walk to the church. Slipping, sliding, often wading drifts, with no conversation between us, the silent white flakes of snow pounding in our faces, we reached the church at last and went in. My heart came up into my throat. In spite of the snow, the little chapel was filled with mountain folks, and the little homemade coffin rested under a wreath of crepe-paper flowers in front of the rough altar.

Such a small, crude little chapel, with its oil lamps hanging on the walls, yet in that moment it seemed to me as vast and awesome as St. Patrick's Cathedral, which I once visited. I thought I'd never reach the front and as I stumbled down the aisle, my frantic brain could only repeat the same prayer. "Dear God, help me, help me. Let me say the words that will help them feel Your presence."

When I turned to face the silent congregation, I had to grip the pine pulpit tightly to keep from just going down. It hit me, too, that there was not even a Bible in front of me and I had not thought to bring mine!

As I realized that, I thought, *Well, this is it. I cannot go any further.* And then my eyes fell on that pitiful little box. Then and there God worked a miracle for me, just as surely as if He had reached out and touched my mind and lips. From somewhere unknown, the words came, disjointed as to correctness of quotation I am sure, but essentially those I had heard from early childhood on similar occasions. "I am the resurrection and the life . . . " "Casting all your care upon Him for He careth for you." "Suffer the children to come unto Me . . . for of such is the kingdom of heaven." On and on the words came, as if a scroll were being unwound before my eyes. Last of all came a prayer—and that was mine, for as I felt my own unborn child stir within me, my petition for a grieving mother in a log cabin on that lonely mountainside found the right words for the final commitment of "earth to earth" at the tiny graveside.

I am now a grandmother, and through the years I have faced many trials and crosses where I have felt like giving up before I started. But always the memory of "my miracle" comes to me and I go on, for surely the loving God who could give an ignorant 21-year-old girl a funeral service can guide a more mature woman through any difficulty. Always, too, in such a crisis I seem to see John's face and hear the simple words he spoke as I turned from that grave toward home.

"Thank you—I knowed you could do it."

**At the bleakest moment in my life, God
chose to comfort me in the most unusual way.**

The Light

by LIL GENTRY

I t all began one Sunday morning when the big old monster of
a refrigerator broke for the last time. That old refrigerator
and I had been waging a battle for a long time, and this time I
just gave up. I had been trying for months to adjust to our new
home, but that morning everything went wrong. The kids were
fighting, none of us had enough room to breathe and then the
refrigerator gasped its last breath.

We had recently moved from a very spacious house near the
ocean, built to my own design, into this tiny, cramped apartment over a garage because my husband had gone into his own
business as a builder and contractor. He felt we needed to be
closer to his business as well as cut down on our expenses. The
children had adjusted beautifully, but I was the one who had
the problem. I just couldn't forget our beautiful home and the
friendly neighbors we had left behind. Today I really missed
everything and longed for my old life-style.

As I peered into that old refrigerator, it looked like a coffin.
Not only was its shape grotesque and out of place in my tiny
kitchen, but it made such loud groaning noises when it was
working. The only thing that never had failed was the little light
inside the refrigerator. We had never yet had to replace it.

Sour milk again, and the kids were yelling for breakfast. I just
couldn't help it. I began to cry. Len, my husband, a happy-go-
lucky Irishman, put his big arms around me. "I understand,
and I promise that first thing tomorrow we will go out and get
you the best new refrigerator in town. For now, let's all go out to
breakfast."

The kids, Sandy, 15, and Larry, 14, and our little guy Bruce who was ten, squealed with delight and off we went. In the restaurant the kids could talk of nothing but school. Tomorrow was the first day, and each had a separate fear about the unknown challenges of the first day in a new school. Len mentioned to me that he had to fly out to Corona and urged me to come along. Len had his own private plane because he had always dreamed of being an air pilot, and this was his way of satisfying that dream. It also helped him in his business, which took him all over California.

I was tempted to go along with him, but I had much to do to get the kids ready for school. I said I'd take a rain check. Len looked a little disappointed but dropped the subject as we began to talk about my newly obtained real-estate license. I was thrilled, but a little scared. I had never worked since I was married, and the very thought of selling someone a large item like a house with all that money involved really scared me. Len assured me again that with my enthusiastic personality and my way of loving everyone I met, I couldn't help but be a success. He would build the houses and I would sell them; that was his dream.

When we arrived back at the apartment I went right to the sewing machine in my bedroom. I had quite a bit of sewing left to do if Sandy's new outfit was to be ready for the first day of school. Len came in to remind me he was leaving and again asked me to change my mind and come along. My attention was on my sewing, so I absentmindedly shook my head. Suddenly Bruce popped up and said, "Daddy, I want to go with you so you won't be alone. Please can I come?"

Len looked at me and I nodded. Bruce was a very special little boy and never made a pest of himself. It would be good for Len to have the companionship. I did make Len promise, however, to have him home early because of school tomorrow.

After they left, I thought of Len and Bruce taking off in that little plane. Len was so happy when he was flying. Being such a free spirit, only in the air did he find peace. He had told me many times, "You know, Lil, honey, up there is where I talk to God. There is no problem God can't solve as long as we let Him." *Thy will be done* was the message Len lived by, and I tried to follow his lead. It always seemed harder for me to do.

Many times during the afternoon I regretted my decision to stay home and sew. It turned out to be a real scorcher. The sun was just setting when I finished and I thought of Len and Bruce again. They would be home soon, hot and bedraggled. I decided to surprise them with their favorite dessert when I remembered the old refrigerator was not working. The special dessert needed to be frozen. I walked into the living room and stared out the window. I looked at the red glow of the dying sun. Len was probably up there somewhere, enjoying being part of God's design. I decided not to let a little thing like a broken refrigerator ruin my day.

As I moved from the window there was a knock at the door. *Wonder who it is?* I thought, I wasn't expecting anyone at this time of day.

As soon as I saw my sister-in-law and brother standing there I knew something was wrong. My brother walked in quickly and put his arms around me. Suddenly I wanted to run, get out. Whatever they were going to tell me was too horrible. I was not ready. *Please, God*, I prayed, *not now*. Then the words came out. The airplane, with Len and Bruce in it, had got caught in a downwind and couldn't pull out. The plane ran right into the side of a mountain and caught fire. Nothing could be done. They were both gone. I heard a scream. It could have been me. I don't know, because I retreated into a new place I had never been before—the place we all go when we can not feel anymore because it hurts too much.

The children and I slept together that night, huddled in the middle of the big bed, not believing what had happened. People were there in the house, but we pulled away, alone on our island of despair. We lay there awake, talking, crying as we searched for some meaning to it all.

After a long time Sandy and Larry finally drifted off to sleep, but I continued to lie there, my mind filled with memories of Len and Bruce. I loved all my children, and each was a unique personality with a special strength. With Bruce, it was the way he could express love so easily. From the day he came home from the hospital he was smiling. He loved people and life so much and was always so thoughtful, always so giving.

If such a child can die, I thought, *then life is meaningless and God is cruel, and I don't want to live in this world.* As the tears began to flow again, I wondered what I had done to deserve this; what had Sandy and Larry done? We had been such a happy, loving family. How could we live without Len, my love, and Bruce, my baby? *I can not do it alone*, I thought, *and God should know that.* I was lost and scared without Len to lean on.

I thought of the time when I was a little girl in Montana and got lost in the woods at dusk. I kept running and calling for someone to save me. Suddenly I saw a flashlight far away in the trees. I kept running and began to cry as I headed toward that light, when suddenly I tripped and fell down. I just gave up and waited, too tired to feel the fear. Then someone picked me up and I was safe. It was my father and he held me in his big arms and carried me home.

Lost and scared, yes, I knew the feeling. In my childhood experience there had been my father to help, but now where could I go? Here I was, lost in the woods again, with no one to help.

The house was quiet and dark. I crept out of bed, trying not to disturb the children. Tomorrow would be the hardest day of their lives and they needed some rest. I walked out into the kitchen. It was so peaceful and quiet. The harvest moon was shining through the window giving the room an eerie and unnatural light. The big old refrigerator cast a grotesque shadow across the kitchen floor. I felt just like that little girl in the woods again—lost and alone. I looked at that old refrigerator, and suddenly we were no longer enemies. I walked over to it and put my hot flushed cheek on its cold hard door. It felt so good and I was so tired. Who could I depend on with Len gone? *Oh, God*, I prayed, *I don't want to be angry with You. Please help me, show me the way.* Automatically my hand reached down for the handle on the refrigerator and I opened that clumsy door. The room was immediately flooded with that everfaithful small light from within. I stood blinking in the unaccustomed light. The breath went out of me in a great sigh and with it, the fear and anger were gone. I was safe. I had found my light because God is the light of the world and His light shines through me. I knew I could depend on God. His light inside of me would lead me as I passed through unknown dark places. All I had to do was keep that door open.

Len and Bruce were gone. Their work here on earth was finished.

But my work here on earth was just beginning. Suddenly life had new meaning for me again. This earthly tragedy was not the end, there was much work for me to do. Sandy and Larry needed me, and so many people out there needed me to help them find just the right home, and if I couldn't, maybe I'd even learn to build them myself. Rather than devoting a life to grieving for Len and Bruce, I would make my life a testimony of my love for them, and a testimony to my love for God and my belief that all things can work together for good for those who put their faith in Him.

God hath not promised skies always blue,
Flower-strewn pathways all our lives through.

God hath not promised sun without rain,
Joy without sorrow, peace without pain.

But God hath promised strength for the day,
Rest for the laborer; light on the way,

Grace for the trial, help from above,
Unfailing sympathy—undying love.
                    Annie Johnson Flint

The Mother's Day I Couldn't Face

by ALICE W. CARLSON

I just couldn't reach out my hand, smile, and say, "A white one, please," as I stepped into the church foyer. I'd never make it.

It was Mother's Day, the first one since my own mother had left us after spending 90 years on earth as a faithful, loving Christian. The church had proved a comfort to me in my time of sadness. I felt confident that grieving over her death would be wrong, in fact selfish, for surely I could not wish her back in the condition she had been for months before the Lord mercifully called her home.

But as I stepped into the church foyer, no one asked me what color carnation I needed. A smiling, gracious young woman simply said, "Good morning!" and extended both hands, one with a red carnation, the other with a white. Acceptance of the white one was made easy for me.

With a deep feeling of relief I sat down in the sanctuary pew. I had cleared that hurdle! The white flower's stem was inserted in my Bible, marking the place of the Scripture reading. I still couldn't bring myself to pin it to the shoulder of my dress. I looked at it questioningly. "Now, why did I consider you such a threat?" I asked silently. "But then, why are you here at all? You're a lovely flower, but you've given me some bad moments. Just what are you supposed to do for me anyway? Your white-ness broadcasts to the world that my mother is dead . . . dead . . . dead, and my heart feels like it is, too."

My silent communication with the carnation continued during the organ prelude. My fingers explored the ruffled petals and as they separated I caught a glimpse of something that made me catch my breath. Deep inside was one tiny petal that suddenly said to me, "She lives!" It was rose red.

I have kept the flower over the years to remind me of that sad Mother's Day turned joyous. I look at its dried petals often, and each time a thrill of reassurance fills my being. I can't risk breaking the petals in an attempt to find again the rose-red dot, but I know it is there.

LOVE IS . . .

Love is not just looking at each other and saying, "You're wonderful." There are times when we are anything but wonderful. . . .

Love is looking outward together in the same direction. It is linking our strength to pull a common load. It is pushing together towards the far horizons, hand in hand.

Love is knowing that when our strength falters, we can borrow the strength of someone who cares.

Love is a strange awareness that our sorrows will be shared and made lighter by sharing; that joys will be enriched and multiplied by the joy of another.

Love is knowing someone else cares, that we are not alone in life.

Love is of God, for God is love. When we love, we touch the hem of the garment of God.
        Patrick Scanlon

What Do I Tell the Kids?

by JOAN SAXMAN

It was April 17, 1968, and Joanne, my good friend from Virginia, had dropped by our Annapolis home with her four children. Together with all my brood—Terry, two, Brian, three, Cindy, five, and Scott, seven—we spent the early afternoon at the weekly Naval Academy parade. The parades were treats for my children—particularly because their father, Capt. John W. Held of the U.S. Air Force, had participated in them while he was a midshipman at Annapolis. Now that he was away, completing his tour of duty in Vietnam, anything that made the family feel close to Jack was important—we missed him so much.

After the parade Joanne and I took the children home and, while we prepared some snacks, we talked about good times we'd had and looked to the future when Jack would be home. Ninety more days wasn't so far away!

A knock at the door halted our conversation, and Scott bounded to answer it.

"Look, Mommy, it's Daddy's friends," he exclaimed as he led three Air Force officers toward us.

I stood up to greet them and, instinctively, Joanne led the children outdoors.

"We have some news about your husband, Mrs. Held," said one of the men, who immediately began to read from a memorandum: "Captain John W. Held has been shot down over South Vietnam . . . " he began.

I accepted the remainder of his words as if in a dream. Jack had been on a mission and had been shot down. His plane had caught fire, and he had ejected. A rescue mission had found his parachute. But there were no traces of Jack—no blood or evidence of a struggle. Thus he was considered missing in action, they said.

For a few minutes I just stared out the window and silently digested the news. Waves of apprehension mixed with relief inside of me. *He's just missing*, I told myself. *It just means he'll be away somewhat longer than expected.* I refused to think that Jack might be dead. But that was necessary for me, a woman who had only recently learned to find strength in the living God.

Just before Jack had received his orders for Vietnam, I had become moody and depressed; I couldn't imagine myself alone with four small children for a whole year. Only after counseling with our pastor and many prayers that helped Jack and me to form our deep trust in Christ were we able to face those orders when they did come through. Now I was building on that trust, and it was holding.

"God, You are with Jack and I trust You to take care of him," I prayed firmly. I assured the officers that I would be okay, and stepped outside to face my family and friend.

In the months succeeding that Wednesday in April when I became an MIA (Missing-in-Action) wife, I kept telling myself that everything was temporary and soon Jack would be home to make things right. Though we were living in Annapolis, our permanent home was in San Antonio, Texas. Because the Air Force Casualty Center as well as many of Jack's friends were in San Antonio, I decided to more the family back there; I wanted Jack to recuperate among his dearest friends when he returned. Many of my friends pleaded with me to stay in Annapolis. "Joan, you were born here; all your family and friends are here to support you," my mother said. But I had prayed for direction and I believed it was God's will for me to move.

Back in San Antonio, the task of tackling my responsibilities alone was overwhelming at first. Jack had always managed our household, even while he was in Vietnam. We had communicated daily by tapes, and when there was a problem with the house or a financial matter, all I had to do was to ask Jack's advice through the tapes. When the mails ceased to carry Jack's support, I awkwardly tried to set priorities and learn what was important for myself and the children.

But I wondered how I could continue to cope with the feelings of self-pity, joylessness and loneliness. Where was the news that Jack was alive and well? What could I tell the kids?

When one year had passed with no word from Jack, I realized that I had to start thinking of occupying my time. I didn't want to just sit around thinking about my problems. So I made an important decision—to return to school to study nursing. I trusted in God to help me in this new endeavor and hoped it was the right thing. But despite my schoolwork, the children came first in my life. Bringing up four lively children often seemed an awesome task. I yearned to have Jack share their growing years with me.

Like the time when Scott, as a Cub Scout, was preparing to enter a pinewood derby with his pack. I didn't know a thing about building that odd little car. But Scott and I stuck with it, determined to create a fine entry. The day of the race came, and our pitifully shaky creation took its place on the track alongside those painstakingly made by fathers and sons. The starter sounded and the other boys shouted gleefully as their cars sped down the track. Scott's racer seemed to fall apart just seconds after the start.

As I walked home with my disheartened son, I knew more than ever that I couldn't be both parents to the children. At home, I gathered them together. Maybe I couldn't do everything for them, I told them. But if we all helped one another, things would work out. We prayed together a long time that evening, for guidance and support.

What with my schooling and my children's lives, time rolled by in our household. Toward the end of 1972, after five years without Jack, I felt that I was making progress, though I was still just one parent in a lopsided family. I also came to know that, as an MIA wife, I didn't really fit in socially.

The few parties I attended only succeeded in depressing me. Little things—like a husband reaching out to touch his wife—

really affected me. I felt so alone as I watched them. After returning from those parties, I would feel overwhelmed by the silence of the house. I never really learned how to deal successfully with the intense loneliness; I just learned to endure it.

Early in 1973, San Antonio began buzzing with talk about a breakthrough in the Vietnam war. When the government announced that a prisoner-of-war list had been assembled, hope began to build in my heart—and I prayed even harder for good news.

On a Saturday in March, I was to learn whether Jack was on the list. The kids and I were just bursting that day; we couldn't wait for the official phone call that evening. Friends visited; some even came to take the kids to an early evening movie. Others called to say they were praying for me. I prayed that God would give me strength to accept His will—regardless of the outcome.

A friend from my nursing class had stayed with me the entire day, and we passed the early evening by talking about school.

The phone call came at ten p.m. I jumped to answer it.

"Mrs. Held?"

I barely responded.

"We regret to inform you that your husband, Jack W. Held, will not be included on the POW list to be released . . . "

The voice had begun, just as the other had done five years before, by reading a memo. Everything seemed to turn oddly quiet, then after a while I heard the voice stop. Then it said, "Is there anything that I can do?"

I mumbled a few questions, but the call just seemed to fade away. I hung up the phone, and I could feel tears filling my eyes. Jack was not a prisoner of war; he was not coming home.

Almost immediately the front door sprang open and my youngsters scampered toward me, begging to hear the news.

Through God's grace, each child had someone to hug them, to wipe away their tears. Even so, Cindy finally pulled away and ran to her room. I followed, torn with love and pity knowing so well how she was feeling. She was lying face down on her bed, sobbing as if her heart would break. I sat down beside her and offered the only comfort I had myself. "Cindy," I said softly, "God will take care of us."

I spent the rest of that night praying and believing that God would continue to give my family courage, even though Jack would surely never be coming home again. We would now have to put that hope behind us and look for whatever it was that God had in mind for us.

In May, 1975, after I had finished my nurses' training and was working in a San Antonio hospital, I visited my family in Annapolis. Returning to San Antonio, I felt upset and spent the whole day praying, trying to find out if God was saying something to me—and what it was. By the end of the day, I felt I had His answer. It was time for me to move back to Annapolis. I felt God wanted us there.

The Air Force approved the move immediately; a suitable home was found for us within a matter of days.

Because my Tuesday night Bible-study with the Officers Christian Fellowship had become so important to me as a spiritual and social outlet, I inquired about joining a similar organization in Annapolis. When I learned I could, I grew even more confident about leaving San Antonio, because I believed that God, as ever, would be with us.

The trip was long and tiresome. I finally drove into our Annapolis driveway with four excited children, two barking dogs, a load of plants and belongings. We had hardly finished our first tour of the house when our first guest drove up to our gate. There stood a tall Navy officer who introduced himself as Lt. Jon Saxman, the Officers Christian Fellowship representative at the U.S. Naval Academy. Could he be of some help? he asked.

In the days that followed, I began to hope that this cheerful, patient man—a bachelor—would be a part of God's plan for me in Annapolis.

For the children, especially, Jon was truly a godsend. He instinctively sensed their need for male attention, and gave it warmly. He would come over in the afternoons to jog with Scott or go to watch the other children at swim meets. He was always there for them and gradually, he began to be there for me, too.

In July, 1975, on a quiet Sunday afternoon, Jon asked me to

be his wife, asked if he could become a father to my four children. A great surge of joy swept over me. Could God be giving me such a gift? I told Jon yes, which was a bit presumptuous since legally I was still married.

Because Jack was still officially listed as missing in action, I had to petition the Defense Department to review Jack's case for me. I had long ago come to terms with the fact of Jack's death, but now it all seemed so painfully fresh. I prayed for guidance, asking God to speak through the Defense Department's decision.

Within three weeks, the government changed Jack's MIA status. I accepted it as God's green light.

At a lovingly prepared memorial service, the children and I said our good-bys to Jack and as I watched my children praying maturely, silently, I knew that God had kept His word. He had been with us all of our days, had taken care of us. And I knew for a certainty that Jack was with Him.

Jon and I were married on September 27, 1975—a bright and joyous day at the Evangelical Presbyterian Church in Annapolis. My children were my attendants—Terri and Cindy looked radiant in our home-sewn, gold creations; Scott, who was Jon's best man, and Brian were proud and handsome in their tuxedos.

Through tears I gazed at the people who had prayed and cried with me over the past seven years—200 strong. Later, as the pastor presented Lieutenant and Mrs. Saxman and family, they exploded with applause. God's faithfulness was apparent to all of us on that special day. God, I know now more than ever, will never leave us or forsake us.

When this kind of love binds a family together, nothing else matters.

Tommy Is Home

by JACK HUNTLEY

The letter from Dad and Mother asking me to give up my inheritance came when I was a college student.

I handed it to my wife, JoAnn, to read, then leaned back in the old chair of our furnished room and thought back to that house in Alliance, Ohio, in which I was raised. Some people called it the oddest-looking house in town.

It all started because Dad and Mother could not have children of their own. And so, in 1924, they adopted a little boy baby.

"But he can't just grow up alone," they said. So in another year they adopted a baby girl. This started a chain reaction of love with Mother and Dad adopting another child each year. Not only did they just plain love kids, but Mother had a compulsion to help young girls who were pregnant "out of wedlock," as she called it, and rejected by their families. That's how I came into the family.

Sometimes they adopted two babies in the same year; thus I have a brother and sister who are the same age.

I was the fourth child and was taken in by Mother and Dad when they were in their 40s. Three girls came after me.

Love from Mother and Dad surrounded and supported us. They called us their "Sears and Roebuck babies." "That's because," Mom said, "we carefully shopped for you and picked you out special because we loved you so."

And so, though each of us knew our background fully, we all grew up feeling we were especially important to them.

Dad didn't earn much as a railroader, but Mother did a lot with the little he was able to bring home. She grew vegetables in our back lot and canned them.

159

And as each new child came into the family our house expanded. I don't know how they managed it, but our little house on Seneca Street sprouted rooms until it looked like some Rube Goldberg creation.

But what it may have lacked in architectural design was more than made up for by the love that blossomed within it. And it was a love that was given us in unusual ways.

For instance, Dad's family had come from England. And with him he brought many of his homeland's customs. Most memorable was our "Family Night." That happened every Friday evening and was so special to all of us that if my senior prom had been held on that night, I would have skipped it in favor of that time around the table with my family.

Mother always set our dining-room table with a linen cloth and arranged the silver and dishes just so. Candles glowed, and Mother and Dad would dress formally. Dad would wear his tuxedo and Mother a long gown. She looked like an angel, and we forgot that she had been peeling potatoes only an hour before.

Dinner would last two or three hours. These were, in part, "training" nights in which we'd learn table manners. More important were the long discussions in which we'd each bring up our problems and questions. Perhaps it was a school situation or a disagreement with a brother or sister or a friend. Dad and Mother counseled us with advice, but we were always guided to make our own decision.

Now, as we sat in the little room called home, my wife and I were facing an important decision. I knew Mother and Dad had made the same request of my six brothers and sisters.

The letter was about Tommy. He was our family's eighth child and had joined the family after most of us had moved on. A year old, Tommy had been found unconscious on a rain-swept highway, evidently thrown from a speeding car by someone who didn't want him. His skull was fractured, and he was bruised and battered. The local hospital did not have the facilities to give him the constant 24-hour care he needed, and the welfare agency brought him to Mother "for a few weeks" until they could find a permanent place.

The weeks stretched into months as Tommy recovered. The welfare agency still hadn't been able to place him, but already he had won a place in my parents' hearts. There was something special about this blond, cuddly boy with the fair skin and bright blue eyes. Those eyes always seemed to be looking far into the distance. By now diagnosis showed permanent brain damage. Though Tommy would develop normally physically, he would never grow beyond the mental capability of a three-year-old.

By this time Mother and Dad had fallen completely in love with him. Dad particularly. And there was something special about the relationship that flowered between him and Tommy.

After several months, Dad decided the little fellow would be theirs. He went to the probate court and spoke to the judge who had handled all of our adoptions.

"It can't be done," the judge said. "Look, Roy," he added gently, "you and Florence are in your sixties. You're too old to adopt a child. Besides, that child does not meet the mental requirements to be put out for adoption. He will be a permanent ward of the state."

Dad went home upset.

When I came home for Christmas vacation, I heard the whole story from Dad as he held Tommy on his lap. Already I could see how much he cared about the little fellow.

"Talk to a lawyer," I suggested. "There must be a loophole somewhere."

When Dad did this, the lawyer thought that something in the way of a "permanent foster parent" relationship might be worked out.

"Well," said Judge Hardy when the case was presented to him, "we could entertain such a proposal if all of the Huntley assets were placed in trust for Tommy. After all," he added, "the parents don't have too many years left and the child's future must be considered."

There was a modest Huntley estate at this time. Mother's frugality had resulted in some pieces of land, the house and some savings that would see them through their older years.

Thus the same letter I received that April was also sent to my brothers and sisters: Joseph, 29, then pastor of the Broadway Tabernacle Church in New York City; James, 27, a registered nurse in New York; Donna Jean, 27, married in Nebraska; Mary, 23, married in Ohio, and Judy, 13, and Jane, 11, still at home.

The letter asked us all the same question: Would we be willing to give up our inheritance, our right to share the family's property and estate?

As I held the letter I thought long and hard. What inheritance? The treasure that Mother and Dad had already given us was not one of this earth that moth and rust could corrupt. (Matthew 6:19)

"Of course," I wrote back. "You have already given me everything a son could ask for."

The folks received similar letters from each of my brothers and sisters.

And so the court accepted the arrangement. They took title to the Huntley property and everything was put into a trust fund so the income would care for Tommy after my folks passed on. Then Mother and Dad were given permanent custody of Tommy.

On our visits home we all saw the joy Tommy now gave our parents in their older years. Dad and Tommy had become inseparable. Dad carried him with him wherever he went, on walks downtown, on visits to old cronies. Though Tommy could only make guttural noises, Dad understood his every want. And this included daily ice-cream cones.

Dad loved watching baseball on television. Tommy would always sit with him, wriggling excitedly at every base hit. We never could tell whether Tommy really understood what was going on or was just attracted by the movements on the screen. But that didn't matter. He was with Dad, and Dad was with him.

When Dad died at age 69, Tommy was ten. But not only did his loving presence help Mother through her grief, he also became her close companion and helpmate. We marveled at God's wonderful plan. For as Tommy grew, he became tall and strong. And though his brain did not develop, he was able to help mother with many simple chores. As she became older and more infirm, it was his sturdy arms and legs that cared for the lawn, got the mail and enabled her to continue living in the family home on Seneca Street.

Mother wrote us how Tommy loved to attend church with her. He always seemed to know when it was Sunday and would come downstairs dressed and ready. At church he would kneel when she did. He seemed to listen to the sermon and would make musical noises during the singing, even though he often held the hymnal upside down.

"I'm sure," Mother wrote, "that Tommy has a communication with the Lord that none of us can even imagine."

The phone call came late one rainy night in June, 1974.

The Lord had given Tommy 22 years on earth. The doctors explained that with his type of brain damage, the center that controls body temperature had ceased functioning. Tommy came down with a fever that soared. In two hours he was gone.

At the time, I was an Army chaplain in Washington, D.C. I got home as soon as I could. As we drove up in front of the old shingled house on Seneca Street, I worried about Mother. I knew she would be deeply upset and grieved. I opened the door and walked in, ready to comfort and console her. But what I found was totally unexpected. Mother was sitting in her wheelchair. She looked up at me, her face full of peace.

"Tommy's home," she said. "He's with Dad now." She took my hand, her eyes shining with assurance. "Tommy's no longer limited, Jack," she said. "Isn't it wonderful? He is healed."

Greater love hath no man than this, that a man lay down his life for his friends. (John 15:13)

**Every time a tragedy entered her life, God
has shown her it was not a dead end, but only a detour.**

Just a Bend in the Road

by HELEN STEINER RICE

Twice in my lifetime I thought my world had come to an end. I thought that all meaning and purpose were gone and that there was no reason to go on living. Yet, in both cases, what I did not know was that God had something excitingly new in store for me, that He would actually use those devastating personal losses to lift my soul into new spiritual consciousness and lead my life into new areas of service I never would have dreamed possible.

Of course I couldn't see any good in either of those heartbreaking experiences at the time. We never can. But now, with the luxury of a full life's experiences behind me, I am no longer looking at the back side of the tapestry, and I see much more clearly how all sorts of adversity—defeat, loneliness, disappointment, rejection, illness—can be used as a springboard to spiritual triumph.

The bitterest pills I've had to swallow both deal with the death of loved ones. The first came when I was 16 and a senior in high school. It was doubly traumatic, first because it came so suddenly and second because it was set against the backdrop of an unbelievably secure and happy childhood.

I grew up in Lorain, Ohio, a bustling steel town on the shores of Lake Erie. My dad was a railroad engineer for the Baltimore & Ohio, which was a good job, but not so good that it elevated us above our neighbors. Dad was a warm, gentle man with an amazingly wide sphere of friends.

Mother was a dedicated homemaker and a gifted seamstress. Mother, my sister and I were usually candidates for the fashion magazines when we strolled Reid Avenue on our way to 20th Street Methodist Church each Sunday.

Then suddenly, in the fall of 1918, Dad became ill. A flu epidemic was sweeping the country, taking many lives. In a matter of days, he was gone, another flu victim.

The great emptiness I felt the night of his death still causes something to stir inside me. I was so young, so vulnerable, so unaccepting. Standing on the back porch of our Reid Avenue house that cold, windy October night, I can remember sobbing over and over, "Why, why, God?"

Instead of going off to Ohio Wesleyan to study law as I'd planned, I went to work. Though we were not destitute, I wanted to stay close to home to help. My job was with the Ohio Public Service Company, doing an odd assortment of assignments at first, until I was asked to become public relations director.

I really worked hard learning everything I could about the company, determined to know the electric-power business inside and out. I also became active in the National Electric Light Association and was named chairman of its women's committee on public relations.

I'll never forget the day I was asked to speak at one of our conventions at Cedar Point. I went to the platform full of confidence, but with not much speaking experience. Suddenly, while I was being introduced, my mind went blank. I had no idea what I was going to say. I panicked. Shakily I walked to the lectern. There was that awkward silence. Suddenly a voice inside told me, "Your Heavenly Father knows what you are going to say." "Well, take over then," I answered, and without hesitation I swung into my talk.

There were several things I wanted to talk about. Many of my teachers had been suffragettes, and I believed with all my heart that women were capable of more responsibility and should be given a chance. I told the mostly male audience that many of them had made the mistake of choosing "blue eyes over gray matter" when it came to their hiring practices. After my speech

I got a big hand. It resulted in several more opportunities to speak, and before long I was going all over the country addressing various groups of businessmen.

One speech I'll never forget was one made to the American Electric Railways Convention in Washington. After my talk, I had my picture taken with President Coolidge and received the praise of B. C. Forbes, publisher of *Forbes Magazine*. He said I should leave Lorain and come to New York where "there is so much more room for doing big things."

Though I didn't move my base of operations, I did form my own lecture bureau and my speaking assignments increased. One took me to Dayton in 1928 to address a group of bankers. Afterward, a handsome young man named Franklin D. Rice, an officer with Dayton Savings and Trust, invited me to have dinner with him. I found him a wonderful person, warm and sensitive. We saw a lot of each other and within a year we were married.

The wedding was conducted by the Rev. Daniel Poling in New York City's historic Marble Collegiate Church. Franklin was a prominent businessman, intelligent and wealthy. We honeymooned on a ship in the Caribbean and returned to a big house with Tiffany chandeliers and servants to polish them. And for my wedding present, Franklin gave me a watch surrounded by 100 diamonds. It was one big make-believe ball but, like Cinderella's, it was not to last.

Much of my husband's wealth was invested in stocks. During the great Depression, when the market crashed, he lost heavily. However, he did what wise investors do in bad times—he bought more. After all, he reasoned, the prices would look cheap when the market rebounded. But, of course, it didn't rebound—not until much, much later. Finally everything we owned was gone, and without any warning, so was Franklin. He had broken from the strain. A note he left me read, "Darling the only thing I'm sorry about is that I never could give you all the things I meant to . . . You'll always go on. I only knew one world. I just can't become a bum—I have to go out with the band playing."

It was like the shock that came with my father's death. I had no idea what I would do, if in fact I wanted to do anything. Then out of the blue, the Gibson Greeting Card Company in Cincinnati asked me to come to work for them. "Make a survey of our cards and tell us how to improve them," the officers instructed me. I did as they said and came back with hundreds of recommendations. They accepted most of them, implemented them, and when the editor's job became vacant I was appointed to fill it. That was in 1934.

For several years I edited the company's cards, but did little writing. I did create my own little greetings for friends, writing a verse on some special occasion, but those messages were not salable. According to the experts, my thoughts were too sentimental, too religious. In the 1950s, though, Gibson did publish some of my verses, offering them in a few markets with modest results.

Many people wrote me, however, and the spiritual help they received from the things I wrote greatly encouraged me. The response of people has always been my greatest reward. Then, in 1960, a performer named Aladdin read a verse I'd written called *The Priceless Gift of Christmas* on *The Lawrence Welk Show*. The response of the public was overwhelming Thousands of people wrote to ask where they could find other poems like that one.

Since then God has opened a whole new world of friends to me. The simple verses I've written have been reproduced by the millions. They have been read on network TV, appeared in thousands of periodicals, in dozens of books.

All I do is put down the words God places on my heart, and then He does the rest. He even finds the people who need to hear them. I'm the world's worst promoter of my verses. I leave the distribution of the words I put on paper to the Author, the One who inspires them.

"So where do you go from here?" someone asked recently, knowing full well that I'm already beyond three score and ten in years. My answer is, "One day at a time as He directs." I know that at my age, time is getting short, but I've faced what I

thought was the end of the road before, and each time I've
discovered what I wrote in this poem:

> *When we feel we have nothing left to*
> *give,*
> *And we are sure that the song has ended,*
> *When our day seems over and the*
> *shadows fall,*
> *And the darkness of night has*
> *descended,*
> *Where can we go to find the strength*
> *to valiantly keep on trying?*
> *Where can we find the hand that will*
> *dry*
> *the tears that the heart is crying?*
> *There's but one place to go and that is*
> *to God,*
> *And, dropping all pretense and pride,*
> *We can pour out our problems without*
> *restraint,*
> *And, gain strength with Him at our side*
> *And together we stand at life's*
> *crossroads,*
> *And view what we think is the end,*
> *But God has a much bigger vision*
> *And he tells us it's only a bend.*
> *For the road goes on and is smoother,*
> *And the pause in the song is a rest,*
> *And the part that's unsung and*
> *unfinished*
> *Is the sweetest and richest and best.*
> *So rest and relax and grow stronger,*
> *Let go and let God share your load,*
> *Your work is not finished or ended,*
> *You've just come to a bend in the road.*

**I think God had placed His hand on my Gramp's
shoulder, and the light in his eyes was the peace he felt.**

I Remember Gramp

by JULIE FULTON

My grandfather lived with us for ten years. His name was Thomas Francis Brown, and he would say it often with pride. Sometimes during those years I would get angry with him, sometimes annoyed; sometimes I scoffed at his clumsiness and his shuffling gait. But most of the time I just loved him and listened to his stories and told him things that were going on in school. Every day he would be waiting for me to come home. He'd sit, squinting at the paper, on the porch, where he could trap the mailman with some news or a piece of gossip.

Everybody knew him. Tom Brown always wore a yellow fishing cap (though he never fished) and gray pants that bunched around the belt. He had many friends of all ages; people were attracted to him. He had a curiosity about everything and was ready to listen to everyone with warmth and wit. Thomas Brown also had a keen memory and a sharp mind; math figures were his specialty. They were leftovers from the long years of adding up bills for his business. My grandfather used to be a milkman long ago.

He had a storehouse of memories that he would share with me. We would spend hours poring over the yellowed scrapbooks of his war days, and he would sometimes tell me about his years with my grandmother. A hushed note of reverence would creep into his voice. But the memories were just a part of the past to Thomas Brown, and he never let them get in the way of the present. Every day he would drive (the driving got slower and slower as the seasons changed) up to the boardwalk· to visit his friends: the fishermen. I think he especially admired fishermen. He liked their patience and their humor—and their private communion with the sea.

When he was alone in his room, my grandfather would make things for his friends. He taught himself how to weave and sew, and he fashioned rugs and blankets and bags during those hours alone. He gave them all away. He could measure the passing of time by the rise in price of the materials he used. He measured age by the friends who died. As time went on, he stopped mentioning their names. He would just open the paper to the obituary columns and sit very quietly for a long time with the paper on his knees. "Well, Jule," I remember he would say, "I guess your old Gramp ain't gonna be around much longer. Guess he ain't long for this world." I never knew what to say. I would change the subject. I know that he was very proud of me. He was always the first to see my marks, or an award. He always came to see the plays I was in, although he couldn't hear the dialogue very well. It wasn't the dialogue that mattered.

I remember winter afternoons when Gramp would shuffle down the street to the lake and stand in the icy wind to watch the sunset. He would stand there, his yellow cap gleaming in the rays of the setting sun, and just take it all in. I would watch him from my window, and something would rise in my throat and catch my breath all of a sudden. I would leave the window and do something else just to get rid of that choking feeling.

I love the beauty of spring, and it hurts to see the autumn leaves lose their life and turn brown and old. It hurts to see them fall, and wither, and blow away. I knew, and Gramp knew, that Time was nodding to him. And Gramp nodded back.

The summer before he died was special in different ways. He was in fair health, although he would get tired easily. But he sat in the sun, and he fixed old chairs; he wove baskets and trapped the mailman every day at noon. It was a summer of beautiful sunsets. My grandfather felt something deep inside of himself that summer; I could see a new light in his eyes. I think God had placed His hand on my Gramp's shoulder, and the light in his eyes was the peace he felt. He told me that he had had a good life. He smiled. I smiled, too.

So in the fall, when the leaves turned yellow under the first chill of frost, my grandfather was not surprised to feel that Time had come for him. He was not surprised, and he was not afraid. He was just a little tired. When he left for the hospital, I was the one who cried, who felt angry. I was the one who was afraid of death.

My grandfather taught me differently. In him I could see the beauty of the fall, and the ending as a new beginning. I visited him often in the hospital. We would watch the football games on television, and my family would joke and laugh and try to overcome the deadening vacuum of silence. One day, though, Gramp said to me, "Well, Jule, I just don't know the score any more. You know what I mean? I just don't know the score any more." For my grandfather, knowing the score was everything. *Okay, Gramp*, I thought. *If you don't know the score any more, you can't play the game.* That was what he wanted to tell me. It was time to go.

So I talked about other things—school and dances. I described the sunsets I had seen at the lake and the many birds resting there from their long autumn flights. I held his hand, and watching those bleached-blue eyes, I saw the light in them gradually blow away.

I felt at peace. I knew he had gone home. He had gone home to the lovely lady I never really knew. Home to his buddies. Home to the springtime and the warmth of strong green trees. My love for him is part of my heart, as his death is part of my life. I have learned from both. So sleep well. Sleep well, Gramp. Because I know.

EDITOR'S NOTE: For this story Julie Fulton became a Guideposts' Youth Writing Contest winner.

5.
Love for Those Who Need Forgiveness

Forgive, and ye shall be forgiven.
(Luke 6:37)

The Interfering
In-Law

by ANNE THOMSON

I could never do anything right in my father-in-law's eyes. He was always critical of me, never satisfied with anything I tried to do for him. For this reason, I kept my distance from him and his wife, Marion, for the first ten years of my marriage, devoting myself to my husband, our five young sons and our home.

Then Marion died. Weeping over her open grave, I found myself wishing that I had been a more thoughtful daughter-in-law, more loving, more Christian. "I'll make it all up to her now by looking after Fitz," I silently promised myself.

Fitz lived twenty minutes from our house. The day of the funeral he surprised us by saying, "I certainly hope you don't expect me to live with you. I'd rather be dead than live in the confusion and noise of your house."

Although Fitz didn't want to live with us, he spent every afternoon at our house. He brought me his laundry, expecting me to iron his shirts and be a willing audience while he reminisced about the past or lectured me about the state of the world. Always remembering my graveside promise, I would postpone my own chores until he left, and I was frequently folding clothes at midnight.

Before a month passed, I came to dread the sight of my father-in-law. His demands on my self-control always left me exhausted. But I kept telling myself that I had to be a loving and forgiving daughter-in-law, if only to make up for the previous years of neglect.

175

Fitz arrived one day while I was fixing lunch for the kids. "I'm making omelets for lunch, Fitz. Won't you stay?" I said brightly, knowing he would stay anyway, but hoping that he wouldn't.

"Don't mind if I do," he said. He set the familiar laundry bag on a chair and peered over my shoulder. "Shake the pan, Anne. No, not that way. Let me show you."

He jerked the pan away, deftly swirling the froth of egg while the usual knot of anger gathered in my stomach. But I kept quiet. Then he handed the pan back, but continued coaching until I flipped the omelet onto his plate.

"Give that one to the children. I'll make my own," he said in a pained voice. "A proper omelet should not have even a fleck of brown. I cannot tolerate brown." I wanted to tell him that I couldn't tolerate him, but I kept quiet.

After Fitz left with his clean clothes, I burst into tears. I knew I couldn't stand him for one more day, but I also felt guilty for being such a flop as a Christian, that I was unable to keep a graveside promise for more than a couple of months.

My nine-year-old, Billy, interrupted my tears. "Here, Mom," he said, pushing a wilted bunch of dandelions toward me. "Why are you crying?"

"I guess because I'm tired and so far behind in my housework," I said, "and no matter how hard I try, I can't seem to please Grandpa."

"Gee, Mom, why don't you just tell Grandpa when you have other things to do? It's the truth. Anyway, we like the way you cook omelets," he said loyally.

I hugged him quickly for both the dandelions and the simple wisdom. Could it be that, in trying to behave like a model Christian, I had become a phony? I knew that the Bible tells us to turn the other cheek and to do good for those who persecute us. But then I remembered how Jesus had angrily thrown the money-changers out of the temple. And I remembered the stern rebukes Paul often wrote in his epistles to wayward Christians. Could a good Christian nevertheless be self-asserting?

The next day I was cultivating a small garden patch near the back door when Fitz pounced on me unexpectedly, jerking the tomato seedling out of my hand and speaking so sharply that I dropped the trowel.

"No, no, Anne," he scolded, "your garden isn't ready yet. You can't cover a tiny seedling with that kind of soil." He filtered the soil through his fingers in disgust before stomping back to his car and returning with a bag of fertilizer. "A good gardener is never in a hurry, Anne," he lectured as he turned the fertilizer into the fresh dirt. "It takes time and care to prepare the soil properly."

"Fitz," I said quietly, remembering Billy, "I don't have time anymore. Now, I want you to be part of my family, not some guest to be entertained or a critical parent I must obey. My way of doing things may not be perfect, but it has worked for me for the past ten years. I'm getting tired of being asked to change all the time."

Fitz put down the cultivator, tipped his hat, scratched his head, took off his glasses and blinked myopically at the sun. The silence stretched taut between us. He looked so old and sad that almost automatically I started to apologize. "I'm sorry, Fitz," I said. "I was up half the night with the kids, and I'm tired and edgy."

"No, Anne. I'm the one who's sorry." he said, and he touched my shoulder gingerly with his fingertips. "I've been so lonely and angry since Marion died that I guess I've been thoughtless. Marion used to tell me that I was a pretty insensitive cuss. Always been that way. Guess I'm too old to change now." He planted the remaining seedlings in silence.

Fitz did not visit the following week. I talked to him on the telephone to reassure myself that he wasn't sick, but he was noncommittal about his activities. I was sure that he was avoiding us because my bluntness had hurt his feelings. So when I saw his old black car coming up the driveway the following Friday, I ran to greet him.

"We've missed you, Fitz," I said. "What have you been doing? And where is your laundry?"

A wisp of a smile touched his pale lips. "I discovered the laundromat, Anne," he said, pleased with himself. "Even met an old codger like myself there. We had a cup of coffee together. Plan to do it again next week. I bought my first permanent-press shirts, too."

I watched him, seeing him really for the first time, as he took his gardening tools and a large flat of seedlings out of the back of his car. "I'm going to plant a real garden for you and the kids this summer, the way I used to for Marion," he said. "The weeding will keep me busy, and it will be good to see my plants grow."

Throughout the long, still summer days heavy with the scent of honeysuckle, Fitz spent hours tending the garden, weeding, watering and cultivating. Often when I finished my housework or the laundry, I took a pitcher of iced tea out to the garden and sat in the grass, the baby in my lap, chatting while he worked.

Our whole relationship had changed since that first day in the garden, and I now looked forward to seeing him. When Fitz died suddenly and unexpectedly in November, I knew that I had lost a very special friend. And I might never have got to really know Fitz if I had not learned that being a good Christian does not mean being a weak person, that Christian self-assertion is the best way to get to know others— and ourselves.

Love worketh no ill to his neighbor: therefore love is the fulfilling of the law. (Romans 13:10)

Could You Have Loved This Much?

by BOB CONSIDINE

This is the story of a woman's love for her husband. Whether he deserved that love—and why he acted the way he did—are questions I can't answer. I'm not going to write about Karl Taylor, this story is about his wife.

The story begins early in 1950 in the Taylors' small apartment in Waltham, Massachusetts. Edith Taylor was sure that she was "the luckiest woman on the block." She and Karl had been married 23 years, and her heart still skipped a beat when he walked into the room.

Oh—there'd been tough times during those years, times when Karl had been depressed, unable to keep a job; but she had helped him through the low times and she only loved him more because he needed her.

As for Karl, he gave every appearance of a man in love with his wife. Indeed, he seemed almost dependent on her, as if he didn't want to be too long away from her. If his job as government warehouse worker took him out of town, he'd write Edith a long letter every night and drop her postcards several times during the day. He sent small gifts from every place he visited.

Often at night they'd sit up late in their apartment and talk about the house they'd own . . . someday . . . "when we can make the down-payment . . ."

In February, 1950, the government sent Karl to Okinawa for a few months to work in a new warehouse there. It was a long time to be away, and so far!

This time, no little gifts came. Edith understood. He was putting every cent he saved into the bank for their home.

Hadn't she begged him for years not to spend so much on her, to save it for the house?

The lonesome months dragged on, and it seemed to Edith that the job over there was taking longer and longer. Each time she expected him home he'd write that he must stay "another three weeks." "Another month." "Just a couple of months longer."

He'd been gone a year now—and suddenly Edith had an inspiration. Why not buy their home now, before Karl got back, as a surprise for him! She was working now, in a factory in Waltham, and putting all her earnings in the bank. So she made a down-payment on a cozy, unfinished cottage with lots of trees and a view.

Now the days sped past because she was busy with her wonderful surprise. In two months more, she earned enough to get the floor laid on one of the bedrooms. The next month, she ordered the insulation. She was getting into debt, she knew, but with what Karl must have saved . . .

She worked feverishly, almost desperately, for now there was something she didn't want to think about.

Karl's letters were coming less and less often. No gifts she understood. But a few pennies for a postage stamp?

Then, after weeks of silence, came a letter:

"Dear Edith. I wish there were a kinder way to tell you that we are no longer married . . . "

Edith walked to the sofa and sat down. He'd written to Mexico for a divorce. It had come in the mail. The woman lived on Okinawa. She was Japanese, Aiko, maid-of-all-work assigned to his quarters.

She was 19. Edith was 48.

Now, if I were making up this story, the rejected wife would feel first shock, then fury. She would fight that quick paper-divorce, she would hate her husband and the woman. She would want vengeance for her own shattered life.

But I am describing here simply what did happen. Edith Taylor did not hate Karl. Perhaps she had loved him so long she was unable to stop loving him.

She could picture the situation so well. A penniless girl. A

lonely man who—Edith knew it—sometimes drank more than
he should. Constant closeness. But even so (here Edith made
an heroic effort to be proud of her husband)—even so, Karl had
not done the easy, shameful thing. He had chosen the hard way
of divorce, rather than take advantage of a young servant-girl.

The only thing Edith could not believe was that he had
stopped loving her. That he loved Aiko, too, she made herself
accept.

But the difference in their ages, in their backgrounds—this
couldn't be the kind of love she and Karl had known! Someday
they would both discover this, someday, somehow, Karl would
come home.

Edith now built her life around this thought. She wrote Karl,
asking him to keep her in touch with the small, day-to-day
things in his life. She sold the little cottage with its view and its
snug insulation. Karl never knew about it.

He wrote one day that he and Aiko were expecting a baby.
Marie was born in 1951, then in 1953, Helen. Edith sent gifts to
the little girls. She still wrote to Karl and he wrote back: the
comfortable, detailed letters of two people who knew each
other very well. Helen had a tooth. Aiko's English was improv-
ing, Karl had lost weight.

Edith's life was lived now on Okinawa. She merely went
through the motions of existence in Waltham. Back and forth
between factory and apartment, her mind was always on Karl.
Someday he'll come back . . .

And then the terrible letter: Karl was dying of lung cancer.

Karl's last letters were filled with fear. Not for himself, but for
Aiko, and especially for his two little girls. He had been saving
to send them to school in America, but his hospital bills were
taking everything. What would become of them?

Then Edith knew that her last gift to Karl could be peace of
mind for these final weeks. She wrote him that, if Aiko were
willing, she would take Marie and Helen and bring them up in
Waltham.

For many months after Karl's death, Aiko would not let the
children go. They were all she had ever known. Yet what could
she offer them except a life like hers had been? A life of poverty,

servitude, and despair. In November, 1956, she sent them to her "Dear Aunt Edith."

Edith had known it would be hard to be mother at 54 to a three-year-old and a five-year-old. She hadn't known that in the time since Karl's death they would forget the little English they knew.

But Marie and Helen learned fast. The fear left their eyes, their faces grew plump. And Edith—for the first time in six years, Edith was hurrying home from work. Even getting meals was fun again!

Sadder were the times when letters came from Aiko. "Aunt. Tell me now what they do. If Marie or Helen cry or not." In the broken English Edith read the loneliness, and she knew what it was to be lonely.

Money was another problem. Edith hired a woman to care for the girls while she worked. Being both mother and wage-earner left her thin and tired. In February she became ill, but she kept working because she was afraid to lose a day's pay; at the factory one day she fainted. She was in the hospital two weeks with pneumonia.

There in the hospital bed, she faced the fact that she would be old before the girls were grown. She thought she had done everything that love for Karl asked of her, but now she knew there was one thing more. She must bring the girls' real mother here too.

She had made the decision, but doing it was something else. Aiko was still a Japanese citizen, and that immigration quota had a waiting list many years long.

It was then that Edith Taylor wrote to me, telling me her story and asking if I could help her. I described the situation in my newspaper column. Others did more. Petitions were started, a special bill speeded through Congress, and in August, 1957, Aiko Taylor was permitted to enter the country.

As the plane came in at New York's International Airport, Edith had a moment of fear. What if she should hate this woman who had taken Karl away from her?

The last person off the plane was a girl so thin and small Edith thought at first it was a child. She did not come down the stairs, she only stood there, clutching the railing, and Edith knew that if she had been afraid, Aiko was near panic.

She called Aiko's name and the girl rushed down the steps and into Edith's arms. In that brief moment, as they held each other, Edith had an extraordinary thought. "Help me," she said, her eyes tight shut. "Help me to love this girl, as if she were part of Karl, come home. I prayed for him to come back. Now he has—in his two little daughters and in this gentle girl that he loved. Help me, God, to know that."

Edith and Aiko Taylor and the two little girls began to live together in the apartment in Waltham. Marie became the best student in her second grade class; Helen's kindergarten teacher adored her. And Aiko—she began studying nursing. Someday, she and Edith would like a house of their own. At night they sit up late and make plans. Today Edith Taylor knows she is "the luckiest woman on the block."

Love ever gives—
Forgives—outlives—
And ever stands
With open hands.
And while it lives,
It gives.
For this is Love's prerogatives—
To give, and give, and give.
          John Oxenham

Letter to a Stranger

by JULIAN B. MOTHERAL

Dear Someone Out There:
 I wonder if you remember the night of June 9, 1967, in Mayfield, Kentucky. I promise you I will never forget it.

You see, until that night, I could walk on moonlit nights with my wife. Until that night, I could run and play with my 14-month-old son. Until that night, I could support my family. I have been unable to do any of these things now for almost ten long years—ever since you put a bullet in my spine.

I'll never forget how nervous you were that night in the service station. The barrel of the pistol you held in your hand was shaking so hard. I remember saying to myself, "You're mighty nervous. This must be your first job."

I can't recall all the details of what happened after I gave you my day's receipts. I seem to remember picking up your gun from the floor where you had dropped it and struggling with you. Did you give me the concussion when you hit me with the pop bottle? Or have I just pieced these things together in an effort to explain all that happened that night?

I do remember being shoved toward the back room with my left arm twisted behind my back. I remember looking up at the clock as you shoved me into the back room. And I still can almost feel the gun barrel as you knocked me in the head again, and I fell to the floor.

I was through fighting. I lay there on the floor hoping you would leave. Why did you feel you had to bend over, place the gun barrel under my left arm and try to kill me?

I remember that crashing sound and the blinding flash of light. Then darkness. When I woke up, you were gone. I tried

184

to get to my feet, but from my neck down there was no feeling whatsoever. There was no pain at all. I was totally paralyzed. I was totally helpless. I was dying.

Only a few minutes had passed when three young boys came in and found me. I thought I had been screaming for help. They said I was only whispering.

I don't remember the 150-mile ambulance ride to the Baptist Memorial Hospital in Memphis. I only remember in bits and pieces the 18 days I stayed there.

My 17-year-old wife had to face the doctors and be told, "We cannot remove the bullet. There is nothing we can do." She brought me home to die.

I relived that night of the robbery over and over, and I would often awaken my family with my screams. I couldn't even feed myself. I was a vegetable.

As I lay there in the hospital bed in the back bedroom of my parents' home, I knew the feeling of crushing despair.

I remember once, when I had just taken 14 of my daily 42 pills, I looked over to the table by my bedside. On top of the table lay a pair of shiny scissors. If only I could reach them and plunge them into my heart it would be all over. Then I realized I couldn't lift my hands to grab them. I couldn't even kill myself.

Did you know I carried your bullet in my neck for over four months? Finally, I was taken to the Jewish Hospital in Louisville, and on November 3, 1967, the .22 caliber slug was removed from the center of my spinal column.

After the bullet was removed I returned to Mayfield. The doctors in Louisville told me I would never walk, that the most I could hope for was eventually to sit on the bedside with a special back brace and possibly be able to feed myself. I wanted more. I felt God could give me more. I left Louisville against doctor's orders.

With a very painful scar on the back of my neck where the bullet had been removed, I began the long road back to normal life. If I wanted to turn in bed, I had to be rolled over and a pillow propped behind my back so I could remain on my side. I could sit in a chair for only a few minutes at a time, and then I had to be tied in place to remain upright.

I would have my wife and my parents roll me to the back yard and place me on wrestling mats laid on the ground. I would try to crawl and drag myself along the ground, and although it would take me 30 minutes to crawl 30 feet, at least I was moving on my own.

Now the pain was to begin. Pain such as I had never before experienced. My physical therapist told me I would begin to have all kinds of weird feelings in my arms, and later in my legs. He was right.

Even today, though I am now able to use a walker and drive my car with special hand controls, I still have little sense of touch in my hands and arms and none in my legs. Yet, there are times when I feel as though someone has just drenched me in scalding water. At other times my arms will itch until I feel I am going to climb the walls. And the constant pain I carry in my arms and hands helps me to pray.

I promised God, a few months after you shot me, that if He would only let me have enough feeling to know pain, I would never again complain. Even pain was better than no feeling at all. I'm afraid a few times I have failed to keep my promise. But then, I try to stop and realize where He has brought me from.

Since that night I have had a chance to really search through the Book I thought I knew so well. I found that in the Bible there were truths I had never before seen. And when I applied to my life what those truths taught me, I was no longer a hopeless cripple, but a cripple with hope.

Do I forgive you for putting a bullet in my spine? By myself I couldn't do it. Will power will not always work. But when I remembered Jesus on the cross, I found that I could pray as He would: "Father, forgive the boy who shot me, for he didn't realize what he was doing."

I believe that, and although I do not know your name, and may never know it, this letter is written to you. I want you to know you need have no fear of retaliation from me. With His help, I have forgiven you. I knew no other way to reach you. But know this. Not one day goes by that I don't pray for you, that you may know the peace and happiness I now know.

The "Galloping Gourmet" and his talented wife made the art of cooking seem glamorous and exciting on television. But something was lacking in their recipe for a happy marriage.

The Missing Ingredient

by GRAHAM and TREENA KERR

S cissors are a wonderful invention, two blades that pivot on a pin. God made man and woman in the same way—two blades. And He put them together with a union called marriage.

We were married, put together by God, on September 22, 1955, but our marriage scissors never worked. The only exposed edges were the points, and points are for stabbing, not cutting.

We loved each other, we always have—ever since we were 11 years old and held hands briefly at a party where we had strawberries and cream and played badminton and listened to the bees.

Treena: My father was a genius, a portrait painter who alternately followed his own will and his clients' whereabouts. We never knew from one year to the next where our home would be.

Graham: My parents ran a hotel and I grew up experiencing a "champagne existence on a beer income." I never made a bed or had to wash a dish; the hotel staff managed all those incidentals. My parents were always busy. The holidays were working days, and we never shared with the community.

I was a loner when I first met Treena in England. She was the loveliest thing I had ever seen and we became close companions. She had younger brothers, but I was an only child.

We used to listen to the radio while the rain ran down the diamond-shaped leaded panes and debate the sinister motives of a bystander in a trench coat as he innocently waited for a bus.

We rang each other on the phone and read poetry or just listened to the other breathe.

Treena: My family finally left England and went to the Channel Islands. I used to write to Graham occasionally, and I day-dreamed about our early "love." I grew up in a difficult home. My parents were not loving parents, and I sought a release from painful reality by becoming an actress.

I was quite good, at least the critics used to say so. I loved the cameo parts where I could steal the show but still feign non-competitiveness with the rest of the cast.

I got love from the audience on my terms; when the curtain went down I was satisfied and didn't have to trade love on a one-to-one basis.

Graham: While Treena was acting, I became a soldier. One day in camp, I opened a newspaper and there, spread over the center pages, were photographs of Treena, my first love. She had won a beauty contest and she looked radiant.

I wrote and she answered. The thread remained unbroken.

Treena: In 1954 I returned to England and wrote to Graham. He replied and within a month we had met and found that after nine years of separation our love was still alive.

Graham: Within ten hours of being with her I proposed, and Treena said yes. We were living our early love again, but this time there was drama, urgency, drive; we were adults, now, though we didn't always act like it.

Treena: I had a violent temper and a very acid tongue. I was more seriously hurt by my early environment than I—or Graham—knew.

Graham: While Treena was the spark, I seemed to be the drive in our marriage. When her moods were electric I would "take it," but also build resentment at the same time. I found release in working. As the work element increased, my available time and attention for Treena decreased. I began to set my sights on possessions—Italian cars, homes by the water, luxurious yachts. And a burgeoning TV career in Australia proved the wherewithal to turn some of those materialistic dreams into reality.

Treena: By this time I was in the theater again, happy and contented, feeling I'd finally got things together. We had two children and I could manage the housework and the theater and Graham . . . when he was home.

Graham: Treena would try to time her stage work to coincide with my TV recording dates, but it never seemed to work. The plays she did always ran longer than expected and it seemed that we were never together. The theater became my rival; her work seemed to give her more joy and satisfaction than I could. Finally we lost control. Success, exposure to luxury and to that smart show-business set, coupled with the pursuit of two separate careers, were too much. The time came when I sought sympathy and attention from another woman. I cannot possibly express the absolute hell that followed that senseless, brutal act, the tearing at both our hearts with the points of the scissors.

Treena: I was filled with righteous anger; I felt dirty and ashamed. It was so unfair. "Why? Why? Why?" I demanded.

Graham: "I don't know," I would reply. All I knew was remorse for our lost love, and a furious desire to make up for it somehow. I would *do* things, *buy* things, *go* places; it was all external patching up when an internal healing was what was needed.

We were submerged in a sea of recrimination, unforgivingness and eventually retaliation. We hacked away at each other with separated blades.

In 1968 we were discovered by American television interests and brought from Australia to perform *The Galloping Gourmet* series.

In an effort to save our failing marriage we agreed that we would co-operate in the production. Treena would be the producer and I would be the clockwork cook. The pressure of the nonstop pace of 200 new shows a year was agonizing. The enemy now became the work load that we shared.

Professionally, we were a tremendously successful team. All the thwarted power of love was converted into drive and ceaseless competition to see who could do the most before collapsing. By April, 1971, we had well over a million dollars in the bank.

In that same month we were hit by a huge truck on Highway 101 outside of San Francisco. Our careers were ended.

Treena: I had violent visions and fell into deep periods of despair and fear. Eventually this depression induced illness—tuberculosis—and I had one lung removed.

Graham: I hadn't suffered mentally but my neck and back had been injured and I couldn't take the recording pace any more, especially without Treena producing the shows. Together we had managed, but on my own the burden became impossible. So we walked away from that life and went to sea in a beautiful yacht called *Treena*. She was 71 feet long and flew 5300 square feet of canvas. She was one giant investment aimed at recapturing our family unity and our love for each other.

But the boat was too big and too fancy and nobody except its owner-skipper wanted to go sailing anyway! It was a 66-ton love-substitute that ate up all our reserves.

Treena: Twenty-five-thousand miles and twenty-two months later our fragmented family, strained even more by the isolation of the shipboard life, came to rest in Maryland at the small port of Oxford. There we purchased an 1814 white clapboard Southern colonial mansion with acres of lawn and graceful colonades and wide river views.

In this tranquil spot I finally hit rock bottom. Nothing had worked at sea and now there was no peace ashore. I began to take pills—"uppers," "downers," painkillers, sleeping pills—anything to try to control the violent moods that had caused our doctor to discuss with Graham the possibility of my voluntary commitment.

Our children were in serious trouble; life was unbearable.

We had a black maid working for us at that time. Her name was Ruthie and she shimmered with joy every day. I turned to her one day and said, "I just don't know what to do, Ruthie." She simply said, "Why don't you give your problems to God?" to which I brusquely replied, "Okay, God, You take them. I can't handle them any more."

God took them! Seven days later I went to Ruthie's small

church in Bethlehem, Maryland. As the singing, handclapping congregation prayed for their "new sister" I felt an undulation in the pit of my stomach that rose to nearly suffocate me; I screamed and fell to my knees, crying tears that flowed like waterfalls.

"I'm sorry, Jesus. I'm sorry, Jesus," I repeated again and again.

I was baptized in water and felt glowingly clean. Then they asked me if I wanted to tarry for the Holy Spirit. I didn't know who the Holy Spirit was, let alone what tarry meant.

"What do I do?" I asked.

Ruthie told me to say, "Thank You, Jesus," so I did—over and over. The church was hot and I felt ridiculous. *Really*, I thought, *you are a sophisticated woman of forty going right out of your mind!*

Then a bright light fell on my face and I thought, *Now they've turned up the church lights to make me think that I've got it—whatever "it" is!*

I opened my eyes and there I saw a Man. He was dressed all in white and He had the most wonderful smile I have ever seen. It held all the love in all the world. He stretched His hand toward me and He touched my heart. He said, "You have it," and I laughed tears of joy as I said, "I know . . . I know . . . I know."

I believed in Jesus at that moment. He is alive; I've seen and spoken with Him, so I truly know.

I left that church a totally new human being filled with the great certainty that, if I just kept quiet, my husband and family eventually would share this love.

Graham: I had tried unsuccessfully to get our lives back together with everything that money could buy. But now Treena was utterly and completely changed. It was a miracle!

There were no more rows or recriminations. She forgave me and seemed to mean it. Our children were happier; the house was peaceful. But I still worried. How long would this last? When would this Jesus thing disintegrate? If I got too close, I'd get hurt when it blew, so I kept back and watched and waited.

Treena: While Graham waited, I prayed. I prayed everywhere, especially in the broom cupboard. (The Bible had said to pray in a closet!) (Matthew 6:6) I fasted and prayed, but never urged Graham to follow.

Graham: After three months I was totally convinced Jesus was real and that He was alive in Treena. It was then that I went on my knees and told Him, "Jesus . . . I love You." And with that confession, He loved me right back.

Graham and Treena: When we pray together we hold hands, and through us now flows the love of Jesus. We are forgiven, so now we have the ability to forgive. There are no old hurts left, only the hunger to serve Him and His people with our lives.

We are a new pair of scissors put together by God. He, at last, is the pinion at the center of our marriage.

And be ye kind one to another,
tenderhearted, forgiving one another,
even as God for Christ's sake hath
forgiven you. (Ephesians 4:32)

The Bondage of Hate

by LAWRENCE H. DAVIS

The moment my friend stepped through the door, I knew this was no social visit. "L.H. . . . ." he said, staring out into the schoolyard, "there's been a meeting of the School Board. . . ."

I laid down my pen and said, "What are you trying to tell me?"

"He's done it at last, L. H., you're out. Harvey's forced the Board to vote for a new superintendent."

I finished out the day mechanically and walked slowly home. Verna met me at the door. One look and she knew something was wrong.

"What's happened" she said.

"I'll tell you later, after dinner."

"No, I want to know now. Children, you run upstairs and wash."

Above the racket of our four children's feet on the stairs, I told her:

"Harvey's got control of the Board—I'm out."

Verna sat down heavily on a kitchen chair. I probably shouldn't have told her so suddenly: neither of us was that young any more. "What are we going to do?"

"I just don't know."

In earlier years, my chances of finding another job might have been better. I'd been in school work since 1902 when I began teaching in a little one-room school house on the Indiana plains. Thirty years of teaching and managing experience. Plus the less measurable fact that schools were my life, my love.

These were my qualifications. But this was 1932 when the Depression was in full swing.

All that spring and all that summer, each time I ripped open a reply to an application, it was *No*.

One job in a little Iowa school drew 165 applicants.

"That makes some contest, Verna," I said handing her the letter. "Maybe I shouldn't have told them I'm 51."

When it became evident that I would not find a job in my profession, I began to look for other work, any work. I walked the streets and knocked on doors and always the answer was the same: "Sorry."

My age, the Depression... but there was still another reason for my not finding work; more subtle, but just as devastating. People instinctively kept away: they sensed that I was charged with hate.

Have you ever known what it is to hate a man: the feeling works away at you, inside, gnawing like a hunger pain. With me it was so intense that whenever I had to go uptown, I took the back streets because I was afraid of meeting Harvey. I was afraid of what I might do.

There's a perverse kind of satisfaction in returning over and over to the source of pain. In my case I relived the events that led to my dismissal. They began, I told myself, the day we didn't buy that refrigerator. . . .

Harvey, the president of the Board, was in the kitchen appliance business. Shortly after I was named superintendent, he said, "It seems to me, Davis, that our Home Economics class needs a new refrigerator." He winked. I didn't understand that wink and answered that I would ask the Home Economics teacher. At the next meeting of the Board I had her reply: she would rather have two sewing machines.

"Fine. Fine," said Harvey jauntily. But I noticed that his hands were clenched into tight fists. Later as we were leaving, he spoke to me again. "Some day, Davis, I'm going to control this Board." He was smiling when he said it; it took me four years to understand that smile.

How I loved to chew on that story as I walked about looking for work. I think without realizing it, I was glad not to find a job.

Because the harder things were, the more Harvey became a villain.

Many of the townspeople were on "my side." There was one thing, however, that puzzled me. Late one evening our minister called and after visiting on the porch for awhile he arose to leave. "I know you're having a hard time," he said. "Just keep close to God and you will see your way clear . . . "

Keep close to God! God? It was almost as if He stood against me; I could understand feeling far from Him if I had been the one to hurt Harvey. But Harvey had hurt me: why should I feel so unable to pray?

The summer leaves turned to brown and dropped and we were down to the last few pennies of our reserve. By the first killing frosts, we were living on skim milk, an occasional egg and bread. The children got the eggs and milk. Verna and I lived on bread.

I mean it literally. Morning, noon and night Verna and I each took one piece of bread and then said the usual blessing: the Lord's Prayer.

And yet it was this prayer which gave me freedom from my slavery to hatred.

I will never forget the day. It was cold: snow already had fallen. The night before a friend had paid us a visit and when he found us all sitting around in our heaviest clothes, he offered to let me cut two large elms from his farm for fuel.

Before daylight the next morning I shouldered my ax and saw and was off to his farm down the river. The snow made the five mile walk difficult. Inside the pocket of my jacket was my one slice of bread: it was all I would have to eat until I returned home that evening.

When I reached the fields and saw those two giant elms my heart sank. I was a schoolteacher, not a woodsman! Still . . . I picked up my ax and took a mighty, hate-filled swing. Four hours later the trees lay stretched across the snow. Then I took out my piece of bread and sat down on one of the tree trunks.

Mechanically I began to recite the words Verna and I always said before meals. "Our Father which art in heaven, hallowed be Thy name. Thy Kingdom come . . . "

I looked over the gray, icing river, not really paying attention to my words: " . . . forgive us our trespasses as we forgive those who trespass against us . . . "

I stopped short.

What was this I had just said? Forgive us in the same way *we* forgive? Suddenly I was shaking from head to toe, and not from the cold. It was a physical reaction to a gripping and powerful insight that swept over me. I saw with a brilliant kind of clarity why I had felt so far from God. I was blocking my own path to Him with my own unforgiven sins. I saw that in His prayer Christ put a condition on forgiveness: first we had to forgive others, *then* we could straighten out our own relation to God. Specifically, I would have to forgive Harvey before I could shed the depression of my own unforgiven sins.

"Father," I prayed, almost joyously, "help me to learn to forgive."

After a while the most penetrating peace settled over me. I was relaxed and spent. But I felt wondrously clean too. In the gathering shadows of darkness that afternoon, I started home. I sang all the way.

I do not feel it was coincidence that I found work shortly after this experience. Nor do I feel it was coincidence that in the years which have passed since this incident, I have never again allowed myself to hate. I know what damage it can do.

There was a particular moment when I *knew* I was free. For several days I worried about meeting Harvey. I thought I had forgiven but I was just not sure. How would I react when I saw him again?

Then one bright, cold day I deliberately put myself to the test: I walked uptown—by the main streets. There must have been a new spring in my step, because people turned to stare as I walked past. Up ahead was Harvey's store. My pulse beat faster as I drew near.

And suddenly there he was.

He came out of the store and turned to close the door behind him. Thus he had his back to me. I could easily have turned around. But—I will never forget this next moment—I did not *want* to turn around. I walked up to Harvey and greeted him like an old . . . well, "friend" would be too strong a word. But the point is I held no ill will toward him.

"Harvey?" I said.

He swung around abruptly and saw me. His jaw dropped. A startled puzzled look came on his face.

I held out my hand. Harvey grasped it hesitantly, then firmly—and in that moment I knew the last barrier had been removed between God and me.

Lord, make me an instrument of Your peace.
Where there is hatred, let me sow love;
Where there is injury, pardon;
Where there is doubt, faith;
Where there is despair, hope;
Where there is darkness, light:
And where there is sadness, joy.
O Divine Master, grant that I may not so much seek to be
    consoled as to console;
To be understood as to understand;
To be loved as to love;
For it is in giving that we receive;
It is in pardoning that we are pardoned;
It is in dying that we are born to eternal life.
        St. Francis of Assisi

Help Will Come, Richie

by BOB YOUNG

The gangling, black-haired teen-ager stood before me, his eyes cast downward. Every once in a while he'd glance up, arrogantly. Just 18, Richie* had been arrested for vandalism and he'd also been cutting school.

The look on Richie's face—a look hovering on the brink of delinquency—reminded me of someone. Then suddenly I knew who. Me.

"You know, Richie," I said slowly, measuring my words, "I was a lot like you once."

The boy peered up at me.

"Yup, I was one bad dude. I did some pretty weird things when I was a kid, and went to prison for them. Let me tell you something; prison is a heavy scene."

Richie stared, dumbfounded. I really couldn't blame him. Dressed in the black robes of a judge, I'm sure I didn't seem the sort to have been a convict.

But I once was, and now Richie was one of the first cases brought before my court since I had become a judge early this year. I wanted to handle him carefully. Not just because I was new to the job, but because I had a feeling that what I would say to this boy was going to be important to him—and to me.

In Richie's eyes I saw a familiar look—a searching look I knew all too well. Trite as it sounds, what I wanted to tell Richie would be the voice of experience. Not just the experience of my background, but experience that came from finally understanding what my own search meant, and maybe how it could help him. Here's what I told him:

Name has been changed. 198

Back when I was your age, Richie, I was a member of the Galloping Gooses Motorcycle Club, an outlaw gang in Los Angeles not unlike the Hell's Angels. Like you, Richie, I thought I knew all the answers, but I was really just mixed up. At 19, I was arrested for stealing a credit card from someone's mailbox. The police offered me probation if I pleaded guilty. "Nah," I said, figuring I was smart enough to beat the rap. "I want a trial."

Even now, many years later, I can still see that judge's face as he pronounced sentence. "Six years," he snapped.

I couldn't believe it. My mother, a woman with a strong religious faith, was shocked to know I'd done something that would put me in prison. "What went wrong?" she asked me tearfully.

"I don't know," I said. And I really didn't know. My brother and sister had never got into any trouble—just me.

But my mother, as usual, refused to give up on me. "Bobby," she said as the bailiff took me away, "I'm going to pray for you while you're in prison."

"Sure," I said, shrugging, feeling it wouldn't do any good. As it appears you have, Richie, I had given up on God, too.

After 20 months in Lompoc Prison, I was paroled, but I got hooked up with the Gooses again. Soon I was back in jail.

Surprisingly, my parole officer, Walter Lumpkin, didn't berate me after the arrest. Nor did he a year later when I was present at a knife fight and was charged with attempted murder.

But he did sit me down and talk to me, in the same way I'd like to speak to you, Richie—with genuine concern.

"Bob," he told me, "take a look at yourself. Your life is going down the drain. You've got to do something to get a new start. Have you thought about college?"

I had thought about it a lot while in prison, and wondered if I should go back. As it probably does to you, Richie, school seemed to be an enemy. However, I stubbornly re-entered at Cal State in Los Angeles, and, incredibly, this time I found I enjoyed studying.

Toward the end of my senior year in college I took an aptitude test. Like the judge who once sentenced me, the man who counseled me afterward was a man who showed me very little concern.

"Mr. Young," he said, "you show a high aptitude in three professions—judge, attorney, or commercial pilot. But your criminal record precludes you from being either of the first two. We'll have to find something else for you."

No we won't, I decided. I would be a lawyer. Filled with the same kind of unrelenting craziness that had always got me into trouble before, I applied to—and was rejected by—11 law schools. My jail record was the determining factor.

Here, Richie, is where I'd like to show you a lesson in not giving up. I decided to visit those 11 law schools personally. My mother was there to see me off—and again she was leaning on what I thought of as her religious crutch. "Bobby," she said, "my prayers are with you."

For two months, Richie, I traveled over three states visiting law schools. Each confirmed its rejection.

Finally there was only one left—McGeorge School of Law in Sacramento, California, my last hope. I was ushered into the office of Charles Luther, the assistant dean. Like all the other law-school administrators, he seemed surprised to see me. But as soon as we started talking, I noticed he was different. Like my parole officer, Walter Lumpkin, Dean Luther seemed to really care about me. He, like Mr. Lumpkin, was much more interested in my future than in my past.

"Bob," he said finally, "I'm going to recommend that you be admitted to McGeorge." My heart leaped wildly. "However," he said, "you must understand that your acceptance does not mean you'll ever be admitted to the bar."

Three years later, with a law degree and honors behind me, I found out what Dean Luther meant. Even though I passed the bar exam on my first try, the state examining committee said my criminal record meant I would have to have a thorough background investigation.

For two years I waited while the investigation dragged on. Whenever I got depressed, Dean Luther, and especially my mother, always seemed to call at the right moment to cheer me up. Then, in August 1972, I was notified I had been admitted to the bar.

"See, Bobby," my mother said when I called to tell her the good news, "the Lord does take care of His own."

In 1974, I took a job in Auburn, California, as deputy public defender. Part of my work there involved the Loomis, California, Justice Court. One day a colleague told me the Loomis court judge was retiring.

"Why don't you run for his office, Bob?" he asked.

"Me?" I said, laughing. Then, I stopped. I had come pretty far. Why not see what I could really do?

I started off the election campaign with my criminal history, just as your arrest will follow you the rest of your life, Richie. At one point, campaign rumors got so vicious I was termed a murderer, rapist and worse.

Just about everyone assured me I had no chance to win. But hard work, the kind I had become used to in college and in law school, the kind of hard work you've got to be prepared for, Richie, became my battle plan. I think I and my campaign helpers rang nearly everyone's doorbell, showing the Loomis residents who I was, but more importantly, showing them I cared.

Election Day 1976 was the happiest day of my life. By a margin of 300 votes, I was voted judge of Loomis Court, and that's how, Richie, I came to be here before you.

Actually, there were some other reasons for my being in this court. I got here because people cared about me—Walter Lumpkin, Dean Luther, my mother. They cared about me even when I didn't care about myself.

But it's my mother I think of when I look at you, Richie. A dear, sweet woman of 64, she has lived all her life in the strength she gets from the Lord. Over and over she had impressed upon me the need to trust in Him. She prayed for me, even when those prayers meant so little to me.

A lot of incredible things have happened to me, Richie, but now I know that those prayers of my mother were the most important things.

That's why, Richie, I'm going to recommend to your parents

that in addition to going to family counseling, you and your folks visit you church's pastor. I'm going to recommend to your parents, too, that they show you more concern, more attention, more love.

And I'm going to tell your parents, Richie, to forget what you've done. Just because you did some wrong things doesn't mean you can't change.

Like a lot of young kids, Richie, your getting into trouble was a way of crying out for help. I know the feeling, believe me. But now that your cry has been heard, you've got to get ready to accept—from your family, your friends and from God—help when it does come.

And help will come, Richie, I know.

I believe in you
no doubt because you believe in me,
which is another way of saying,
whatever I have is yours,
or I'm your friend,
or I like your way of thinking,
or thanks for standing by me,
or you are something special,
or I love you.
                    Fred Bauer

Wedding vows are easily broken. Mending them is harder.

How Could He Do This to Me?

by MARGARET CAMPBELL*

They say the wife is always the last to know, but when David hung up the telephone that night I knew before he spoke a word what I was going to hear. We were dressing to go out to the faculty New Year's Eve party, and although I sensed there would be no party for us that evening, I nevertheless walked over to David and turned my back. Automatically he pulled up the zipper on my dress.

"Who was that on the phone?" I asked carefully. David didn't reply. I turned to face him and he returned my look with one of stony impassivity.

"I don't know how to tell you," he said.

And so I told him. "It's Gloria, isn't it?" I said. Cute, tiny, feminine Gloria, young enough to be David's daughter, the wife of one of David's assistants. Clinging and sweet, wide-eyed with admiration for David's work in the Science Department, Gloria also, I thought bitterly, had treated me with deferential respect, had asked my advice and help in her housekeeping and cooking, had asked me to be her friend.

"Yes, it was Gloria." David hesitated, then plunged on. "She says Roger's found some love letters I wrote to her. Margaret, I want a divorce. Gloria and I love each other, and we want to be married."

In a crisis I am always calm and competent; it is only later that I go to pieces. "I'm sorry, David," I said evenly, "no divorce. We've got to think of the children. Besides, I don't think you really want a divorce."

*All names have been changed.   203

My intuitive feeling was that David, caught up in circumstances he had created, felt obliged to carry matters
through to the only conclusion he could envision.

Gradually I learned the whole story. Gloria was an only
child, the petted darling of elderly parents who had died in a
car accident six months before she met and married Roger. She
had been left enough money to support her and Roger comfort-
ably, but Roger, she had confided to David, cared more for
science than for spending happy, lazy hours with her. She
leaned more and more on David, until one day she came to his
office and tearfully confessed that she had stopped loving Roger
the day she met David. And David rushed headlong into the
thrills and excitement of a love affair.

Intellectually I could understand it. When I was able to think
rationally, I could see life from David's point of view. At age 50
he had reached the top in the small denominational college
where he teaches; less than a year before he had been made
head of the Science Department. Without ever mentioning it,
we both knew this was the end of the road for him. There would
be no offers from one of the big universities—he simply didn't
have the writing or experimenting credentials—and there was
nothing left to work for where he was. He was at the last stop
before retirement.

Was it any wonder, really, that when desirable and available
Gloria appeared, David jumped at the chance to escape from
his self-doubts and anxieties?

In my head, I knew that David and Gloria had nothing to do
with David and me, nothing to do with our marriage, which
had always been strong and good. But knowing a thing in one's
head and feeling it in one's heart are two different matters.
Never in my life could I have imagined the depth of my hurt,
the sense of total rejection, the daily reminders of betrayal.

And it wasn't only *my* rejection and betrayal that hurt me.
David had rejected all of us during the last three months when
his attentions were centered on Gloria. Luckily young David,
19, was away at college and was unaware of the change. But his
17-year-old brother Andrew complained to me, "Gee, what's
the matter with Dad? He doesn't even seem to care that I

finally made the varsity basketball team." Our daughters, Rebecca, 15, and Elizabeth, 13, were actually reduced to tears over their father's lack of interest in their activities.

I thought back over the 21 years we had been married, the life we had shared together. How I had kept the kids out of David's hair so he could prepare for classes and grade papers and handled money matters in order to spare him from financial worries. How I would read and digest material to help him in his job.

That's why my hurt was so deep. And out of my hurt I struck back at David. I wanted to make him suffer, too. "You're a nothing," I snarled at him. "You've gone as far as you can go. And now all you have to show for your life is one disgusting affair with a neurotic spoiled girl."

Apparently my reminder of his responsibility to his family had made an impression on David because he never attempted to move out of our home. And after thinking things through for several days, he tried to make amends.

"I'm sorry, Margaret," he said finally. "I was a fool. It's you I love. I always have." But I rejected everything he said. I didn't believe him when he said he was giving Gloria up. The time came when David simply endured my vicious tirades in silence—a silence I took to mean he was longing for the sweetness and joy that Gloria had brought him.

Gradually anger and bitterness turned me into a person dominated by hate. Ruthlessly I went through the house. David had given me a beautiful Chinese vase for Christmas, but the real pleasure of David's Christmas, I believed, had been in picking out a present for Gloria. So I took the vase out onto the front porch and smashed it with a hammer, and left the fragments where David would have to see them when he came home. Gloria had mailed little gifts to David at his office. Very well, I would mail "gifts" also. I got out our wedding album, removed each picture and carefully tore it into pieces. I put the pieces in a box, gift-wrapped it, wrote on the card, "For my *loving* and *faithful* husband," and mailed the package to David.

Throughout that terrible time, my thoughts were turned constantly to God. Where was He? *He is just, He is merciful,*

He keeps His promises to all who turn to Him in faith and trust,
I thought. "Help me, God," I begged. "Heal my wounds, make
David sorry he did this terrible thing to me. Make my life good
again."

I understand now that God helps and comforts only those
who commit their problems and hurts to Him without reservation. Yes, I wanted God to help me, but it had to be on my
terms, not His. "Where are You, God?" I would sob—but God
was silent, because while I wanted Him to comfort me, I also
expected Him to punish David. I decided that God, too, had
rejected me.

And then an "ice age" set in between David and me. We
ceased talking to each other. David aged. He was no longer a
vigorous man in the prime of life—he was a stoop-shouldered,
gray-faced, defeated 50-year-old. I lost 30 pounds and couldn't
bear to look at myself in the mirror.

Shut away in my world of desperate hurt, I became exter-
nally bright and brittle—"keeping up appearances." I joined
volunteer groups, and one of my activities involved visiting our
local old-people's home several times a week. I began with the
intention of escaping from my pain by assuring myself that even
though David had rejected me, I could still be of use to others.
But instead of giving, I received.

One of the old folks I visited regularly seemed just an ordi-
nary old woman, at first sight no different from any of the others
one sees in such places. But as I came to know her, I discovered
a firm patience and a deep compassion that cut through human
behavior to see the needs behind it.

Katie's wise old eyes saw through my bright chatter soon
enough, and eventually the day came when she spoke up.
"Margaret, there is despair behind every joyful word you utter.
Can an old woman help?"

And so I told her. I told her everything—of my hurt, of my
awareness that I was destroying David, whom I deeply loved,
because of my inability to deal with the hurt. "It's so unfair," I
protested. "I did nothing to deserve all this."

"In other words," Katie said, "you want revenge."

"Revenge?" I echoed stupidly.

"Yes, you want to punish David. I've seen other people just as malevolent as you in similar circumstances. But vindictiveness doesn't accomplish anything. Of course David did wrong, but does that really matter? Does love set conditions? Do you want David to come crawling back on your terms? If you truly love David, Margaret, remember this: *Real love doesn't have to win*. And if you want God's help in this, I think you've got some work to do—recognizing your anger and putting it on the line with God."

Katie paused for a minute to let me think about what she had said. Then she continued, "By making David miserable you're also making yourself miserable. Just look at yourself in my mirror over there."

As I looked at my gaunt, bitter face in the mirror, I knew what Katie said was true. All those weeks when I had been praying to God to help me I knew deep down that He wanted me to be loving and forgiving—to give David another chance. But I had rejected that—I felt God was giving me too great a test.

It was strange, but this old woman, close to the end of her own life, finally helped me to understand. Love gives, without demanding repayment. Christ on the cross hadn't "won," yet in His forgiveness and love for the people who had turned against and rejected Him, He set a victorious example that no human can match, but all can try to imitate. Love accepts and understands. Love heals its own wounds by ministering to the hurts of others.

I could see now that David was hurt far more than I—he had lost his self-respect, his self-confidence. He had to live with the knowledge that his actions had turned me into a haggard, hate-filled shrew. If I loved David—and I *did* love him—then I must replace his terrible hurt with my total and undemanding love. My own hurt could be turned over to God.

It was not easy at first. I had formed the habit of tearing David down with bitter, ugly words, and I had to learn to break that habit by substituting loving phrases every time I was tempted to say something cruel. And perhaps God was helping in another way. Roger left David's department to take a job at another college in another city. And Gloria went with him.

There were moments of great discouragement for me because I naively expected David to respond at once. He didn't. But Katie told me to give him time. "Be patient," she said. "He's still too hurt to respond."

At first it was awkward for both of us—just being together for increasingly lengthy periods in the same room. Then one evening when David and I were silently together in his study—he correcting papers and I working on some mending—he got up to go for a drink of water. As David walked by me, a sudden impulse made him touch my cheek with an affectionate caress. My hands were full, so all I could do was tip my head toward his hand in recognition of his gesture. But tears welled up in my eyes as he went toward the kitchen. I sensed that David was wordlessly reaching out to me, that he realized my attitude had really changed—that my vindictiveness was gone.

When he returned, I said, "David, I'm sorry I've caused you so much misery." And with that simple apology the final bricks of the wall between us tumbled down and we began to discuss all sorts of things again, just as we had before.

That spring and summer we worked contentedly side by side in the vegetable and flower gardens we had been so proud of in former years, but had neglected the year before. And David resumed taking an active interest in what our children were doing. In the fall I began to help him once again with his reading.

Not only has time healed us both, but for me, and I think for David too, our marriage is stronger and more loving than ever before. We have both learned to give love without reservation, without demanding a return, and in doing so, we have received the love that comes from God. I thank Him for that, and as I pray, I ask him to bless Katie for showing me what true love really means.

6.
Love for Those Who Feel Unloved

Eye hath not seen, nor ear heard, neither have entered into the heart of man, the things which God hath prepared for them that love him.

(*I Corinthians 2:9*)

Though this story first appeared in Guideposts several years ago, time hasn't dulled its message—that's because it speaks with an ageless language of the heart.

Someday, Maria

by EDDIE ALBERT

Someday, Maria, someone is going to say a silly thing to you. "Maria," he'll say, and he'll be very solemn, "you must always be grateful to Mr. Albert for choosing you out of all those children."

And the trouble is, Maria, that you just might believe him. Because you are beautiful, because I adore you, because your hair is long and your eyes enormous, because you are seven years old and have me completely wrapped around your little finger, you might actually believe that I stepped into that orphanage, looked around at all the children and selected you. But I didn't, Maria. I wasn't the one who chose you at all.

It was three years ago that I had dinner in Paris with Art Buchwald. It was the first time I'd been away from Margo and young Edward, and I missed them terribly. Only one thing cast a shadow when I thought of my family—there wasn't enough of it! Margo and I never dreamed of having just one child. After Edward's birth, when no brothers or sisters came, we placed our name with adoption agencies all over the country. Years went by, but no child came to live with us.

That evening in Paris I was sounding off to Art on the slow pace of adoption. He laid down his fork. "We have three adopted kids," he said, "and we didn't wait years and years to get them. We found one in England, one in France and one in Spain—and you couldn't ask for finer youngsters."

He leaned across the table. "It would break your heart to see some of those orphanages. Why, we saw one in Spain that had over two thousand children."

211

It was one of those strange moments when everything seems to make sense, even the language. Margo was born in Mexico and speaks Spanish fluently. I went to the telephone and talked to her in California. The next day I was bound for Madrid and that orphanage with its 2000 children.

Once on the plane, the enormity of what I was doing swept over me. How was I going to pick the right child from 2000?

Psychiatry, I thought. I'd pick a child who looked healthy and bright and then take him or her to a psychiatrist for tests. I lowered the seat back; I was tired.

But sleep wouldn't come. Suddenly I realized that psychiatry could not really define the special magic that makes one person belong with another.

I remembered what I'd learned long ago, that the only valid position for viewing a decision is eternity, that the only One who sees from there is God. I'd asked Him to guide me in lesser matters; why not in this one? Did I really have more confidence in myself than in Him? The children in the orphanage were His children, just as Margo and Edward and I were. He knew which one belonged with us.

But how would *I* know? How would I be shown His choice for our family? As soon as I asked the question, I knew the answer. God's choice would be the first child I saw.

There in the plane I bowed my head. "Lord," I said, "I'll take that first child."

This time, I got to sleep.

Early the next morning I was sitting in the office of the director of the great gray-walled orphanage.

"And what kind of child do you have in mind?" he asked in English.

"I would not be so impertinent as to say," I told him.

The director stared at me, then at the paper he'd been writing on. "You have one son, age seven. So I suppose you would like a girl?"

"A girl would be fine."

The director scrutinized me for a moment. Abruptly he picked up the phone and spoke a few words in Spanish. I wondered if he heard my heart pounding as we waited.

The door opened and a nun led in a little girl. I stared at her, gulped and closed my eyes.

"Lord!" I prayed. "You don't mean it!"

For there in front of me you stood, Maria—the toughest, most defiant, dirtiest four-year-old I had ever seen. You stood with your feet planted wide apart, your eyes on the floor.

I looked from you to the director. He was watching me nervously, apologetically, retaining the nun to whisk you away when the American exploded. I suddenly knew that this was not the first time you had been shown to a prospective parent. Suspicions stabbed me. You might be a behavior problem . . .

"How do we go about adopting her?" My words came quickly.

The director stared at me as if he hadn't heard right. Then he sprang from his chair so hastily he almost knocked it over and plunked you into my lap. And so, with your feather-weight on my knee, I heard the director outline procedures—the Spanish government required certain papers; the United States, others.

I hardly listened. For—was I imagining it or—was there a gently pressure against my chest? I leaned forward half an inch; the tiny pressure increased.

My proud Maria, before you responded to me you were testing me to see if I would respond to you. It was a kind of unspoken proposition with no loss of face. "I could love you if you loved me." My brave Maria!

I didn't see you again for two whole weeks, while the slow, legal part of the adoption got started. My first job was to tell Margo that we had a daughter. I'd call her and talk about mechanics—she would have to deal with the immigration authorities, find a welfare agency to sponsor us . . . Then there was Margo's voice from California, asking the one question I'd been pretending she wouldn't ask.

"Oh, Eddie, describe her to me!"

I suppose that was the longest pause ever run up on a transatlantic phone call. Then I remembered a photograph I'd once seen of Margo as a child; she was all skinny arms and legs.

"Honey," I said, "she reminds me a lot of you."

One day, while we were waiting for final papers, the orphanage gave me permission to take you out for lunch. At the restaurant you scraped your plate clean while I was unfolding my napkin. Then you ate my lunch, too.

In the taxi going back you sat close to me, studying my face. That is why you didn't see the orphanage until we had stopped in front of it. You looked out at the gray walls, then back at me.

Maria! How could I have known? How could I have guessed?

Somehow no one in the orphanage had explained to you that this was only a visit, only out to lunch. So many children, overworked Sisters, and no one to read in your eyes that you thought *this* was the day of adoption, the final leave-taking. And now I had brought you back!

You flung yourself, shrieking, to the sidewalk. And I, with my miserable lack of Spanish, could not explain. I knelt beside you, begging you to believe me. "I'm coming back! *Mañana*, Maria! Tomorrow!" When a nun came out to get you, we were both sitting in the middle of the sidewalk, crying our eyes out.

I did come back, the next day, and the next, until the unbelievable day when you were ours.

It was 24 hours from Madrid to Los Angeles. You sat on my lap the entire plane trip; you would not sleep.

We were a pretty groggy pair when we stumbled off the plane in California and into Margo's arms. She let loose a machine-gun volley of Spanish. The only word of which I understood was "Mama."

Going home you sat in her lap, and for weeks afterward I was a lucky man if I got so much as a glance.

At home Margo tucked you into bed. And still you would not close your eyes. You'd been without sleep 36 hours, but you didn't want to let Margo out of your sight. At last you pointed to her wedding band.

"Give me your ring," you said.

Margo slipped off the ring and placed it in your hand. "Now you can't leave me," you said. A second later you were asleep.

And Edward—how did he feel about this possible competition for our love? We soon found out. You had lungs that could summon the fire department, but whenever, I asked you to speak more quietly, Edward would give me a look of deep reproach.

"Papa! Of course she shouts! There were two thousand kids making a racket; she had to yell to be heard."

Any correction you received had to be while Edward was out of the room. And you felt the same way about him. I'll never forget the day the school bully knocked Edward down and you knocked down the bully. They tell me you were banging his head on the floor when a teacher pulled you off.

I love the toughness in you. I love your loyalty. I love your quick mind. I even love your noise (but not while Papa's napping, all right, honey?).

I think you are the most beautiful little girl in the world, and sometimes, watching you, I think, *How in all the world did I find you?*

Then I remember. I didn't find you. I didn't do it at all.

Editor's Note: Maria Albert today is attending Immaculate Heart College in Los Angeles. She is interested in working with children, perhaps combining her artistic talents (she studies singing and dancing) with a psychology major.

How to Show Your Parents That You Love Them

by MILDRED TENGBOM

How do you say "I love you" to your parents?

An ancient letter tells us how. It describes a most unusual love affair. The chief character in the story was a wizened, scarred old man—a jailbird, in fact. The love affair was being sustained through letters, one of which has survived. We know it as the epistle Paul wrote to the congregation at Philippi, and it is to that letter we now turn to learn how to say "I love you."

I **Say it.** To say, "Of course they know I love them" is not enough. Paul revealed his affection for the Philippians in his letter. "I hold you in my heart," he wrote. And again, "I yearn for you." "My beloved." "My brethren, whom I love and long for."

When we are not limited to communicating through letters, we can say "I love you" not only with words but also touch and looks. Put your arms around your aging parents. Hug them. Pat them. Kiss them. Stroke their hair. Joke with them. Tease them gently and lovingly. Make sure they know you care.

II **Love not only in word but also in deed.** In the case of Paul and the Philippian Christians the love between them was not simply an exchange of sentimental words either. Paul had suffered to see the Philippian Christians introduced to God. They, in turn, tried to understand what Paul's needs were.

At the time he wrote the letter Paul was an imprisoned man. Some Bible scholars believe respected prisoners like him were

216

not put behind bars but were confined to quarters. For Paul, this very likely meant renting a house. The Philippian congregation sent money for rent. They also sent one of their own, Epaphroditus, to be with Paul. Money could pay the rent and buy groceries. But feet and hands were needed to bring the groceries home. And a cheerful, courageous heart was needed to encourage the aged Paul.

Our gift-giving to our aging parents should be equally thoughtful. For years my mother has pleaded with us not to buy her any more "things." "The house is full," she explains. "There's no room to put any more things."

But she welcomes shrubs and flowers for the garden, an airline ticket to visit us, trips to new, unexplored places as well as old familiar ones. Mother also loves to entertain—even at 80-plus. She was delighted one year when my sister-in-law gave her a big box of gaily decorated napkins for all occasions.

III Express appreciation to your parents for all they have done for you and have meant to you. Gratefully Paul acknowledged the gifts from the Philippians. "I am thankful for your partnership." "It was kind of you to share my trouble." "The gifts were a fragrant offering."

What do you appreciate most about your parents? As a young person I was restless, and my wanderings took me far from home. One day, 2000 miles from home, my heart welled up with love for my father and appreciation for all he had meant to me. Impulsively I sat down and wrote a letter. When he received it, Mother told me later, Dad read and reread it. And then, holding it in his hand, he said, "We should frame this." A few months later my father was dead. I've always been glad I wrote that letter.

IV Try to understand what is important to your parents. The Philippian Christians understood that it was not only material things that were important to Paul. He admonished them to "Stand firm in the Lord." They stood firm.

And they were successful also in keeping their children true
to the Lord.

What is important to your parents? That the family name
continue to be held in high esteem? That family solidarity
continue? That family members love and support their country? Have your parents worked hard to support certain philan-
thropic causes? Have they been devout Christians, concerned
that all their children live godly lives?

As you consider their interests and concerns, do what you
can to perpetuate them. An aging person needs to feel not only
that he has made a contribution to society, but that his influence will continue to be felt.

If your parents are gone or if you live away from them, there's
still a way to honor them—that's by being kind and helpful to
someone else's aging parents. God's family is a large one, all
inclusive, without boundaries, unlimited.

V **Build and nourish confidence and faith.** Our aging parents need to have their faith and trust nourished and
strengthened. The dying of friends and relatives and their own
failing health and declining strength will remind them that
death, the great final test, is drawing near. To face death coura-
geously and cheerfully calls for faith, confidence and assurance.

We can help our parents build faith. If we haven't done so
previously, we can talk with them as to whether they are at
peace with God and man. If they need transportation, we can
make arrangements so they can get to worship services. We can
read and pray with them, give them records and tapes. Our
parents perhaps were the first ones to teach us to trust in God.
Now, in gratitude, we can reach out in love to strengthen their
faith.

As trust in God grows, peace and joy will garrison their
hearts. Read through the epistle to the Philippians and count
how many times the words "joy" and "rejoice" appear. Remember those expressions of joy came from a man chained to a
guard day and night, from one who never knew when the
summons to death would come. But he could rejoice because
he was assured of God's love. He knew of God's love through

the death of God's Son on the cross, true, but he also experienced God's love through the Philippian Christians.

God loves people through people. God can love your aging parents through you. So tell them you love them. Show them you care. Express your appreciation. Value their contributions to life. Reaffirm their faith in God. And hope that someday your own children will do the same for you.

A Fragile Moment of Love

My husband Charles has a special way of making his love known. As a lawyer, it is often necessary for him to leave me notes since I work as his secretary. I find them in the most unusual places—written on the bottom of a report I must copy, on a letter I must file, on a napkin under my coffee cup—just a few scribbled words. Sometimes the words written are "Sweetheart, I love you." Sometimes, "Darling, you are so sweet." Sometimes, just simply, "I love you."

I tear off these precious words and slip them into the pocket of my skirt, or my robe, into a desk drawer or in my recipe box—wherever I happen to be when I come across them.

His love has been constant through the years. We are both in our 50's now.

I always am finding his notes—when I run my hand into my pocket for a tissue or open a drawer for a pair of scissors—there they are—endearing jewel words, making a bright day happier, dark day brighter.

Suddenly my troubles seem less important, any sadness is softened, the happiness more complete. Charles' little note has wrapped me in the warmth and magnitude of his love. And I am reminded of God's love—all around us, whenever we're happy, whenever we're sad—a bulwark, never failing, caring for us today and loving us always.

Allene R. Sullivan

We all learn about love in different ways.
For her, it was the night of . . .

Homecoming

by JERI NIELSEN

Two weeks after the Junior Prom I was still walking around saying that I'd never again help plan a dance. So when they asked me to be a chairman of the Homecoming dance my mouth dropped open in disbelief, and I firmly said no! But by the middle of the summer I was asking myself what I was doing having meetings to plan the Homecoming dance.

Throughout the entire summer all the plans were talked over, verbally organized, talked over again, priced and talked over some more. We were confident about our plans, but it was only after school started that we realized that we had just three weeks left and that time's life would soon run out. There could be no more talk—just action.

Differences of opinion arose and personalities clashed. The original plans were unworkable—two weeks before the dance we started over. Meetings before and after school. Tickets misprinted—thus a delay on sales. Start over. Hurry. Mom, could you help me cut out these frames for the windows? Mom, save some dinner for me—I have another meeting and I'll be late.

The day before the dance we put up the window decorations. It took nearly five hours to transform 16 cafeteria windows into light blue ovals. The next day we started our decorating at 7:30 a.m. I didn't go to any classes at all that day.

When the school day ended at 2:30 I had a terrific headache. We had run out of tape three times and had encountered other problems I would never have imagined could come up. I was hungry and dizzy and I just wanted to go home, curl up in bed and go to sleep.

But there was far too much to be done in·only a few hours' time for anyone to take even a short break. None of us who were decorating even got to see the football game. As it grew later and later, individual committee members disappeared. So much was yet to be done and I was almost alone. I looked around at that half-decorated cafeteria and cried.

The dance was supposed to have started at eight p.m. At 8:00 I was sweeping the floor and rearranging chairs and benches. Finally I realized that the dance would just have to happen. If, at this point, something wasn't right, I hoped no one would notice.

It was after 8:00 when I got home and my date was coming at 8:30. I was flying—and at 8:25 when I put my dress on, I discovered that the zipper was unsewn in one place. I tossed the dress to Mom and put on some desperately needed make-up while she fixed the zipper. I put the dress back on, looked in the mirror and almost cried again. My eyes were red, my hair was uncurled and I looked tired and terrible. I *couldn't* go to this dance. Everything should have been perfect, but it was as far from being ideal as it could have been. Naturally my date was right on time—and of course, I wasn't ready. I heard him tell Dad he'd go pick up some tapes and come back. Moments later my parents left for the dance, where they were to be honored guests.

I was finally ready. The house was empty. I sat down on my parents' bed. All day, and especially while I was getting ready, it had been like a downtown street at rush hour inside my head and now the honking ceased. Everything stopped moving and it was silent—strange, blissful silence.

As I sat there absorbing the peace and quiet, my eye caught sight of a note on Mom's dresser. Seeing my older sister's handwriting, I leaned over and read it. "Living is like licking honey off a thorn . . . but sometimes, Mom, it seems like you get the whole rosebush. But that means there's got to be flowers, too, right? Good luck with your tests today. I'll be thinking of you—wish I could go for you . . . "

There was more, but I didn't finish it. Something grabbed at my heart and squeezed hard and tight. I knew Mom hadn't been feeling well, but . . . tests? I felt frightened at first, but then fright turned to guilt. I had been so caught up in my own affairs that I didn't even know what was going on in my own family. I had been so "busy" I hadn't given anyone the chance to tell me what was happening. And the ironic thing was that at a time when my mother needed my help, I was asking—or demanding—she do things for me, which she did without a complaint. In that loud, silent moment, I realized how selfish and ungrateful I had been. And when I wanted to tell my mother how much I loved her, she wasn't there. She was at my dance.

Editor's note: For this story Jeri Nielsen became a Guideposts' Youth Writing Contest winner.

But the very hairs of your head are all numbered. Fear ye not therefore, ye are of more value than many sparrows. (Matthew 10:30,31)

**I found myself caught between the relationship
we had and what I thought a marriage should be.**

Is Love a Tender Trap?

by PATRICIA HOUCK SPRINKLE

It was a stormy summer afternoon in the mountains of North Carolina. I stalked through the woods of a Christian conference center carrying a paintbox and a pad, but my mood wasn't the least bit artistic; it matched the clouds—gray, heavy and threatening.

You see, I thought I was tired of marriage. Oh, I still loved my husband and felt he was the most marvelous man I knew. But I had gone into marriage two years before with all sorts of notions (culled from years of digesting romantic books and movies) about what marriage would be like. And by those standards, Bob and I scarcely had a "marriage" at all.

We were in our mid-twenties when we married, both happily pursuing careers we felt God had placed us in. We even talked excitedly about our marriage as a merging of our Christian missions. I envisioned it as a sort of constant togetherness for God. We were also both highly independent, but I assumed that a lot of our independent ways would change after marriage.

Yet our particular missions still demanded that frequently we be apart. My being here in North Carolina this very week was an example of what our life was like. I had been invited to a Christian women's conference to teach a class and give a series of meditations. Meanwhile, Bob was back home two states away working on a crisis center for an inner-city neighborhood. Each of us felt God wanted us where we were, and each affirmed the importance of what the other was doing. "But is *that* marriage?" I asked myself. Not as I expected it to be.

I had expected other specific kinds of togetherness in marriage—things I had always been told were important.

For instance, I had always thought that marriage meant two people going to bed at the same time, lazily sharing their day before falling asleep in each other's arms. But Bob and I both liked to work at night, and most nights one or the other of us lagged behind to finish a paragraph or a speech.

To me, marriage meant leisurely meals, candlelit dinners. But many of our meals were hastily eaten before we dashed out—together or separately—to some important meeting.

To me marriage meant doing things together—painting furniture, working in the yard, washing dishes. Yet we seldom were in the mood for painting or yardwork at the same time, and both of us liked to use dishwashing time for meditation instead of conversation.

The list went on and on, and with each item the gap seemed to widen. I found myself caught between the relationship we had and what I thought a marriage should be. I felt all pulled to pieces—and so tired of the struggle between enjoying Bob himself and constantly trying to improve our marriage so it met my preconceptions.

"Oh, God," I said aloud suddenly, as I stamped through some ferns toward a clump of rhododendrons, "please show me what to do about our marriage."

I bent to pick a tiny yellow flower and added it to a handful I had unconsciously gathered. As I straightened up I suddenly glimpsed a small brown gazebo hidden among the rhododendrons on the edge of a stream. It was so unexpected and beautiful that it startled me out of my self-pity.

I had brought my watercolors and pad along that afternoon hoping to find a subject to paint. In the morning I had enrolled in a creativity class, in spite of years of evidence that art is not my medium. People who paint alongside me in art classes always wonder if we inhabit the same planet. My roses look like chrysanthemums' cousins while my crystal pitchers turn into lopsided stone jugs. That very morning my turkey-shaped swan had gone from white to dirty gray and finally to black as I tried to improve it. Yet within my soul burned a Walter Mitty conviction that if I only had a fitting subject and the time, I could create a watercolor masterpiece.

Filling an abandoned paper cup with water, I set up my paints on the gazebo floor and sat down crosslegged before them. Just at that moment the clouds fulfilled their threats, and torrents of water streamed around me. The gazebo, with its wide eaves, was dry enough, but unless I wanted to paint cobwebby beams, my subject matter was limited.

My eyes fell on the forgotten flowers lying beside the water cup. Still fresh, they were the only spot of color in that veiled world, a perfect subject for my first creation. Remembering an arrangement the teacher had made that morning, I carefully placed them in my left fist. "There," I sighed, forcing the violet once more to hold up its head, "that ought to be perfect." I painted furiously for half an hour, then sat back to compare my painting with the real thing.

Poor flowers. They were totally wilted, their little heads drooping for lack of water. I stuck them in the paint water to revive while I added a few finishing touches to my work of art, then stood back to admire it.

But neither the fist nor the flowers bore much resemblance to any God ever made. In fact, what struck me most about the painting was how stiff and unnatural it was. I looked from the painted violet poking erectly through my rigid fist to the real violet, drooping over the cup. "Poor baby," I murmured, bending to pick it up, "you didn't like that pose, did you?"

The violet nestled into my palm, and to it I added a small yellow bloom and an even smaller pink one. Idly I began to paint them like that. They looked pretty good. Freely, without models, I added blossoms to the picture until flowers covered my palm and floated toward heaven. What fun! Soon a riot of flowers spilled across the picture, open and free and, above all, unique.

I looked from one painting to the other, and an idea seemed to float into my mind. Was that first rigid and lifeless painting an echo of my preconceptions about marriage and what it should be? I heard myself complaining to Bob:

"You ought to go to bed when I do."

"If I go to a football game with you, you should take me to the ballet."

"You ought to go to bed earlier so we could get up and eat breakfast together." (Me picturing myself in a fluffy robe stirring homemade biscuits.)

All these pleas to conform to a model as rigid as the instructions in our art class!

I guess it was that last item that convinced me I was getting a message. Neither Bob nor I had paid much attention to breakfast *before* we were married. What made me think we should both change who we were and what our habits were to fit a box labeled "marriage?"

As I looked at the second painting, I found myself breathing deeply, feeling a sudden sense of peace. Slowly I began not to care about *marriage*, but only about *us*. In my childish paintings I saw a lesson from God—that if I insisted on trying to create a "marriage" according to the book, I was going to squeeze our unique, precious, unusual but loving relationship until it was stiff, ugly and dead. Only by being willing to let Bob become the best Bob (not "husband") he could be, and only by letting him help me become the best me (not "wife") I could be—both of us trying to fathom God's will—could we build the life together God wanted us to have.

Today we still have a strange marriage by a lot of my old standards. We go to bed, eat meals and spend time together at odd hours between dashing off to things we feel are important. We never rise in time for a leisurely breakfast, and sometimes we skip dinner until 11. Many times we find ourselves going places alone when most folks are in couples.

But do you know what? It's an exciting, wonderful marriage just the same, and it is particularly ours. Which is why I only smile when people make fun of two pictures by my dresser. *I* know they represent a lot more than two handfulls of flowers.

> "I'm Ka Yeung Kwan from Hong Kong. I
> think English is a real bore. My main
> hobby is harassing stupid teachers, and
> English teachers are the stupidest of all."

Go Ahead, Hate Me!

by MARILYN HELLEBERG

It was the first day of classes at Kearney State College, and I'd asked my freshman English students to tell a little about themselves. I hadn't been teaching in the department very long, and so, even though he said them jokingly, Kwan's words splattered against my ego like a rotten tomato.

The other students looked embarrassed. During the rest of the period, Kwan snickered, mumbled under his breath, dropped books on the floor and squirmed in his seat.

Later, when I told my husband about it, he said, "You'd better crack down on him right now or you'll have trouble all semester." That night I prayed for strength to be firm. But then, as I was drifting off to sleep, the words, "See Christ in him," floated across my mind.

About halfway through the next class period, I heard a loud, "Ho-o-o hum! How boring!" It was Kwan, with a sly smirk on his face. I was ready to say, "If you're bored, Kwan, you can leave." But there was something in those dark eyes behind the thick glasses that stopped me. I ignored him and went on with my lecture.

After class, I noticed Kwan standing in the doorway, I expected another smart remark, but he asked me a question about the literature we'd been discussing and walked back to my office with me. He now seemed a very intelligent, good-humored young man, and I was sure I'd have no more trouble with him.

I was wrong. In the classes that followed, Kwan seized every opportunity to practice his "hobby"—coming in late, making wisecracks, arguing with everything I said, interrupting other students. Yet every day he stayed after class, asking perceptive questions.

I couldn't figure Kwan out. He was really two different people—the childish, irritating boy who disrupted class, and the mature, thoughtful young man who was becoming my after-class friend.

His first essay was extremely well-constructed, but it was sprinkled with obscene language, obviously intended to shock me. How could I see Christ in someone who used such un-Christlike words?

One day after class, Kwan confided that all his life he'd been playing a game called never-let-anyone-know-you're-hurting. I understood, because I sometimes played that game, too.

I hoped that with our growing student-teacher friendship, the problem in class would dissolve. But if anything, it got worse. When we were studying the poem, "God's Grandeur," by Hopkins, Kwan monopolized the class discussion by arguing with the other students about their beliefs. It was upsetting to many of the students and doubly so to me. See Christ in Kwan? Was it really possible to "see Christ" in someone who wasn't even a Christian? *Maybe I should just squelch him, once and for all,* I thought.

Instead, I closed the class with a quotation from "Outwitted" by Edwin Markham and prefaced it with the words, "This is for Kwan."

"He drew a circle that shut me out—
 Heretic, rebel, a thing to flout
 But Love and I had the wit to win:
 We drew a circle that took him in!"

There was a warm silence in the classroom, and even Kwan seemed subdued. After class, he said, "I can't understand you. Why don't you just give up on me?"

I felt like telling him how many times I *had* almost given up. I thought of telling him that I was trying to see Christ in him, but I didn't because, in spite of my efforts and prayers, I still couldn't quite do it. Christ, to me, was beautiful and loving and compassionate—all of the things Kwan's behavior showed *he* wasn't.

During our quiet talks, I had told Kwan about Christ's love, but I knew he was far from accepting it. Whenever I prayed about the problem, I seemed to get the same answer—not "tell him about Christ," but "see Christ in *him*." Still, the more I tried, the harder he seemed to try to make me reject him.

Then came the essay in which Kwan wrote: "There are three kinds of teachers—those who are interesting but stupid, those who are intelligent but boring, and those who are both boring and stupid—like my English teacher." First I was angry, then hurt. Till now, I hadn't realized how much I really *cared* about this student. What about the friendship I thought we'd built? Did he really despise me so much?

I couldn't put a grade on his paper. When I handed it back without a mark on it, he waited for me after class.

"I'm sorry, Kwan," I said. "I can't play the game of never-let-anyone-know-you're-hurting. I just lost." Then, to my horror and embarrassment, I started choking back tears. I hurried into my office and tried to eat my lunch, but I couldn't swallow. "Oh, God," I prayed, "why have I failed so badly with Kwan?"

I don't know how long I'd been sitting there, aching with rejection and failure, when Kwan walked in. Without a word he put a note on my desk and left. It said, "I am truly sorry for what I have written. I did not know until now that you are just as vulnerable as I am. I meant the essay as a big, teasing joke. Instead, I hurt you, the only true friend I have . . . I've been rejected so often in my life that I've learned to protect myself by hurting other people first. But you wouldn't let me do it! You 'drew a circle that took me in.' If this has something to do with your Christ, then I think I'd like to know more about Him . . . "

Something to do with your Christ. Hurrying out of my office, I found Kwan standing near the stairs. Blind to the students all around us, we stood looking at each other, unable to speak. Then my insolent student took off his glasses, dried his eyes and handed me his handkerchief.

And in that moment, for the first time, to me Kwan *did* look Christlike.

In this special excerpt adapted from his
best-selling book, Dr. James Dobson,
well-known psychologist and marriage
counsellor, discusses common complaints
wives make about their marriages.

What Wives Wish
Their Husbands
Knew About Women

by DR. JAMES DOBSON

Not long ago, I conducted a personal survey among young
married women between the ages of 27 and 40. The
majority were mothers with children still at home, and they
were mainly women who professed a commitment to the Christian faith. While the inquiry lacked the rigors of the scientific
method, it did verify some observations I have made over the
years in counseling married couples.

I asked the women to rank ten leading causes of marital
depression, according to their personal experience. In other
words, I instructed them to select the problem that had been
the most difficult and indicate it with a number one, followed
by the other nine in descending order.

The categories were: Absence of *romantic* love in marriage;
In-law conflict; Low self-esteem; Problems with the children;
Financial difficulties, Loneliness, isolation and boredom; Sexual problems in marriage; Menstrual and physiological problems; Fatigue and time pressure; and Aging.

The most frequently named causes of depression by women I
surveyed were: Low self-esteem; Fatigue and time pressure;
Loneliness, isolation and boredom; and absence of *romantic*
love in marriage. I'd like to discuss these leading causes of
depression here.

230

What does it mean to have low self-esteem? What does a person experience when struggling with deep-seated feelings of inadequacy? Perhaps I can express the troubling thoughts and anxieties that reverberate through the backroads of an insecure mind. It is sitting alone in a house during the quiet afternoon hours, wondering why the phone doesn't ring, wondering why you have no "real" friends. It is longing for someone to talk to soul to soul, but knowing there is no such person worthy of your trust. It is feeling that "they wouldn't like me if they knew the real me." It is becoming terrified when speaking to a group of your peers. It is wondering why other people have so much more talent and ability than you do.

It is feeling ugly and sexually unattractive. It is admitting that you have become a failure as a wife and mother. It is disliking everything about yourself and wishing, constantly wishing, you could be someone else. It is feeling unloved and unlovable and lonely and sad. It is lying in bed after the family is asleep, pondering the vast emptiness inside and longing for unconditional love. It is reaching up in the darkness to remove a tear from the corner of your eye. It is depression.

There will be a few readers with no true understanding of the experiences I am describing. They are, perhaps, the women who were "superstars" as children: They were cute babies, bright in the early school years, cheerleaders and homecoming queens and everybody's favorites in high school. For these individuals, this primary source of feminine depression, inferiority, will remain a bit mysterious. For the greater majority, however, personal identification with this emotional dungeon will be instantaneous.

I certainly do not want to give the impression that low self-esteem is exclusively a feminine characteristic. Many men feel just as insecure and worthless. In fact, low self-esteem is a threat to the entire human family, affecting children, adolescents, the elderly, all socio-economic levels of society and every race and ethnic culture. It can engulf anyone who feels disrespected by other people.

If low self-esteem is so pervasive throughout our society,

then why have I emphasized its impact specifically on women? Because the "disease" of inferiority has reached epidemic proportions among females today. Their traditional responsibilities have become matters of disrespect and ridicule. Raising children and maintaining a home hold very little social status in most areas of the country, and women who are cast into that role often look at themselves with unconcealed disenchantment.

Advertisements have contributed immeasurably to the notion that the slightest physical flaw is cause for alarm and despair. Have you seen the magazine ad for a magic cream that promises to remove "horrid age spots"? It shows a picture of four middle-aged women playing cards, and one is cringing in shame because she has an "age spot" on her hand. The word "horrid" is always used to describe her condition. Now seriously, folks, in view of the world's grave problems, a freckle on the paw shouldn't rank very high, yet every middle-aged woman who sees that advertisement will look down at her hands with a gasp of anxiety. How can she bear the disgrace? It is horrid, no less. By cultivating this kind of nonsense, Madison Avenue has taught us to feel inferior and inadequate over the slightest flaw.

Another source of low self-esteem among American women relates to basic intelligence. Simply stated, they feel dumb and stupid. Psychologists have known for decades that there is no fundamental difference in the overall level of intelligence between men and women, although there are areas of greater strength for each sex. Men tend to score higher on tests of mathematics and abstract reasoning, while women excel in language and all verbal skills. However, when the individual abilities are combined, neither sex has a clear advantage over the other. Despite this fact, women are much more inclined to doubt their own mental capacity.

Low self-esteem among women may be traced to dozens of causes, most of them linked with early home life. The adult who felt unloved or disrespected as a child will never forget the experience.

Withdrawing at one extreme and fighting at the other are two of the most common responses to inferiority, but it is an unfortunate pattern, too, because they are both extreme approaches to the problem. Neither is very healthy.

The wives and mothers who participated in this inquiry did not appear to be suffering from low self-esteem. They were outwardly sociable and pleasant, laughing and interacting with one another. Yet when given an opportunity to reflect their true feelings in confidence, self-doubt rose to the surface. One of those young women later came to me for counseling and wept for more than an hour as she tried to express the inexpressible anguish of inferiority. Near the end of our session I asked her if she had ever shared these feelings with her husband. Her reply was typical. "I have been married for eight years, but my husband has no idea that I feel so inadequate!"

I suggested she tell him her feelings, which she did. Later, she told me that the day she shared this inner need with him marked the beginning of a new and improved marriage. It is no mere cliché to say that poor communication and poor marriages go hand in hand. More commonly, however, feelings of inferiority stand as the best-kept secret of the year.

How can a husband help his wife cope with longstanding feelings of low self-esteem? Without question, his greatest contribution can be made by keeping the romantic aspect of their marriage alive. If I had the power to communicate only one message to each man in America, it would specify the importance of romantic love to every dimension of feminine nature. It typically provides the foundation for a woman's self-esteem, her joy in living and her sexual responsibilities. Unfortunately, the pressures of earning a living and coping with day-to-day responsibilities often destroy this vital marital relationship.

This need for romantic love is one of the primary understandings that "wives wish their husbands knew about women." It is consistent with the Biblical principle expressed in I Peter 3:7:

"You husbands must be careful of your wives, being thoughtful of their needs and honoring them. Remember that you and your wife are partners in receiving God's blessings, and if you don't treat her as you should, your prayers will not get ready answers." *(The Living Bible)* Obviously a man's concern for his wife's welfare is so important that it even influences his own relationship with God!

T he second most depressing irritant in marriage, according to my poll, is fatigue and time pressure.

How frequently does your head whirl and spin with the obligations of an impossible "to do" list? "I simply must get the bills paid this morning and the grocery shopping can't wait another day. And my children! I've had so little time to be with them lately that we hardly seem like a family any more. Maybe I can read them a story tonight. And we really should be taking more time to maintain our spiritual lives. That's one area we cannot afford to neglect. And what about our social obligations? We can't expect to have friends if we never get together. The Johnsons have had us over twice now, and I know they're waiting for us to reciprocate. We'll just have to set a date and keep it, that's all. And there are so many things that need fixing and repairing on the house. And the income tax is due next month . . . "

So we're too busy; everyone can see that. But what does a hectic pace have to do with depression? Just this: Every obligation that we shirk is a source of guilt. When there are more commitments than we can possibly handle, then self-esteem is further damaged by each failure. "I'm really a lousy parent; I'm too exhausted to be a good wife; I'm disorganized and confused; I'm out of touch with the world around me and I don't have any real friends; even God is displeased with me." Truly, over-extended lives contribute to emotional pathology in numerous ways.

For some strange reason, human beings (and particularly women), tolerate stresses and pressure much more easily if at least one other person knows they are enduring it. This principle is filed under the category of "human understanding," and it is highly relevant to housewives. The frustrations of raising small children and handling domestic duties would be much more manageable if their husbands acted as if they comprehended it all. Even if a man does nothing to change the situation, simply his awareness that his wife did an admirable job today will make it easier for her to repeat the assignment tomorrow. Instead, the opposite usually occurs. At least eight million husbands will stumble into the same unforgivable question tonight: "What did you do all day, dear?" The very nature of the question implies that the "little woman" has been sitting around watching television and drinking coffee since arising at noon!

Everyone needs to know that he or she is respected for the way he or she meets his or her responsibilities. Husbands get this emotional nurture through job promotions, raises in pay, annual evaluations and incidental praise during the workday. Women at home get it from their husbands—if they get it at all. The most unhappy wives and mothers are often those who try to handle their fatigue and time pressure in solitude, and their men are never sure why they act so tired.

Husbands *and* wives should constantly guard against the scourge of overcommitment. Even worthwhile and enjoyable activities become damaging when they consume the last ounce of energy or the remaining free moments in the day. Though it is rarely possible for a busy family, everyone needs to waste some time every now and then—to walk along kicking rocks and thinking pleasant thoughts.

You must resolve to slow your pace; *you* must learn to say "no" gracefully; *you* must resist the temptation to chase after more pleasures, more hobbies, more social entanglements; *you* must "hold the line" with the tenacity of a tackle for a professional football team blocking out the intruders and defending the home team. In essence, three questions should be asked about every new activity that presents itself: Is it worthy of our time? What will be eliminated if it is added? What will be its impact on our family life? My suspicion is that most of the items in our busy day would score rather poorly on this three-item test.

The viewpoint of a child can sometimes be refreshing and full of insight. The following theme entitled *What Is a Grandmother?* was composed by a nine-year-old girl. It suggests a pattern for behavior we might all consider when we have no time for "trivia."

What Is A Grandmother?
by a third-grader

"A grandmother is a lady who has no children of her own. She likes other people's little girls and boys. A grandfather is a man grandmother. He goes for walks with the boys, and they talk about fishing and stuff like that.

Grandmothers don't have to do anything except to be there. They're old so they shouldn't play hard or run. It is enough if they drive us to the market where the pretend horse is, and have a lot of dimes ready. Or if they take us for walks, they should slow down past things like pretty leaves and caterpillars. They should never say, "Hurry up."

Usually grandmothers are fat, but not too fat to tie your shoes. They wear glasses and funny underwear. They can take their teeth and gums off.

Grandmothers don't have to be smart, only answer questions like, "Why isn't God married?" and "How come dogs chase cats?"

Grandmothers don't talk baby talk like visitors do, because it is hard to understand. When they read to us they don't skip, or mind if it is the same story over again.

Everybody should try to have a grandmother, especially if you don't have television, because they are the only grown-ups who have time."

The third and fourth ranked causes of depression among women who completed my questionnaire were the categories of loneliness, isolation and boredom and absence of romantic love. The two problem areas did, in fact, finish in a dead-even tie.

A closer look at the women's responses reveals a highly significant trend among American housewives. The ladies were saying in effect: (1) I don't like myself; (2) I have no meaningful relationships outside my home; (3) I am not even close to the man I love. These young, attractive wives and mothers admitted to being emotionally isolated from all other human beings!

Feelings of self-worth and acceptance can be obtained from only one source. They cannot be bought or manufactured. Self-esteem is only generated by what we see reflected about ourselves in the eyes of other people. The vast majority of us are dependent on our associates for emotional sustenance each day. What does this say, then, about those who exist in a state of perpetual isolation, being deprived of loving, caring human contact year after year? Such people are almost certain to experience feelings of worthlessness and deep depression and despair.

Certainly there are many reasons why housewives can find themselves lonely, isolated and bored, even if they live in the midst of six million other lonely people. And what agitation is caused by their emptiness. One writer said, "Everybody must be somebody to somebody to be anybody!" I agree. Dr. William Glasser explained this same psychological principle in his popular text *Reality Therapy:* "At all times in our lives we must have at least one person who cares about us and whom we care for ourselves. If we do not have this essential person, we will not be able to fulfill our basic needs."

At this point I offer a message of great importance to every husband who loves and wants to understand his wife. Whereas men and women have the same needs for self-worth and belonging, they typically satisfy those needs differently. A man derives his sense of worth primarily from the reputation he earns in his job or profession. He draws emotional satisfaction from achieving in business, becoming financially independent, developing a highly respected craft or skill, supervising others, becoming "boss," or by being loved and appreciated by his patients or clients or fellow businessmen. The man who is successful in these areas does not depend on his wife as his *primary* shield against inferiority. Of course she plays an important role as his companion and lover, but she isn't essential to his self-respect day by day.

By contrast, a housewife approaches her marriage from a totally different perspective. She does not have access to "other" sources of self-esteem commonly available to her husband. She can cook a good dinner, but once it is eaten, her family may not even remember to thank her for it. Her household duties do not bring her respect in the community, and she is not likely to be praised for the quality of her dusting techniques. Therefore, the more isolated she becomes, as we have discussed, the more vital her man will be to her sense of fulfillment, confidence, and well-being. He must be that "one person" of whom Doctor Glasser wrote, and if he is not, she is "unable to fulfill her basic needs," and that spells trouble.

Men derive self-esteem by being *respected*; women feel worthy when they are *loved*. This may be the most important personality distinction between the sexes.

This understanding helps explain the unique views of marriage as seen by men and women. A man can be contented with a kind of business partnership in marriage, provided sexual privileges are part of the arrangement. As long as his wife prepares his dinner each evening, is reasonably amiable and doesn't nag him during football season, he can be satisfied. The romantic element is nice—but not necessary.

However, this kind of surface relationship drives his wife utterly wild with frustration. She must have something more meaningful. Women yearn to be the special sweethearts of their men, being respected and appreciated and loved with tenderness. This is why a housewife often thinks about her husband during the day and eagerly awaits his arrival home; it explains why their wedding anniversary is more important to her, and why he gets clobbered when he forgets it. It explains why she is constantly "reaching" for him when he is at home, trying to pull him out of the newspaper or television set; it explains why "absence of romantic love in my marriage" ranked so high as a source of depression among women. Men, I suspect, would have rated it much lower.

But women often find it impossible to convey their needs for romantic affection to their husbands. One man said, "I just don't understand my wife. She has everything she could possibly want. She has a dishwasher and a new dryer, and we live in a nice neighborhood. I don't drink or beat the kids or kick the dog. I've been faithful since the day we were married. But she's miserable, and I can't figure out why!" His love-starved wife would have traded the dishwasher, the dryer, and the dog for a single expression of genuine tenderness from her unromantic husband. Appliances do not build self-esteem; being some-body's sweetheart most certainly does.

There is still no substitute for the Biblical prescription for marriage, nor will its wisdom ever be replaced. A success-ful husband and wife relationship begins with the attitude of the man; he has been ordained by God as the head of the family, and the responsibility for its welfare rests upon his shoulders.

Am I recommending that men dominate their wives, ruling with an iron fist and robbing them of individuality? Certainly not. God, Who created the entire universe, should be able to tell us how to live together harmoniously. He has done just that in Ephesians 5:28-33:

"That is how husbands should treat their wives, loving them as parts of themselves. For since a man and his wife are now one, a man is really doing himself a favor and loving himself when he loves his wife! No one hates his own body but lovingly cares for it, just as Christ cares for his body the Church, of which we are parts. (That the husband and wife are one body is proved by the Scripture which says, 'A man must leave his father and mother when he marries, so that he can be perfectly joined to his wife, and the two shall be one.') I know this is hard to understand, but it is an illustration of the way we are parts of the body of Christ. So again I say, a man must love his wife as a part of himself; and the wife must see to it that she deeply respects her husband, obeying, praising and honoring him." (*The Living Bible*)

There is certainly no room for masculine oppression within that formula. The husband is charged with loving leadership within the family, but he must recognize his wife's feelings and needs as being one with his own. When she hurts, he hurts, and takes steps to end the pain. What she wants, he wants, and satisfies her needs. If this one prescription were applied within the American family, we would have little need for divorce courts, alimony, visiting rights, crushed children, broken hearts and shattered lives.

But what about women? What can they do to improve mar-riages that are less than idyllic? Certainly not by nagging, pleading, scolding, complaining or accusing!

This is how it often sounds to an exhausted man who has come home from work moments before: "Won't you just put down that newspaper, George, and give me five minutes of your time? Five minutes—is that too much to ask? You never seem to care about my feelings, anyway. How long has it been since we went out for dinner? Even if we did, you'd probably take the newspaper along with you. I'll tell you, George, sometimes I think you don't care about me and the kids any more. If just once . . . just once . . . you would show a little love and understanding, I would drop dead from sheer shock," etc., etc.

If a wife wants to get through to "George," it might be helpful to consider the three suggestions that follow:

1. Timing

Select the moment when your husband is typically more responsive and pleasant (perhaps that opportunity will occur immediately after the evening meal, or when the light goes out at night, or in the freshness of the morning). The worst time of the day is during the first 60 minutes after he arrives home from work, yet this is the usual combat hour. Don't lumber into such a heavy debate without giving it proper planning and forethought, taking advantage of every opportunity for the success of the effort.

2. Setting

The ideal situation is to ask your husband to take you on an overnight or weekend trip to a pleasant area. If financial considerations will cause him to decline, save the money out of household funds or other resources. If it is impossible to get away, the next best alternative is to obtain a babysitter and go out to breakfast or dinner alone. If that, too, is out of the question, then select a time at home when the children are occupied and the phone can be taken off the hook. The farther you can get him from home, with its cares and problems and stresses, the better will be your chance to achieve genuine communication.

3. Manner

It is extremely important that your husband does not view your conversation as a personal attack. We are all equipped with emotional defenses that rise to our aid when we are being vilified. Don't trigger those defensive mechanisms. Instead, your manner should be as warm, loving, and supportive as possible under the circumstances. Let it be known that you are attempting to interpret *your* needs and desires, not *his* inadequacies and shortcomings. Furthermore, you must take his emotional state into consideration, as well. Postpone the conversation if he is under unusual stress from his work, or if he isn't feeling well, or if he has recently been stung by circumstances and events. Then when the timing, setting, and manner converge to produce a moment of opportunity, express your deep feelings as effectively as possible.

There is one final fact wives need to face: Your husband will *never* be able to meet all of your needs and aspirations. Seldom does one human being satisfy every longing and hope in the breast of another. Obviously this coin has two sides: You can't be his perfect woman, either. Both partners have to settle for human foibles and faults and irritability and fatigue. A good marriage is not one where perfection reigns; it is a relationship where a healthy perspective overlooks a multitude of "unresolvables."

Simply stated, the family was designed by God Almighty to have a specific purpose and function: When it operates as intended, the emotional and physical needs of husbands, wives and children are met in a beautiful relationship of symbiotic love. But when that function is inhibited or destroyed, then every member of the family experiences the discomfort of unmet needs. That is my message. When the family conforms to God's blueprint, then self-esteem is available for everyone—which satisfies romantic aspirations—which abolishes loneliness, isolation and boredom—which contributes to sexual fulfillment—which provides security for children—which gives parents a sense of purpose—which contributes to self-esteem once more. The chain has no weak links. It reveals the beauty of God's own creation, as does the rest of His universe.

What do women most want from their husbands? It is not a bigger home or a better dishwasher or a newer automobile. Rather, it is the assurance that "hand in hand we'll face the best and worst that life has to offer—together."

Take Hold of Love

by HENRY CARTER

I was working feverishly on my Christmas sermon—the hardest time in any minister's year to find something fresh to say—when the floor mother appeared at the study door. Another crisis upstairs. Christmas Eve is a difficult day for the emotionally disturbed children in our church home. Three-quarters of them go home at least overnight and the ones who remain react to the empty beds and the changed routine.

I followed her up the stairs, chafing inwardly at the repeated interruptions. This time it was Tommy. He had crawled under a bed and refused to come out. The woman pointed to one of six cots in the small dormitory. Not a hair or a toe showed beneath it, so I addressed myself to the cowboys and bucking broncos on the bedspread. I talked about the brightly lighted tree in the church vestibule next door and the packages underneath it and all the other good things waiting for him out beyond that bed.

No answer.

Still fretting at the time this was costing, I dropped to my hands and knees and lifted the spread. Two enormous blue eyes met mine. Tommy was eight, but looked like a five-year-old. It would have been no effort at all simply to pull him out. But it wasn't pulling that Tommy needed—it was trust and a sense of deciding things on his own initiative. So, crouched there on all fours, I launched into the menu of the special Christmas Eve supper to be offered after the service. I told him about the stocking with his name on it provided by the women's society.

Silence. There was no indication that he either heard or cared about Christmas.

And at last, because I could think of no other way to make

242

contact, I got down on my stomach and wriggled in beside him, bedsprings snagging my suit jacket. For what seemed a long time I lay there with my cheek pressed against the floor. At first I talked about the big wreath above the altar and the candles in the windows. I reminded him of the carol he and the other children were going to sing. Then I ran out of things to say and simply waited there beside him.

And as I waited, a small, chilled hand crept into mine.

"You know, Tommy," I said after a bit, "it's kind of close quarters under here. Let's you and me go out where we can stand up."

And so we did, but slowly, in no hurry. All the pressure had gone from my day, because, you see, I had my Christmas sermon. Flattened there on the floor I realized I had been given a new glimpse of the mystery of this season.

Hadn't God called us, too, as I'd called Tommy, from far above us? With His stars and mountains, His whole majestic creation, hadn't He pleaded with us to love Him, to enjoy the universe He gave us?

And when we would not listen, He had drawn closer. Through prophets and lawgivers and holy men, He spoke with us face to face.

But it was not until that first Christmas, until God stooped to earth itself, until He took our very place and came to dwell with us in our loneliness and alienation, that we, like Tommy, dared to stretch out our hands to take hold of love.

How would our small house ever accommodate seven more people? And what would Bob think?

A Home in the Heart

by GINNY WOMBOUGH

The only link we had with the Bromleys* was our Robbie and their Bryan, who had met in kindergarten. When they moved out of their rented farmhouse and into an apartment in a nearby town, Robbie wondered what had happened to his friend. He asked me if he had died.

"I'm sure Bryan's all right," I said. "His family just moved, and he's going to a new school." I promised I would get their phone number and call Bryan's mother some Saturday soon to see if they could spend the day together.

When I finally did phone, on a Saturday morning, I found I had intruded on a calamity. The Bromleys had serious troubles—they were flat broke, with no job or income, all five children were sick with a virus, they were to be evicted from their apartment that very day and had no place to go.

It was late spring, the time of year in our resort-area community when most rental property was either already taken for the summer or outrageously expensive for a family of seven. Cathy Bromley, the young mother, told me she had exhausted every possibility of a rental within 50 miles. She was at her wit's end. If they hadn't found anything by six p.m., she said, they would all be out on the sidewalk—sick kids, furniture, everything.

I offered to help. I told her I would look further, thinking I would surely hit on a house or apartment that Mrs. Bromley had missed. For the next three hours I was on the phone finding out what Cathy Bromley already knew: There was nothing for them to rent. Sheepishly, I called her back to report my failure.

There simply was no way that words of sympathy or encouragement were going to help. They needed more than that. And so, in the middle of my trying to reassure her that things would work out, I blurted out, "Cathy, if you still can't find a place, you can move in with us for a few days."

She was so desperate I didn't have to say it twice. "Oh, Ginny," she said, "you're a godsend."

After I had hung up, the realization of what I had done struck me like an aftershock. My husband, Bob, and I lived frugally with our two youngsters in a small, two-bedroom, one-bathroom house, just about big enough to accommodate our quiet family of four. How would seven more people fit into it? And what would Bob think? He was off at work and wouldn't be home till late afternoon. When he got home, I would have to tell him that seven complete strangers were moving in, that I had made a promise without even talking to him about it.

My anxiety grew when I found out later that Mr. Bromley had some kind of an emotional problem that he tried to relieve with alcohol. The effects of what I had done immediately began to surface. Those closest to us, outside our tiny family circle, were appalled, fearing that I was making an awful mistake.

"Dear Lord," I murmured, "if I've done the right thing in trying to help these people, please let me know it."

Bob got home from the plant, and after he'd had a chance to wash up and get comfortable, I nervously told him what had happened. He listened attentively. When I finished, his face remained calm and serious. Then his eyes moved to mine. "Whatever you want to do," he said, "is all right with me." I sent up a little prayer of thanks.

Bob not only accepted the idea of their moving in, but volunteered to help move their furniture. He and Cathy spent most of the afternoon putting things into our basement while I minded the children and went about the task of preparing supper for 11 people.

Bob and I were in the habit of shopping once a week—on Wednesday, Bob's payday—and I would freeze our meat in separate packages, one for each night's meal. For this night's meal I had to defrost all the meat for the next four nights. I felt like I was feeding the 5000, as Jesus had miraculously done—

and that I would need a similar miracle to keep 11 people fed on our budget.

The furniture was all moved in, supper was ready, Bob and I were ready, but our guests still hadn't shown up. After waiting till the food was cold, we decided to find out what was wrong. We put our two children into our car and drove to the Bromleys' apartment. There they all sat on the sidewalk. Ed Bromley was having extreme difficulty accepting our invitation. Finally, he reluctantly consented.

So with fresh misgivings, on that May evening we welcomed the Bromleys into our lives. There were Millie, seven, Bryan, six, Scott, five, Mike, four, Paul, two, plus Cathy and Ed Bromley. And to top it off, they brought their huge German shepherd dog, who turned out to be pregnant. All of us would have to learn to cope with one another. I prayed we would, with God's help, work it out somehow.

Even while I was still praying on Sunday, some of the "somehow" was being provided. Bob and I hadn't known it, but Ed's mother worked for a large, nearby hotel, where the banquet season was on. The banquet leftovers became ours for the asking! Our menus, beginning Monday morning, consisted of: pounds of chicken livers; prime ribs, cooked but never served; barbecued spare ribs; baked potatoes; fresh fruit juices by the gallon; vegetable soup by the gallon and vegetables by the gallon.

The hotel may have called them leftovers, but Bob and I felt we were dining like royalty, far better than what we were used to. Ed's mother was to supply food like that every week. We would be able to feed the 5000, I decided, and when we said grace at mealtime, a new experience for the Bromley children, we really meant it when we gave thanks.

After a while, we settled into a routine. The week after they moved in, Ed Bromley got a job at a junk yard, and he and Bob would leave for work around eight in the morning. So I would first get the workers fed, then feed the children and send the three who were school age off to school. Cathy drove hers to school in their old station wagon. Since the end of the school year was close, the school authorities allowed them to finish with their class in their old neighborhood's school.

The younger kids watched television and played while Cathy and I cleaned up the breakfast dishes. That done, I'd start preparing for lunch, as Cathy straightened up the house and did her family's laundry. She kept her children spotless, and ran the washer four times to my one.

Putting their furniture in the basement turned out to be a great idea, for it let all the Bromleys sleep in their own beds and have their things around them. The basement became like a tiny apartment, brimming with Bromleys.

After lunch, Cathy and I would wash and dry dishes again, and I'd start on supper, then try to squeeze out some time for myself before the kids got home from school at three o'clock.

Dinner began about 5:30, children first, all grouped around the kitchen table, elbows flying, laughing, fighting and talking all at the same time. While the kids played, did their homework or watched TV, we four grown-ups ate. Then we would get the children to bed and clean up the kitchen again.

It was during those hours after dinner that Bob and I got to know our guests. Ed and Cathy were both about 25. He was short and stocky, and she was small and thin, but strong and full of energy. Ed was an auto-body mechanic and had previously operated his own repair shop. He was a perfectionist, though, and would spend hours planning to do the job right when others would simply go ahead and do it.

The four of us would play Canasta at the kitchen table and talk long into the night. Many times we'd invite our neighbors in to play, too. The chance to talk with someone who would listen to him seemed to help Ed and relieve the tensions he felt. We'd play cards and talk till midnight, then quit and head for bed and keep talking. Often Ed and Cathy would stand at the top of the basement steps and we'd keep talking till one or two in the morning. Oddly enough, neither Bob nor I felt tired when we got up in the morning.

As summer came on, local real-estate offices began to list a few houses available for rent. That was a break, but it created other problems and pointed out one in particular. To rent a place, the Bromleys needed to pay two months' rent in advance. And with a large part of Ed's earnings being spent on alcohol, they weren't able to save enough to make that payment. So Cathy decided she would go to work, too, and found a part-time job as a housekeeper at a motel.

That meant that for a big part of the day I had all the children to mind by myself. They were out of school now. There were so many of the Bromleys that they seemed to take over everything—toys, time, space and, most worrisome of all, attention. They constantly interrupted and preempted conversations and activities. Robbie, our six-year-old, and Denny, who was four, were willing to share their toys, house and yard—but sharing Mom and Dad was different.

The realization of the Bromley children's seeming takeover came to me one evening while I sat quietly after supper, toying with a metal key as I tried to relax. Denny came over to me and climbed onto my lap. As I held him, he wanted to see the key, and I gave it to him. Pointing the key at my heart, he pretended to open it up. He peered in and told me sadly, "I don't see very much love for me in there." I just about cried.

After that, I noticed that Bob, too, was showing more attention and affection to the Bromley youngsters than to our own. I knew well, though, that neither of us could help it. With Ed working seven days and Cathy away so much of the time, too, Bob and I had to show our love for the Bromley children. The situation demanded it. Still, I felt resentment and fear creep into me. I prayed that God would help me overcome such feelings, and that Robbie and Denny would somehow understand and not be harmed by the experience. God was to answer that prayer a few days later.

It had been a particularly tiring and trying day, and I was both weary and angry at the end of it when I went to get my boys into bed. I felt they were dragging their feet, and making things harder for me than they should be. I told them both sternly, "I am going to blow a fuse if I don't get your full cooperation!"

"Don't blow a fuse, Mommy," Robbie said, his eyes bright with a child's wisdom and humor, "or you'll put out the light."

Wow! I thought. *That's right. When I lose my cool, I actually put out the light of Christ's love in my heart.*

Then the words of Christ came back to me: "Every one that hath forsaken . . . brethren, or sisters, or father, or mother, or wife, or children . . . for My name's sake, shall receive an hundredfold, and shall inherit everlasting life." (Matthew 19:29)

Some of our friends and relatives couldn't understand the kind of giving that Jesus was talking about and therefore did not approve of what we were doing. Those relationships were strained temporarily. But Bob and I knew that God was with us and He would provide the help we needed, a hundredfold.

The help sometimes came in small ways, like letting us be wise enough to figure out ways to get along. Cathy and I worked out a plan to alternate afternoons away from the house, to give us time off from each other's family. One day she would take her youngsters to the beach or picnicking or shopping and let Robbie and Denny and me have the house and yard to ourselves for a few hours. The next day, I would do the same for her.

Sometimes we were helped in odd ways. Lady, the Bromleys' German shepherd, seemed to be nothing but trouble. She scared the kids—ours and the neighbors'. When she ran loose, she wouldn't bother the children, but when she was chained, she was a barking terror. She wouldn't let strangers come near her—and almost everyone was a stranger. When the dog was chained to Bob's tool shed, she wouldn't let Bob get to it; she was "protecting" it. So Bob had to build an eight- by 16-foot pen for Lady, from which she would occasionally escape by climbing the six-foot fence. While in the pen, she gave birth to 13 pups, which added to the confusion and made Lady a little more nervous.

But toward the back of our two-acre lot, where Bob kept his garden, things were calmer than usual. The dog, with all her barking and running around, frightened away the rabbits, moles and groundhogs that usually played havoc with Bob's garden. And that summer, the garden yielded five times the vegetables Bob ordinarily got from it.

After eight weeks with us, the Bromleys found a place to

rent, Ed found a new job with an auto-body company, and the family moved out of our house. They left us on a Sunday. And as if to dramatize the fact that the good Lord had provided according to our needs, on Monday morning, our clothes washer, which had kept our two families in clean clothes daily, broke down and flooded our basement—now emptied of all the Bromleys' belongings—with six inches of water.

That wasn't the only demonstration, though. We all saw God's caring in our lives as we tried to share His caring with people in need. Ed Bromley was overwhelmed by the fact that strangers had taken him and his family into their home for no reason other than they thought it was the right thing to do. "Gee, Bob," he told my husband on more than one occasion, "I never dreamed there were people who would do something like this."

Bob realized that Ed had truly been affected when one evening he overheard Ed, while trying to repair our car's troublesome radiator, say, "Please, Lord, let me fix this thing so I can do something for this guy who's done so much for me."

Our children got a demonstration, too, of how to share. Robbie and Denny, as well as the Bromley youngsters, saw that people really can care for and help one another, as God intended. In all my years of working in Sunday school, I don't think a better lesson in Christian love was ever taught.

And the love that grew between us during those weeks has grown deeper over the years since we shared our home. The Bromleys have moved to another state, but we still stay in touch and visit each other during holidays.

Although they moved out of our house after eight weeks, they've never moved out of our hearts. And, praise God, they feel the same way about us.

7.
Love for Those Who Feel Lonely

*Lo, I am with you alway, even unto
the end of the world.*
(Matthew 28:20)

The Voice in My Heart

by NORMA ZIMMER
Star of the "Lawrence Welk Show"

The memory of that terrible afternoon haunted me for years. I had just trudged home from school and, passing under an open window, I heard my mother telling the landlady about me.

"We really didn't want to have Norma," my mother said matter-of-factly. "Two children were enough. In fact, I tried to lose the baby by riding my horse every day."

I winced as my mother's words knifed into me. I slipped into the house to my room where I threw myself on the bed, sobbing convulsively.

Not until evening shadows darkened the window was I able to sit up. I walked to the cracked mirror. It was easy to see why no one wanted me, a homely, short girl with a bad complexion and thick ankles. My older sister and brother had all the looks. When I came along, I was so small they laughed at me as "the runt of the family."

I slumped back on the old bed, despondent and miserable. I felt worthless. And it had been this way ever since I could remember.

We lived in the Seattle slums. Father never held a job very long. He had been a concert violinist, but had lost the use of his fingers in an accident. Disillusioned, he turned to drink, and our family sank deeper into poverty. Mother tried to do her best, remaking clothes, scraping together meals from welfare food. But, crumbling under hopelessness, she joined father in his drinking. Often they'd fight, arguing so loudly that the landlady would ask us to move. We'd find another shack where the wind whined through pine board walls.

At school I was taunted by the girls when one discovered me wearing her old shoes, which had been given to charity. But Father could be perverse about handouts. One Thanksgiving when we had only dry bread to eat, several ladies came to the door. Dad, who had been drinking, answered their knock. "Happy Thanksgiving, Mr. Larsen," one said, "we brought you a turkey."

A turkey! I crept to the door, peeking at them. But Dad took the food-filled basket and threw it violently out onto the ground. "I don't take charity!" he bellowed and slammed the door.

Dad had one dream: to make concert violinists out of my sister and brother. But they didn't care for the instrument. I shared Dad's love of music, and tried to please him by practicing hours each day.

But as I stood squinting at the notes in the dull glow of the smoky oil lamp, I knew I would never make a top violinist. My stumpy hands had trouble with the fingering in difficult concertos.

By the time I reached high school, however, I could play well enough to join the school orchestra. Then an angel entered my life. He was Carl Pitzer, the music teacher. A tall, sandy-haired man with friendly blue eyes, he sensed my lack of confidence, so he concentrated on my good points. One day after coaching me he said, "Norma, you have a marvelous ability to sight-read music!" I floated on air the rest of the day and vowed to try even harder. He encouraged me to try out for the glee club, where I learned to sing the beautiful songs of Victor Herbert, Sigmund Romberg and Jerome Kern. As I sang in school, a strange feeling filled me; I felt as if this was something for which I had been born.

Mr. Pitzer was also choir director at the University Christian Church. One day he asked our glee club assembly how many sang in a church choir. Every hand went up except mine. Our family had never gone to church.

After class, Mr. Pitzer walked over to me. "Norma," he asked, "don't you sing in a choir?"

"No," I said, feeling awkward.

"How about singing in my church's choir?" he asked, smiling. "You'd be a real asset to us."

My heart jumped at the compliment, and I told him I would.

I'll never forget that first Sunday in church. A deep peace and reverence filled me. This was a *home*, the home of God. My eyes feasted on the carved oak pews, the rich red carpeting and the soaring sanctuary. I thrilled most to the glowing stained glass window that showed the Lord Jesus, His hands open in an invitation, a little lamb at His feet.

I felt unworthy and insignificant before such things. But then the minister, Doctor Hastings, preached on how God loves us no matter who we are or what we have done; God had a wonderful plan for everyone's life. *Even for someone like me?* I wondered. I didn't see how God could love me. But oh, how I wanted that eternal life He promised.

Every time we rose to sing in church my heart soared, and I always felt better than I was.

Then a wonderful thing happened in my senior year. Mr. Pitzer said he would like me to become one of his featured church solists. And on a coming Sunday I would sing *How Beautiful Upon the Mountain*. When my parents learned I was going to sing a solo, they insisted on coming. I was pleased at their interest.

Finally the great day arrived. That morning I left the house early. In church, when the organ thundered the processional, we filed into the sanctuary in our blue and gold robes. As we moved in procession down the main aisle, I stole glances at the congregation, trying to find my parents. We slowly made our way up the stairs and back to the choir loft. Finally settled in the loft, I still couldn't find them.

Suddenly I felt my heart contract. Down the main aisle weaved my father and mother, both intoxicated. On they came, searching for a place to sit, my mother's hair disheveled, her lipstick smeared, my father's face flushed, his eyes bleary.

Finally, they stumbled over people to seats in the middle of a row.

I sat paralyzed in shame. I wanted to crawl under the benches and run out of the church. I sat through the invocation, hymn, prayer and offering numb with shock.

Then I got up and sang my solo: "How beautiful upon the mountains are the feet of Him that bringeth good tidings . . ." The song seemed interminable; I tried to think only of the words and averted my eyes from my parents.

I sat down, heart pounding. But I made my decision. I would quit the church and never come back. How could I ever show my face here again?

I was hardly aware that Doctor Hastings had started preaching. But then his words reached me. "God is our refuge and strength, a tested help in time of trouble." Tears filled my eyes. My own trouble seemed more than I could bear. I realized how desperate life in my unhappy family was without God. I had nothing; even my talent seemed ashes.

I looked at the stained glass window of Jesus, glowing with the morning sun. His hands stretched out to me. "Oh, dear Lord," I pleaded, "if I could only be that little lamb at Your feet."

Then I seemed to hear His words: "Come unto Me all ye that labor and are heavy laden, and I will give you rest." (Matthew 11:28)

I looked up, the beautiful colors wavering through my tears. "Lord Jesus," I prayed, "I give You my burdens. I want You to come into my heart."

Then something wonderful happened. As I sat there, it was as if an electric current started flowing through me. My fingers tingled. And my heart swelled like a bud bursting into bloom. I felt thrilled with His glory.

By the time the service was over, I wasn't worrying any more about my parents or myself. As the choir moved down the aisle, I walked with my head high, singing joyfully, I had found my Lord. I had found my life. He was mine, and I was His.

After church, I greeted my parents as people congratulated me. Then I walked home with them. I knew that when God commanded us to honor our fathers and mothers, He did not mean just the perfect fathers and mothers.

Since that day much has happened. There have been joyful times—Dad and Mother becoming sober and happy, my marriage blessed with two fine sons, and a fulfilling career. There have also been sad times—family illnesses, loss of loved ones and some of the other sorrows we must all face in this world. I'm still basically a shy person. And at times I tremble and feel so inadequate. But then I *know* He is standing there, arms outstretched, saying, "Come on, Norma, we can do it together."

Thou wilt show me the path of life; in Thy presence is fulness of joy; at thy right hand there are pleasures for evermore. (Psalm 16:11)

**It's been several years since this story
of a desperately afflicted and lonely young man
first appeared in Guideposts—years that have
given emphasis to the haunting beauty of . . .**

The Friendship

by PAUL SCOTT*

At a time of utter despair, at a time when I could not go on, a
remarkable man came into my life. He came with love. I
had run into disaster six long years before. A high-school senior,
I loved dancing, good times and sports. I was playing halfback
on the football team when the first hint of trouble came. I
couldn't seem to hold on to the ball. The condition grew worse.
Finally I was hospitalized for extensive tests and at last my
problem was diagnosed.

"You have leprosy, Paul," the doctor said.

Nowadays most doctors call it Hansen's disease. No matter
what its name, to me it was a death sentence. My parents were
horrified. Secretly, as if I were a criminal, I was whisked away to
the Federal Public Health Service hospital in Carville,
Louisiana, the only leprosarium in the U.S.

I was confined there for six fright-filled years—years of
separation—lonely heartbreaking years.

Then medical science discovered new drugs—sulfone
drugs—and they worked! But the new medication had arrived
too late to prevent deformity. My life was saved, but my face
was disfigured. I'd lost partial vision in one eye and I walked
with a slight limp. My hands were severely crippled. Dr.
Daniel Riordan performed 16 operations in order to make them
more efficient.

When at last I returned home, my parents could not accept
my disabilities.

---

*Name has been changed.

I was left utterly alone and could not cope with the hopelessness of my situation. Because of my face, I hated to go outdoors to the stares, the shock that followed my appearances. Old friends were uncomfortable with me. I would go out only at night, to walk the New York streets alone. One Halloween, my depression reached the lowest point in my life. Some youngsters, dressed in Halloween costumes and wearing grotesque masks, shrieked, "Look at him—he doesn't need a mask." At first they were joking, but as they looked, they realized it was absolutely true and they drew away.

I felt there was nothing to live for; there was no sense in struggling. I was not a Catholic, but something impelled me to enter St. Patrick's Cathedral on Fifth Avenue that Halloween night. I don't know to this day if I prayed or not. I only remember that there—in the quiet of the huge vaulted cathedral—I began to think of Fulton Sheen. While I was at Carville, Bishop Sheen had visited there. I thought he would understand my feelings.

I saw a priest near the main altar and approached him, asking, "Could I please see Bishop Sheen? It's important."

The priest must have recognized, from my words or manner, the urgency of my request. He told me that the bishop was not associated with St. Patrick's, but that he would see that Bishop Sheen received my name and address.

To me, it was just another failure. Yet soon after that, I received a message inviting me to see the bishop in his office.

"I've come to you because I have no one else to turn to," I said, "I haven't a friend in the world."

"Well, now you have one," Bishop Sheen said, smiling. He invited me to dinner the next night. Soon after we began to eat, I had difficulty handling my knife and fork. Without stopping his conversation, my host reached over and cut my meat for me. That one very simple gesture touched me so deeply that I realized that I did, at last, have a friend. I poured out all the torment in my soul—my despair, my friendlessness, how I could not find a job, my lack of hope . . .

"God has a purpose for your life, Paul," Bishop Sheen told me. "It is up to us to find it." In the weekly dinners that followed as the bishop invited me again and again, I found new hope.

"You won't have many friends," he would tell me. "But those you have will be real ones."

And so it has been. I'm grateful for the friends who have given me so much, and for the two dedicated physicians, Theodore Capeci and Carl Barlow, who provided, free of charge, several operations that greatly improved my appearance. My hands are still deformed, but they are much better than before the operations. Finding work was difficult, but I finally located an office job at a minimum salary.

I am so grateful for the gifts God has sent me. These gifts that have enabled me to persevere were there all the time, but it was through Bishop Sheen that I learned to recognize them. It was he who gave—not as a bishop, but as a human being concerned about another human being.

What were those gifts?

I received the gift of faith. I have been able to accept Christ. The bishop himself baptized me in St. Patrick's Cathedral and confirmed me in his private chapel.

Each day I live is different from the next. Every day is not necessarily good; at times I still am overwhelmed with loneliness. But my faith helps me. I don't wake up in the morning and say to myself, "Today I'll have faith." Faith and belief are with me all the time and I don't have to consciously dwell on it. They're there—just as God is—and I can live in that assurance day by day.

I received the gift of love, spiritually and materially. My friend helped furnish my apartment, provided clothes and once, between paydays, when he discovered I had no food, insisted on taking me to a delicatessen where we filled a shopping basket for me.

I received the gift of acceptance. Although filled with resentment at the things that had happened to me, I learned to accept myself, to be less bitter and to work on what I can offer to others—good manners, cleanliness, neatness, respectability, a sense of humor.

I received the gift of security, of knowing that any time I am too lonely, too depressed, I can reach Bishop Sheen. "If you can't get me by phone, send me a telegram," he told me. After he moved to Rochester, New York, I missed him greatly. Still, I have learned now to rely more upon myself. I have learned the security of faith.

When Bishop Sheen was installed as Bishop of the Diocese of Rochester, he included me in the guest list. I was sitting at the end of a center pew and had a good view as he proceeded down the red-carpeted aisle of the cathedral after the ceremony. There were many well-known people present, but, suddenly, he stopped by me. He put his arms about my shoulders saying, "It's nice to have you here, Paul."

I said something in reply and became conscious of an increased murmur all about me, of necks craning. The lady sitting next to me must have wondered, as others probably did, who I was. She whispered, "Are you a representative from the Vatican?"

Her question amused me. "No," I answered. "Just a friend."

The lady looked at me for a moment and then softly said, "He must love you very much."

She had used the one perfect word—love.

EDITOR'S NOTE: Paul Scott's faith continues to sustain him. He is now unable to work because of his physical condition, but he has given well over 1000 hours of volunteer service at a social-service agency that helps troubled people with their problems. Archbishop Sheen encourages Paul to have this interest in others—"to reach out and see that you can be helpful despite any limitations you have."

Life seemed hopeless for this child, but a
hidden Power was at work.

A Smile for Renay

by MARGUERITE FREEMAN

Renay met me at the door, a tall, slender girl, still shy, but pretty now. She smiled at me, and it was the most remarkable smile I've ever seen, winning and warm and ever so beautiful. I could only hug her, thinking of the child I had known, and of the long, long struggle leading to this day. . . .

Renay was ten when she entered my fifth-grade class in Chickasaw, Alabama, in 1968. She was small for her age, very thin, and too shy to talk. When she did speak, her voice was low I could scarcely hear what she said.

Each day when I stood near the door as the class was leaving, Renay would reach out and touch me with her finger instead of saying good-by. One day I noticed why she wasn't saying anything. There was something wrong with her mouth. Her upper lip had been disfigured in such a way that her mouth was pulled tight and stiff. This made it difficult for her to talk, or even smile.

It wasn't long before I noticed other children making fun of Renay. One day when that happened she ran to me with tears in her eyes.

"My mother says I must forgive people who treat me mean, and my father says if I keep quiet for just a while before I answer I won't be mad at them," she sobbed. "But I'm still mad!"

I pulled her frail body close to mine, and held her on my lap as she told me what had happened to her lip.

"Well, then," I said after hearing it, "we're going to tell the rest of the class that story, too."

262

Renay looked up at me, her eyes widening. "I can't! They'll laugh at me!"

"They're laughing now," I said, wiping her tears. "But maybe if they know about it, they won't."

The next morning I told the students that Renay was going to teach a class in safety. There were whisperings and giggles from some of the girls and one loud laugh from the back of the classroom, but little Renay took her place at my desk and unwound a length of electrical cord that she had brought.

"Would one of you come up here and bite into this lamp cord, please?" she asked.

The children roared with laughter. Renay waited until they settled down, then began her story in a soft voice. The children became very quiet as they listened, visualizing a small baby crawling around the floor, finding a lamp cord and putting it in her mouth. Everyone in the room felt the pain as the baby bit the cord. We saw the flash and heard the baby's screams. We felt sick and weak when Renay finished her story.

"Why didn't somebody do something?" said the voice from the back, not laughing any more.

"The doctors did all they could," answered Renay. "And my parents, too."

And that might have been the end of it if things had been left to busy, fallible people like myself. Fortunately that was not the end of it.

In the days following Renay's talk to the class, I noticed the other children playing with her more, teasing her less and being much more accepting of her. But the child's face was drawn as though she was in pain. When I asked her what the trouble was, she pointed to her teeth. She was badly in need of dental care and suffering from a severe toothache.

I decided to go home with Renay and talk to her mother about taking the child to a dentist. When I did go to the house, I found the family in serious financial difficulties. It was not that they were indifferent or careless. They were simply unable to pay for dental services, and would not ask for help without paying.

I didn't like the idea of meddling. But something kept prod-

ding me and the only solution I could think of was for me to take
Renay to my own dentist. This turned out to be difficult because Renay's parents didn't want my assistance. They were
proud, self-respecting people who resisted the idea of accepting anything that looked like charity. Finally, very reluctantly,
they gave their consent, and I made an appointment. From
then on all I did was sit back and watch a miracle unfold.

The dentist filled the troublesome tooth and refused to take
any payment, but most important, he looked at me and said
sternly, "Why hasn't something been done about this child's
lip? Don't you know there are doctors who can help her?"

"I thought everything possible had been done," I answered.
"And furthermore, the family has very limited means."

Renay sat in the dental chair with her head down, listening to
our conversation. There was a kind of hopelessness on her face
that tore at my heart.

"Would they take her to a doctor if I got an appointment?" the
dentist asked. "There are services available, free, for cases like
hers."

There was a swift change of expression on Renay's face. Her
head came up and her eyes were shining.

"Oh, yes, sir," she said. "Yes, sir!"

The dentist called a plastic surgeon and arranged for him to
look at Renay's mouth. The surgeon arranged for her parents to
put her under the care of the Crippled Children's Clinic. In a
few weeks, an operation was scheduled and the plastic surgeon
performed the first step in a series of operations.

I was shocked after the first operation to see so little progress, but Renay and her family explained to me that the doctor
was building up her mouth. She wore her scars proudly—with
her head up. Everything was different now. Something was
being done for her, and instead of hiding her disfigured mouth,
she talked to everyone about what was happening. She loved
her surgeon and quoted him happily. She loved the hospital
and the nurses. If she suffered any pain, no one ever knew
about it. Each time I visited her I thought of Paul's words,
"Now faith is the substance of things hoped for, the evidence of
things not seen." (Hebrews 11:1) Renay and her family had

formed a clear mental picture of how she would finally look, and once they had begun this long, drawn-out adventure, they never thought of stopping.

The third operation was performed, and after a long wait, the fourth and final one. I had kept in touch with Renay and her family, but I had also been busy with each succeeding group of fifth-graders. It came as a surprise, one evening, when the telephone rang and a happy voice said, "The doctor has dismissed me and I'm through with operations. Come and see me as soon as you can. . . ."

Now here I was, in the presence of this tall, pretty teen-ager. I glanced at her face. The stiffness was gone from her mouth, and there was only the faintest sign of a scar, which would be removed later on.

"She goes around the house smiling all the time," her mother told me. "She never stops. . . ."

I looked at Renay, so moved that I was unable to speak. All I could do was say a silent prayer of gratitude for the builders of that smile: the doctors and dentists who were willing to give of themselves to help, the proud family that was able to be good receivers, the little girl whose faith was so strong she refused to give up . . . and the patient, invisible Power Who had used all of us to complete His compassionate design for a needy child.

A formula for dealing with
days that lack sunshine.

Ten Ways to Beat The Blues

by MARTHA McCHISNEY
WILKINSON

Once, at a time of great sorrow, I found it difficult to over-come the feelings of loneliness, grief and depression that kept enveloping me. Finally, though, I discovered some ways to beat the blue moods. I believe they can work for others, too.

1. It may seem too simple, but ask God to give you the strength to overcome your mood.

2. Say to yourself, "I have felt this way before. It will pass. It did the other times." The grief may not leave, but the present mood often does.

3. Deliberately "turn off" your mind to your unhappiness. In place of sad memories, force yourself to inject pleasant things into your thoughts.

4. If the weather permits, take a walk or engage in some other outdoor exercise. If that isn't possible, *keep busy* at something indoors.

5. Be grateful for all the happiness you have had. List your present blessings.

6. "Be not overcome of evil, but overcome evil with good." (Romans 12:21) Help someone, maybe even a stranger, if you can.

7. Realize that this mood may have a physical basis. Perhaps nervous fatigue or some other bodily ill is at least partly respon-sible. If so, ask your doctor to help you.

8. Be confident that if you are really willing to place yourself

in God's hands, something, or someone, will come along and help you bear the unbearable.

9. Remember that every person at some time in his or her life must make the same adjustments, many with fewer "tools" with which to work than you have.

10. Believe in tomorrow!

A Fragile Moment of Love

The Reverend John Barker tells the story of the time he returned home one evening after a busy day, dropped into an easy chair and concentrated on plotting his next day's program.

His four-year old daughter climbed into his lap. "Daddy, I love you!" she said. He smiled and answered absentmindedly, "Yes, dear." Again she repeated this bit of adoration and again he murmured something.

For a third time she repeated the four magic words but still her father was lost in his world of work. Then the child bounced up, threw her arms tightly around his neck and shouted, "Daddy, it's time you loved me!"

In hundreds of ways God reminds each one of us that He loves us; how often do we tell this to Him?

James H. Buswell

The Day I Stopped
Feeling Ashamed

by JOSEPH LAHEY

I sat there in a white hospital gown—terrified. I was in the infirmary of Morristown School, a boys' private school. A group of boys from my grade, the seventh, were waiting our turns for a physical examination.

Some of the boys were making small, unfunny jokes about what the examination would be like, but I could not join in their laughing and kidding. I was too conscious of what an ordeal the examination was going to be for me. I was fully aware that of all the boys there I was the only one who was very different physically—to put it bluntly, in an ugly way. I knew I was deformed.

Though this could be concealed for the most part with my clothes on, when I was undressed, it was all too clear to see. I lived with a feeling of shame—and hated it. I wished more than anything else I could be like those other boys with their fine, straight bodies. Soon the doctor would be saying, "Now, Joe, take off that robe and let's have a look at you," and I dreaded it. I never, never, never undressed in front of anyone.

The trouble had started with a sled ride when I was four years old. The sled hit a tree and I took quite a wallop on my back. The pain did not go away; it got worse. When the doctor dropped a nickel on the floor and asked me to pick it up, I bent with my legs only, keeping my back stiff. "I think," he said, "we'd better take some X rays." Tuberculosis of the spine was found—and the years that followed are a blur of memories best forgotten. Casts, an operation for a spinal graft, literally years of lying strapped on a canvas board.

That was all over now, though. I was back in school, with a formidable steel brace. The hump in the middle of my back was fairly well concealed when I had all my clothes on, but I could never conceal this defect from myself, and living with this constant feeling of physical inferiority hurt me greatly.

At last it was my turn, and I walked into the examining room. Behind the desk sat a tall, gray-haired man, reading the chart in his hand.

"Umm, Joseph," he said, "you're in the fourth form, I see."

"Yes, sir," I said. Then he looked up at me and I could see his very blue eyes. They had a sparkle to them, but also a look in them that I could feel penetrating the hospital gown and even into my inner feeling of discomfort and shame.

"All right," he said, getting up, "let's get on with it. Hop up on the scale first." He came over and balanced the weights and then lowered the stick over my head to measure my height. He carefully marked these statistics on my chart, and then, without looking up, said, "Now, take that robe off."

I fumbled with the string, my hands shaking, but I finally got the cord at the neck untied and slipped out of the robe. It was an awful feeling standing there.

Suddenly the doctor put down the chart and came forward and gently put his hands on either side of my face, looking deep in my eyes.

"Do you believe in God?" he asked.

I was astonished, but I told the truth. "Yes, sir," I said.

"That's good," he said, "because there's nothing we can do in this world alone. The more faith we have in Him, the greater the faith we have in ourselves."

"Yes, sir," I said again. There was something about the touch of this man's hands on my face and the intensity of his belief in this dependency of man on God that went right into me and made me shiver. Then, just as suddenly as he had shown that side of his character, he became once again the strictly businesslike doctor. He left me standing there while he went back to the desk and wrote some more on my chart. Then he stood up and said, "Excuse me for just a minute—I'll be right back."

I stood there for a moment, feeling chilly and hoping that he would soon be back and the whole ordeal over. Then my eyes traveled to the chart he had left lying on the desk. "I wonder what it really says about me," I said to myself. "I wonder what he has written about my deformity." My throat was tight; I was steeling myself for the worst. But there on the paper, beside the words "Physical Characteristics," I saw clearly written just five words: "Has an unusually well-shaped head."

For a moment I just stared at the words in confusion—they were so unexpected, so completely different from the thoughts that had been obsessing me, preying on my mind. It took a moment for my thinking to turn around, to dwell on something other than my misshapen back.

"Has an unusually well-shaped head." I read the words again. No, there was no mistake, that was what he had actually written—and, most important, nothing else. Nothing at all!

Almost before I knew it, he came back in the room, smiling at me with those blue eyes so full of insight and compassion.

"All right, Joseph, get your robe on and tell the next boy to come in now," he said.

I stood there a moment, half-dazed, but at last I fumbled my robe back on and said, "Thank you, sir, thank you," and let myself out of the room.

It is years since that brief incident—and I know that my head is no better shaped than anyone else's. But I got the message that this great man had to give: to focus on the best, not the worst, in any situation. To believe that with God's help a person can learn to live with any handicap or any difficulty.

I got the message, and I'll treasure it as long as I live.

At Christmas the Heart Goes Home

by MARJORIE HOLMES

At Christmas all roads lead home.

The filled planes, packed trains, overflowing buses, all speak eloquently of a single destination: home. Despite the crowding and the crushing, the delays, the confusion, we clutch our bright packages and beam our anticipation. We are like birds driven by an instinct we only faintly understand— the hunger to be with our own people.

If we are already snug by our own fireside surrounded by growing children, or awaiting the return of older ones who are away, then the heart takes a side trip. In memory we journey back to the Christmases of long ago. Once again we are curled into quivering balls of excitement listening to the mysterious rustle of tissue paper and the tinkle of untold treasures as parents perform their magic on Christmas Eve. Or we recall the special Christmases that are like little landmarks in the life of a family.

One memory is particularly dear to me—a Christmas during the Great Depression when Dad was out of work and the rest of us were scattered, struggling to get through school or simply to survive. My sister Gwen and her school-teacher husband, on his first job in another state, were expecting their first baby. My brother Harold, an aspiring actor, was traveling with a road show. I was a senior working my way through a small college 500 miles away. My boss had offered me 50 dollars—a fortune!—just to keep the office open the two weeks he and his wife would be gone.

"And boy, do I need the money! Mom, I know you'll understand," I wrote.

I wasn't prepared for her brave if wistful reply. The other kids couldn't make it either! Except for my kid brother Barney, she and Dad would be alone. "This house is going to seem empty, but don't worry—we'll be okay."

I did worry, though. Our first Christmas apart! And as the carols drifted up the stairs, as the corridors rang with the laughter and chatter of other girls packing up to leave, my misery deepened.

Then one night when the dorm was almost empty I had a long-distance call. "Gwen!" I gasped. "What's wrong?" (Long-distance usually meant an emergency back in those days.)

"Listen, Leon's got a new generator and we think the old jalopy can make it home. I've wired Harold—if he can meet us halfway, he can ride with us. But don't tell the folks; we want to surprise them. Marj, you've just got to come, too."

"But I haven't got a dime for presents!"

"Neither have we. Cut up a catalogue and bring pictures of all the goodies you'd buy if you could—and will someday!"

"I could do *that*, Gwen. But I just can't leave here now."

When we hung up I reached for the scissors. Furs and perfume. Wrist watches, clothes, cars—how all of us longed to lavish beautiful things on those we loved. Well, at least I could mail mine home—with I.O.U.s.

I was still dreaming over this "wish list" when I was called to the phone again. It was my boss, saying he'd decided to close the office after all. My heart leaped up, for if it wasn't too late to catch a ride as far as Fort Dodge with the girl down the hall . . . ! I ran to pound on her door.

They already had a load, she said—but if I was willing to sit on somebody's lap. . . . Her dad was downstairs waiting. I threw things into a suitcase, then rammed a hand down the torn lining of my coat sleeve so fast it emerged mittened and I had to start over.

It was snowing as we piled into that heaterless car. We drove all night with the side curtains flapping, singing and hugging each other to keep warm. Not minding—how could we? We were going home!

"Marj!" Mother stood at the door clutching her robe about her, silver-black hair spilling down her back, eyes large with alarm, then incredulous joy. "Oh . . . *Marj*."

I'll never forget those eyes or the feel of her arms around me, so soft and warm after the bitter cold. My feet felt frozen after the all-night drive, but they warmed up as my parents fed me and put me to bed. And when I woke up hours later it was to the jangle of sleigh bells Dad hung on the door each year. And voices. My kid brother shouting, "Harold! Gwen!" The clamor of astonished greetings, the laughter, the kissing, the questions. And we all gathered around the kitchen table the way we used to, recounting our adventures.

"I had to hitchhike clear to Peoria," my older brother scolded merrily. "*Me*, the leading man. . . ." He lifted an elegant two-toned shoe—with a flapping sole—"In these!"

"But by golly, you *got* here." Dad's chubby face was beaming. Then suddenly he broke down—Dad, who never cried. "We're together!"

Together. The best present we could give one another, we realized. All of us. Just being here in the old house where we'd shared so many Christmases. No gift on our lavish lists, if they could materialize, could equal that.

In most Christmases since that memorable one we've been lucky. During the years our children were growing up there were no separations. Then one year, appallingly, history repeated itself. For valid reasons, not a single faraway child could get home. Worse, my husband had flown to Florida for some vital surgery. A proud, brave man—he was adamant about our not coming with him "just because it's Christmas," when he'd be back in another week.

Like my mother before me, I still had one lone chick left— Melanie, 14, "We'll get along fine," she said, trying to cheer me.

We built a big fire every evening, went to church, wrapped presents, pretended. But the ache in our hearts kept swelling.

And, the day before Christmas, we burst into mutual tears. "Mommy, it's just not *right* for Daddy to be down there alone!"

"I know it." Praying for a miracle, I ran to the telephone. The airlines were hopeless, but there was one roomette available on the last train to Miami. Almost hysterical with relief, we threw things into bags.

And what a Christmas Eve! Excited as conspirators, we cuddled together in that cozy space. Melanie hung a tiny wreath in the window and we settled down to watch the endless pageantry flashing by to the rhythmic clicking song of the rails. . . . Little villages and city streets—all dancing with lights and decorations and sparkling Christmas trees. . . . And cars and snowy countrysides and people—all the people. Each one on his or her special pilgrimage of love and celebration this precious night.

At last we drifted off to sleep. But hours later I awoke to a strange stillness. The train had stopped. And, raising the shade, I peered out on a very small town. Silent, deserted, with only a few lights still burning. And under the bare branches, along a lonely street, a figure was walking. A young man in sailor blues, head bent, hunched under the weight of the sea bag on his shoulders. And I thought—*home! Poor kid, he's almost home*. And I wondered if there was someone still up waiting for him; or if anyone knew he was coming at all. And my heart cried out to him, for he was suddenly my own son—and my own ghost, and the soul of us all—driven, so immutably driven by this annual call, "Come home!"

Home for Christmas. There must be some deep psychological reason why we turn so instinctively toward home at this special time. Perhaps we are acting out the ancient story of a man and a woman and a coming child, plodding along with their donkey toward their destination. It was necessary for Joseph, the earthly father, to go home to be taxed. Each male had to return to the city of his birth.

Birth. The tremendous miracle of birth shines through every step and syllable of the Bible story. The long, arduous trip across the mountains of Galilee and Judea was also the journey of a *life* toward birth. Mary was already in labor when they arrived in Bethlehem, so near the time of her delivery that in desperation, since the inn was full, her husband settled for a humble stable.

The Child Who was born on that first Christmas grew up to be a man. Jesus. He healed many people, taught us many important things. But the message that has left the most lasting impression and given the most hope and comfort is this: that we do have a home to go to, and there will be an ultimate homecoming. A place where we will indeed be reunited with those we love.

Anyway, that's my idea of Heaven. A place where Mother is standing in the door, probably bossing Dad the way she used to about the turkey or the tree, and he's enjoying every minute of it. And old friends and neighbors are streaming in and out and the sense of love and joy and celebration will go on forever.

A place where every day will be Christmas, with everybody there together. At home.

---

*For God so loved the world that he
gave his only begotten Son, that
whosoever believeth in him should not
perish, but have everlasting life. (John 3:16)*

**He needed me and I loved him—but did I
have the courage to marry him?**

The Love We've
Found

by ANN SAYERS

I really didn't feel comfortable as I walked through the respirator ward. As a volunteer hospital visitor, I certainly shouldn't have had such an attitude, but the utter hopelessness of the patients made me want to cry.

And then I saw the curtained cubicle where the leather bellows of an iron lung ballooned in and out.

The patient, a quadraplegic whose arms and legs were paralyzed, had intrigued me when I had visited this ward previously. There was an independent look in his eyes and something almost defiant in his voice.

"Hi, my name's Ann. Remember me?" I said, urging a cheerful note into my voice.

Bill was reading a book fastened to a rack above his head. "Hello," he mumbled around a rubber-tipped mouth stick with which he turned the pages. Two sky-blue eyes regarded me.

I removed my coat. "Dark in here, isn't it?" I reached for the window shade. "There, that's better, isn't it?"

"Yeah." He sounded convinced he was about to be pestered.

"Would you like your mirror?"

"Okay."

I exchanged the reading rack for his mirror. They both fit into the same bracket on the front of the iron lung.

Finally I was seated, peering up into the respirator mirror through which Bill viewed the world. He had a thin, good-looking face, Roman nose and red hair. "How did you get sick?" I asked.

"I got polio. I'm in an iron lung. That's all there is to it."

I swallowed and tried again. "When did you contract polio?"

"Fifteen years ago. I was twenty when it hit me." Doctor Salk's vaccine had come too late for him.

I felt a chill as I realized that for 15 years a motor impassively had kept Bill's flesh, blood and lungs functioning.

For the next hour, I carried on a monologue punctuated by single syllable answers. It was hard work, but something made me keep trying. Finally, I said, "I guess I'll be going."

"Okay," he said. "Before you go, would you turn on my TV?"

I flipped it on.

"Take care," I said, struggling into my coat.

"Sure. Be good." I felt dismissed. He was intent on the television screen.

My eyes blurred as I rushed into the cold night. But later at home, as I sipped hot coffee, I realized Bill couldn't enjoy such a haven. He could not go to a quiet place and meditate. Bill lived in a fish bowl. He had to be fed, bathed, and assisted to perform the most intimate functions.

I admired him. He was embarrassingly honest, making clear what he liked and didn't like, without apology. His refusal to give in to self-pity showed me he had not succumbed to despair.

I knew how easy that could be. I was 32, unmarried, and like Bill, was putting up a brave pretense of not needing anyone. Despite his crusty attitude, I decided to go back to the hospital to see him again.

I returned the following weekend bringing sandwiches and coffee. Bill dropped his guard a little and our conversation flowed easier. I learned that he was an avid reader and had always wanted to be a writer. Soon our visits became a weekly occurrence. When Bill's meals arrived, it seemed natural that I feed him. I began to look forward to the visits.

Our talk often turned to Bill's writing ambitions. "God left me with a healthy mind," he said, "and a love of books. But I don't know a thing about the mechanics of writing."

"Why not take a short story correspondence course?" I suggested.

His head turned and his eyes brightened. "You think I could?"

"Sure," I laughed. "You can dictate to me and I'll type up the lessons and mail them."

When the course started, I began visiting him every day. They were busy days, full of Bill's dictation and my typing the lessons and mailing them. Through it all I watched his native ability grow. At first his writing scrupulously followed the course instructions, then began to flow as his confidence strengthened.

One day another volunteer invited Bill and me to a party at her home. To my surprise, Bill accepted the invitation.

To leave the hospital, Bill had to wear a portable chest respirator. This was a plastic shell that hugged his body from abdomen to chest. From it a hose snaked to a bulky compressor motor on wheels.

When he was lifted to the stretcher for the trip, I saw his legs. They were encrusted with bedsores, and he groaned when he was moved. Then Bill, strapped to the stretcher, and I, with my legs shaking at the possibility of his respirator failing, were off to the party.

We enjoyed ourselves, or rather, Bill enjoyed himself. The thought of an emergency didn't bother him at all. Once in a while, a grimace of pain crossed his face, but he did not complain.

I was relieved when we returned to the hospital.

"How did you like it, Ann?" His smile was eager.

"Fine," I lied.

"Would you ease my chest strap, please?" he asked. I began to loosen the belt. His face crumpled with relief. "Too tight all day," he said.

"Why didn't you tell me?"

"It was nothing. Everything went great, right?" He smiled brightly. "It isn't hard to get me out of the hospital, see?"

I didn't answer as I continued readjusting the belt. All I could remember was his sore legs, his pain, his helplessness.

"Ann, will you marry me?"

My hands froze. So that was it! He had made the trip to show he could safely leave the hospital.

In a daze I completed his belt adjustment, and forced myself to speak. "I . . . uh . . . I really don't know how to answer, Bill," I stammered. "Give me a little time to think."

I could see the disappointment in his eyes. But then he bravely covered it up. "Don't take it too seriously, Ann . . . guess I had too much grape soda at the party."

In my apartment that night I could only think about Bill's proposal. One thing I knew: I loved him. Deeply, surely. For months now I had known it. And his proposal really wasn't that much of a surprise.

In our visits I could feel Bill's fondness for me growing. I could see him reaching out for life and love after all his bitter years behind the walls of the hospital. He needed me and I loved him.

But could we manage? Did I have the courage to try?

Bill had many physical ailments, any one of which could lead to an emergency situation. From years in the iron lung, his joints had stiffened. His muscles sprained easily and his bones were frail and brittle so that even giving him a bath took hours of gentle, slow handling.

A simple cold could develop into pneumonia. His breathing equipment broke down peridically and required immediate attention by a mechanic. Power failures were frequent in the area where we would have to live, as close to the hospital as possible.

I would have to quit work and we would live on his Social Security disability checks and supplementary welfare. We would move into public housing.

I rose and walked to the window, looking into the rainy night. No, I couldn't do it. It was more than human strength could bear. The life God had asked Bill to accept for 15 years was too hard.

And then I looked back on my last 15 years; carefree, pointless, empty. And suddenly I knew I faced a decision. Life or death.

Marrying Bill would be accepting the cross that is at the heart of all vital living. To be alive is to suffer sometimes.

Suffering isn't all there is to life, but unless we accept misery as an integral part of it, all the other experiences are diminished. And suffering is unbearable only when we feel alone in it.

So I chose life, I chose Bill.

Nine years ago we were married.

Bill is now a happy guy constantly involved in some new project. He's still paralyzed from the shoulders down, but is no longer dependent on the iron lung. He breathes through an air tube. "I can do just about anything." he says, grinning up at me.

And Bill is pursuing his writing career, typing three or four hours every day, striking the keys of an electric typewriter with a mouth stick. He has completed a book about his years in the hospital. A literary agent read the manuscript and said it has merit. After repeated attempts to sell it, we finally found a publisher for it.

Recently I showed a friend some snapshots I had taken of Bill. After scanning them, she said, "You can see the happiness shining out of his face."

"Yes," I said, "I know. I have it, too."

And I do. Oh, yes; I do!

LOVING SOMEONE IS . . .
caring
sharing
bearing
working—changing
TOGETHER
            Jean Lowder

The Lonely Trail

by DON BELL

My horse steadied herself on the slope. I looked up at the sky—and didn't like what I saw. Snow was falling hard, and there was already 18 inches on the ground. Winter always sets in early in the Rockies, especially in the Absorkee Range southwest of Cody, Wyoming. We'd had snow here since September.

It was mid-November now. Up till a few days ago, I'd been one of the guides assigned to a party of hunters going after game meat in the high mountains. At the close of the season, I'd brought 'em back to the low corral. After I'd helped the hunters unload their supplies from the pack animals, though, I'd found we were short three horses from the 40 head we had left with.

A horse can't live through a winter in that country of jagged 12,000-foot peaks. Everything's covered in deep snow, and a horse can't paw down through snow to feed. They might try and work down to lower country till they got rimmed in by snow, but every horse I'd ever known got confused then. Wouldn't backtrack, but just stand and look toward home till he starved. Or froze, maybe.

I made up my mind to go after them horses. I knew every peak and canyon of the Absorkees, so I just might have a chance of finding 'em. I saddled my best horse and loaded another stocky pack horse with my good bedroll, a small tepee tent, and panniers filled with enough feed, bacon, bread and coffee to last a few days. Then I started out with my old dog Shorty taggin' along.

For two days I didn't see any horse tracks but our own. The

281

trip was rough, and the higher I got in the mountains, the deeper the snow became. Sometimes my horse wallowed belly-deep in snowdrifts on the trail. And now, the sky looked bad. I didn't like the ugly way the clouds had piled up. If I turned off the trail here, I figured I could reach the old hunting campsite, about half a mile away.

I reached the camp just at dark. By then, a full storm was blowing in. People who don't live here just can't imagine how bad a Wyoming blizzard can be. I couldn't see but a few feet in front of me, so I couldn't travel much more for fear of riding my horse right over a cliff. I figured the temperature was about zero; the wind sent the cold at my face like arrows.

"Use your head, now," I warned myself. "Life's cheap in a blizzard."

With the wind howling like it was, I couldn't set up the tepee tent I'd packed. The only shelter I could find was a spruce thicket set in a little hollow, so I made for that.

I had about 20 pounds of oats still, so I divided it for the two horses. I took the panniers of grub off the pack horse and loosened the cinch on my own mount. Next I laid my bedroll out in the hollow, and crawled inside it. Shorty came in, too, and curled up, a warm and comfortable companion at my feet.

It would be nice to have God as a companion right now, too, I thought. *I'd like to talk to someone.* But I'd been a cowboy all my life, spending most Sundays out on the range. I wasn't a churchgoer, though I believed in God. I'd just never learned to pray to Him. Didn't seem fair somehow to bother Him with my talk, if I'd never done nothin' to pay attention to Him before. So I just talked to Shorty. -

"Wish I'd eaten more on the trail today," I said. But now I couldn't find firewood, or make a fire in that wind, anyhow. So I just laid still, to wait out the storm.

All night the snow fell.

When I woke up next morning, the wind was still howling. Poking my head out of the snow-covered bedroll, I saw what I was afraid I would see—nothing. Everything was light gray. And I knew the weather wasn't about to change. I had to pass another day here, at least.

Little dry pangs were letting me know where my stomach was. But I also knew, with the snowstorm like it was, I couldn't leave the bedroll. It would be nearly impossible to find my packets of grub under the drifts, and I could get lost a few feet from the bedroll—it happens in blizzards not even this bad. I wouldn't last long exposed to that weather.

So I spent a long day in a bedroll that grew stiff with cold and was mighty glad when the whiteness all around me darkened some. By evening I was no longer thinking of the lost horses I'd come up on the mountain to find. The animals I had with me were cause enough for worry. The horses had long since finished the grain I'd left 'em, and now they gave occasional whinnies to let me know how hungry and cold they was.

My own thoughts wandered to food, too, as night fell. I thought of the hard, chewy bread I'd put in the grub sacks, and the meat and the coffee.

"You don't know how thick and fine coffee tastes, do ya, dog?" I said to Shorty. He shifted a bit against my legs and licked my hand.

I couldn't get to sleep that night, tossing and turning while the wind whistled and roared. Finally, when I figured it was morning, my legs were pinned by the weight of the snow on 'em. But I worked my arms free and dug an opening for my head.

It was eerie. Everything was still lost in the white. I heard my neighing horses through holes in the wind, but I couldn't see 'em at all. I couldn't see anything.

My stomach felt tight; hungry wasn't the word for it any more.

Also, my feet were getting cold. I was plenty scared. It looked like this bed was gonna be my burial ground, too.

The blizzard never let up that whole day. As darkness approached, I knew that the end wasn't very far off. I wasn't gonna get through this alive, not without help.

I started thinkin' about all those churches I'd never been to. I thought hard.

"God," I said at last, "I never did learn to pray. Up to now, we've never been real close, I reckon. I know You don't owe me nothin', Lord . . . but, I'll tell You, I'm awful scared and hungry now. I came up here after some pack horses that strayed off. I don't care about that no more. But, if I'm gonna pull though this alive, God, well . . . I figure it's up to You. That's all I want to say."

I didn't know if I got all the prayer said right. But I was glad I'd tried. I felt calmer somehow. I still didn't know if I'd make it through the night. But I no longer felt so alone.

I only caught uneven patches of sleep that night, tired as I was. In-between dozes, I thought how lost I must seem to the world, all huddled in a bedroll, shiverin' under the snow on a mountainside in a blizzard. And I thought about dyin'.

I could only judge what time morning would come. I'd tucked my head deep into the bedroll, and by this time I could hardly shift about under its weight. The sounds of the blizzard had been cut off a while ago. The walls of my stomach were all squeezed together, it felt like, and I knew I'd have to chance goin' out for food this day. *If only the storm would show some promise of blowing itself out . . .*

Finally I felt it was morning. I wriggled my arms, and pawed against the snow that was collapsing on my head. In a moment, my head was free of the sleeping bag and I opened my eyes. I was blinking in the early morning sunlight!

The temperature was way below zero, but how much I couldn't know. I knew there was still a chance of being hit by another blizzard, so I didn't waste time makin' a breakfast fire. I left the rest of the supplies and my frozen bedroll lying where they was.

My fingers were stiff as wood as I tightened the cinch on my saddle horse, then mounted and spurred her to begin the long journey back. Shorty followed in our tracks. Slow as we were moving, he had a tough time lunging through the drifts after us.

When I reached the point where I figured I should turn off for the main trail, several fresh sets of hoofprints had luckily already broken the trail in the direction I was headed. I wondered who could be up here makin' tracks, and didn't know until we caught up with the animals after a few miles. There were three of 'em—my own missing pack horses! All were wore-out and starved-looking; they were glad to be herded down toward the winter range.

It was a mighty nice sight when I topped a ridge that evening and saw firelight glowing in the windows of a cabin at the home corral. Weak and hungry though I was, I stopped and smiled.

"Well, Lord, I thought You was only in church, but You taught me somethin'," I said. "I wouldn'ta blamed You if You just ignored me. But I sure am grateful to learn You really care about a cowboy's prayer."

And we rode down to the corral.

**Alcohol has wrecked countless marriages.
Was our marriage to be yet another?**

One for the Road

by NOELLE CRAIG*

I didn't know that Ben had a drinking problem until after we were married. I realize now that for the three years we were going together I seldom saw him without a drink in his hand, but that didn't mean much to me then. Our crowd in that little logging town in the Northwest, where we grew up, did quite a lot of drinking.

But even if I had known beforehand about Ben's problem, I'm sure it wouldn't have stopped me. I was in love with Ben from the moment I first saw him. That was in 1966 when I was a senior in high school and he was already working in his brother-in-law's lumberyard. He was 23, five years older than I, very calm, very quiet. Quiet, that is, until he had a drink or two. Then his personality would seem to brighten and he'd open up and be funny and make all of us laugh. Maybe I didn't pay special attention to his drinking because he was not a mean drunk, never crude and insulting.

Ben and I went together, sort of, for three years. Whenever our crowd got together we just seemed to pair off. In 1968, Ben was drafted and sent East to an Army camp in Maryland and later to Korea. But before he was shipped overseas, he came home for a long furlough.

"After I'm through with the Army," he told me, "I want to come back here and buy a logging truck and be in business for myself and . . . " he said in the same incredible breath, "I want you to marry me right now!"

I didn't keep him waiting. We were married immediately. Then, a few days before he was to leave for Korea—we had

*Names have been changed.   286

been married two weeks—Ben did one of the strange things that was to become so familiar in time. We went out for dinner with another couple. We had a couple of drinks and somewhere along the line Ben excused himself and left the table. Minutes passed; he didn't return.

"Where'd Ben go?" our friend Larry asked.

"I don't know," I said, a little anxious, a little embarrassed. "I thought he was going to the rest room. Check it for me, will you?"

Soon Larry was back. "He's not there."

We looked everywhere in the restaurant, but we couldn't find him. There on the table before us were his car keys. I was frantic and bewildered, and the whole evening remained a mystery to me even after we found him in a nearby cocktail lounge, sitting alone, very drunk.

That peculiar evening led to our first fight, a one-sided fight really, for Ben couldn't explain why he had walked out. He could only apologize over and over again, and beg me to forgive him.

Soon after Ben went to Korea, I realized I was pregnant. During the months of waiting for the baby to be born, and for Ben to return, my life changed profoundly. The change—a spiritual one—came about largely through my closeness to Ben's sister Carrie and her husband Ralph. Ralph was the one who owned the lumberyard where Ben had worked. Both Ben and I admired them; they had a strong marriage and a strong faith.

While Ben was away I found myself doing things with them, including church on Sundays and Carrie's Bible class on weekdays. Slowly I picked up my own faith where I had left it as a heartsick teen-ager who had prayed fervently, but in vain, for Jesus to restore her father's eyesight. Though I had stopped attending church, I guess I had never really stopped loving Jesus.

Ben got his discharge from the service in time for Christmas 1969. Our lovely, healthy daughter Mary Ann was waiting for him. Then Ben managed to get his log truck, a big red 1962 Kenworth, and started driving it for a living. We were like three happy people out of a storybook—except for Ben's compulsive drinking.

Whenever we went out during his first three months home, I'd take a drink with Ben, but after that, growing wary about the fights that always seemed to develop later, I stopped. From then on he'd simply pick up and go out by himself, not constantly, not regularly, but always suddenly, unexpectedly. He'd just disappear. It unnerved me. I'd sit up at night in our little house listening to the wind in the fir trees, thinking about car wrecks and fist fights and heart attacks, worrying myself sick about him.

Four o'clock, five o'clock in the morning he'd come back, sometimes with drinking buddies pounding on the door trying to lure him back out for one more. Once he came home at midnight and I hid his car keys. For two hours he was a lunatic shouting, "Give me my keys! Give me my keys!" until, at two a.m., the time the bars closed, he lay down on the couch and went peacefully to sleep. Always in the morning he was so very contrite.

In those days it seemed obvious that Ben's lack was a spiritual one, and I started trying to graft my own new, deeper faith onto him. But whenever I'd talk to him about religion, it became strained and embarrassing for both of us. For a while we did go to church together on Sundays, but apparently the only thing Ben liked about it was the breakfast we would eat out after the service. The minister, Ben said, "bored him to death," and he could always get a rise out of me by saying, "I come out of that church feeling twice as bad as when I went in."

Soon Sundays in our home became anything but days of rest. My first thought upon awakening would be, "How am I going to get him to church *this* week?" I'd give Ben five or ten minutes of calm, rational reasoning as to why he should go, always pointing out that he had Mary Ann's spiritual well-being to consider. If that failed, my temper would flare and I'd end up storming out of the house to brood over the situation throughout the church service.

One day during the late winter of 1971, just to get out of the house, Mary Ann and I went out with Ben in his truck. He was loading deep in a stand of cedar that day; the rain was pouring down. I sat bundled up in the cab, occasionally rubbing the steam off the windshield so I could watch Ben at work— buzzing around without letup, adjusting a chain, shouting to his helper, leaping onto the loader, then jumping down into the mud again. I could see the joy he got from his work.

While the rain poured and Mary Ann slept in my arms, I thought about Ben. How loving he was. What an adoring father he was. Why did he have to spoil it all with his drinking? Yet, I thought, he had never missed a day of work; he was never disagreeable, always even-tempered, certainly not like me. Did I overemphasize his one shortcoming?

At noon that day Ben dropped me off at the monthly lunch-eon of our Christian Women's Club at a nearby inn. This was always a good meeting for me because we always had a stirring out-of-town speaker and lots of discussion and prayer. That Monday, the moment the speaker started I began to feel un-comfortable. She talked about marriage and how her own had fallen apart because of her militant holier-than-thou attitude. "Let this be a lesson to you," she said, and I could swear she was looking directly at me. "I fell into the spiritual trap of trying to change my husband, rather than myself."

I scrunched down in my seat. All through the closing prayer and for the rest of that afternoon and evening I kept thinking about her words until at last it hit me clearly that her story was mine. At long last I had found a key to my own marriage problem. If there was any changing to be done in Ben, it was up to God to do it, not me. From that day on I turned our lives over to Him, completely.

In the weeks that followed, I prayed constantly. I was unable to understand fully how Jesus was working through me, but with no effort at all I forgot what Ben was doing to *me*, and began to worry about what he was doing to *himself*. I developed a genuine sympathy for him, for the problem he could not control or understand. His sporadic drinking sprees continued, although less frequently, but I stopped picking on him when he came home from them and was careful not to accuse or criticize him. As for the matter of Sunday church, many people might still disagree with how I handled that. I stopped going. I stayed home with Ben rather than let that widen the gap between us. But all the while my faith told me that one day we would worship in church as a family.

Ben noticed the change in me. "Why aren't you yelling at me?" he'd say. And as time went on, I began to notice a few little chinks of change in him. Like the time he told me that some of the buddies he'd seen downtown were getting on his nerves with their loud talk and coarse language. Or the strange new thing about his hang-overs. Ben had been able to drink all night without apparent physical harm, but now he suffered nosebleeds, vomiting and headaches for two or three days after a binge.

In the autumn I became pregnant again. I grew big quickly and was sick a lot and felt very unpretty. I worried about that. Ben had never seen me pregnant before. Then winter came, a hard winter for Ben. The roads were packed with ice and snow and he didn't get the trips he'd counted on. The loader he was using broke down frequently. Now he went out to drink more often. I prayed harder.

The crisis came on a weekend in March when Ben went to a trucker's convention at a seashore resort. On Friday night he came home drunk. Saturday night he didn't come home at all.

On Sunday evening, after putting Mary Ann to bed, I got out my Bible. "What's the matter, God?" I prayed. "Have I been wrong?" I prayed until I felt I knew what God wanted me to do. Ben came in late. He crawled onto the sofa in the living room and slept.

The next morning Ben was up and out at his usual six a.m. When he had gone, I arose, fixed Mary Ann's breakfast, and then I went in and packed Ben's suitcase and put it in the living room.

At 9:30 Ben returned unexpectedly. He walked in and saw his suitcase in front of the heater. Pain swept over his face. I began to cry. "Go on, leave," I said. "I don't want you around any more. You won't even let God help you!"

He left. I sat down on the sofa, my eyes dry now, too numb even to cry any more.

Ten minutes later I heard Ben's old red truck careening back into the vacant lot next door, its jake brake blasting through the silent neighborhood. In seconds the front door opened and there was Ben again. He just stood in the doorway, looking at me. We were like two figures frozen to the spot until Ben walked over and put his arms around me. "Where do I find Him?" he said.

That was March 13, 1972. That was the day my strong and gentle husband accepted Jesus into his life and sat at my feet pouring out all the anguish he had been feeling for months, all the confusion and mixed emotions about nosebleeds and trucks breaking down and icy roads and babies on the way, all the guilt about liquor and a waitress who'd been after him at one of the truck stops, all the tensions that had been mounting day by day, tensions he couldn't understand until he'd climbed into his truck and was heading down the road and suddenly, suddenly, he knew. And he turned the truck around and gunned it home.

Anyone who is a Christian knows that my story could end here. Once you sincerely ask Christ into your heart and believe that He is with you, He takes over your life. He took over mine. He took over Ben's. Today Ben says that his desire to get out and drink has not disappeared altogether; it's just that his desire to be with his family is greater. We've worked on it together, discussing it, praying about it, never avoiding the fact that it's a struggle for Ben. But how God has blessed us! He has given us a more spacious home, replaced our old truck with a brand new one, and in July of 1972 he gave us a little boy. When Sunday comes these days, we go to church just as I always believed we would—as a family.

**She discovered that there are
many ways to say, "I care."**

The Loving Line
by ADRIENNE FLURRY BLAND

Each year when Valentine's Day comes around, with its tradition of exchanging affection, I am reminded of a touching display of love that happened when I was a college student—and has affected me ever since. Some of us from our church youth group used to take a bus out to a boys' orphanage on Sundays. We'd play games, lunch with them, help with their farm chores and sometimes just walk and talk with them. The most memorable part of the day, however, was just after our bus arrived at the orphanage. As the bus approached the gate, the boys would be waving and shouting greetings. But just as soon as we had stopped and were getting off, they would be completely silent, forming a quiet line.

Puzzled by it, we asked Mrs. Ryner, the matron, if we were offending them. "Are they waiting for something we're not giving them?"

"They're waiting for something, yes," Mrs. Ryner answered. "But you're giving it. You don't even realize you're doing it sometimes, your feelings are so spontaneous. But that moment when you touch a boy's cheek, hug him, give him a kiss on top of is head, that's what he waits all week for."

"I call the lines the boys make a 'loving line'," she continued, a soft expression on her face. "With your touch, your hand reaching out, you take them out of that line and make them individuals."

Since that time so many years ago I've looked for "loving lines" wherever I happen to go: elderly people in chairs around a nursing-home room; children at a state school; patients in a mental hospital; people alone in my church; the shy or bewildered travelers in airports or bus stations. It is so easy—and rewarding—to reach out to someone waiting on a "loving line," to show a moment of concern, to follow the way Christ showed us when He said, "Inasmuch as ye have done it unto one of the least of these My brethren, ye have done it unto Me." (Matthew 25:40)

8.
Love for Those Whose Faith Needs Strengthening

They that wait upon the Lord shall renew their strength;
they shall mount up with wings as eagles; they shall run,
and not be weary; and they shall walk, and not faint.
(Isaiah 40:31)

Collision Course

by NANETTE JOHNSON

I t was a day in July, sunny and hot, a Monday. My husband
and I and our three children had returned the night before
from a holiday on Cape Cod. There was the unpacking to do,
and loads of wash, but our oldest, 14-year-old Lynne, couldn't
wait to see her friends at Lake Sacandaga, seven miles north of
our place in the Adirondacks. I didn't really want to go, but
finally Lynne and I put on our swimsuits and I drove her up to
the lake.

Looking back, I can see myself so clearly that summer morning: a fairly typical American wife and mother who took her kids
to Sunday school and had even taught it herself, but who was
basically a restless and groping person. I knew there must be a
God somewhere, but He wasn't real to me. I knew there must
be more to life than cooking meals and making beds and having
occasional good times, but I didn't know what that something
was. Outwardly I managed to seem fairly contented, but inside
I was so dissatisfied that sometimes, when I was alone in the
car, I'd drive at reckless speeds just because I didn't really care
much what happened to me.

That day the lake was calm. Lynne and I took our 16-foot
outboard out to Beacon Island. Two of Lynne's teen-aged
friends, Robert and George, were there with Robert's father's
22-foot inboard speedboat. All the kids loved to water-ski. At
that time skiing on one ski was the big thing, and they wanted
me to teach them how to make a "dry start." This is done by
pulling the skier right off from the beach.

With Robert driving his father's boat, and Lynne and George

in the back, and me on one ski behind the boat, we took off to circle the island. The only other boat I saw on the lake was a little rowboat with a man fishing.

I was being towed on a 75-foot line, wearing a lightweight ski belt. I was skiing back and forth across the boat's wake; the lake was as smooth as a bowl of Jello, the day crystal-clear.

Robert began the wide turn around the lower end of Beacon Island. As I swung out to the right, I saw a boat coming toward us, ahead and off to the right. It was a small outboard, about 14 feet long, and low in the water. As we got closer I realized that if both boats stayed on course there might be a collision.

I pointed to the other boat, but apparently nobody understood why I was pointing. I swung back behind our wake, and when next I swung out, the boats were still on a collision course, but I never for a second thought a collision would actually happen. My real concern was that the little boat, which had so little freeboard, might be swamped by the wake of our boat. I could see four people in it. I also had to consider my own safety. If the boats came very close I might be run over.

I swung back in our wake where it was safer, but as I could not see the other boat from there, I swung out to the right again, and at the last instant I saw the little boat swerve directly broadside, right in front of our boat and I knew disaster was upon us.

There was a terrible bang, like an explosion. The front of our boat went up and then the back flew up and George was hurled about 20 feet in the air. I saw him hit the water. I looked for my daughter—and couldn't see her. I thought she, too, must be in the water. As the momentum of the ski boat carried me toward the wreckage, I screamed her name, "Lynne! Lynne! Lynne!"

I skied into the wreckage and threw the ski rope to one side. There was the tip of the bow of the little boat, suitcases, picnic hamper, splinters of wood and plastic. Up came a boxer dog, barking. Up, like a cork, came a baby about 15 months old in an orange lifejacket, crying. Up came a woman with brown hair, dazed and screaming. Up came a man, yelling "Are you all right? Are you all right?" to the woman. They were on the other side of their boat's wreckage, and, holding the baby, they clung there.

I went underwater, and when I came up, two boat-seat cushions rose alongside me. On one cushion a teen-aged girl lay on her stomach, unconscious, terribly lacerated by the propeller blade. On the other cushion was another teen-aged girl lying on her back. She, too, had been badly injured.

I sank as I removed my ski. When I surfaced, the man who was out of sight on the other side of the wreckage was yelling to the girls, "Hang on! Hang on!", the baby was crying, the dog was barking, the man's wife was crying out, the wreckage was bubbling and gurgling—and at this point the girl who was lying on her stomach said in a very clear, pleading voice: "God, help me."

At that exact moment something happened to me. Suddenly I had a tremendous feeling of serenity, of calm, of assurance—a kind of inner tranquility that I cannot put into words. I felt we were in the presence of God. Not that God was going to reach down and save us; but I knew that whether we lived or died, He was with us. For the first time in my life I knew with absolute certainty that there really is a God and we are not alone. No matter what happens, He is watching over us every minute, every second, all the time.

This tiny spell of illumination must have taken only a brief moment, then I was back to the dreadful reality. Both girls were slipping off the cushions and sinking. I am not the greatest swimmer in the world, I am not even a good swimmer, but I knew I had to do something. I reached over and grabbed one girl by the hair, but the other girl had gone down too deep for me to reach her. So I let go of the first girl and took off my ski belt, went down and grabbed the other girl's hair. By then the first girl had come down, too, and I caught her by the hair. Raising them both over my head, I kicked with all my might to get us to the surface. The girls were unconscious and I was afraid they would breathe in water. When I broke the surface I yelled and screamed for help as loud as I could, and then we sank again. We went under and came up repeatedly.

The ski boat was dead in the water a hundred yards away

with no one in sight. Where was Lynne? Was she drowning, too? I realized we were all drowning. I had swallowed so much water, I couldn't yell for help any more.

Underwater I heard a propeller coming closer and closer. A boat with a man and a woman in it came to the edge of the wreckage. I heard the man say to the woman, "Don't look!" He threw some flotation cushions in our direction. Then he left us! I couldn't believe it. I was so enraged that my anger gave me a shot of adrenaline that kept us alive until the small fishing boat I had seen when we first started out came to our rescue.

With great difficulty the fisherman and I got the injured girls into the boat without capsizing it. Robert swam over from the ski boat and helped us. Then George, who had been thrown in the air, swam to us, and the man and woman from the struck boat swam over with the baby, and we helped them get in the little rowboat. There was no sign of Lynne. One of the injured girls was still unconscious, but the other girl now regained consciousness and began shaking with convulsions.

The boat was badly overloaded, with only a few inches of freeboard. The fisherman chugged off as fast as his little engine would allow. George, Robert and I clung to some wreckage until a speedboat came and picked up Robert and me. George swam back to the ski boat.

In the much faster boat we reached shore first and called for an ambulance and the state troopers. By the time the ambulance arrived, both girls were in convulsions, but both were alive. I thought it was a miracle that any of us were alive.

As I sat on the grass under a tree in the awful aftermath of the tragedy, another miracle occurred. I was sure my daughter Lynne was dead. I hadn't seen her, no one had said a word about her; I hadn't even dared to ask. I looked up and there was Lynne, walking up from the docks. We rushed into each other's arms, and she was as astounded as I because she had thought I was dead. Someone had found her wandering around Beacon Island in a daze and had brought her to shore. It was like God delivering my daughter back to me.

We went to the hospital and the girl who was so badly injured was in the operating room. I went in to see the other girl.

"You don't know me," I said to her.

And she looked up at me and said, "I know you.

The older of the two girls, Mary Jane Murray, died the next day. She was 16 years old. Her father is a minister. She had been on a retreat only the week before. The other girl, Kathleen Hayes, eventually made a complete recovery.

It took me months to recover from the emotional shock of that day on Lake Sacandaga, and when I did recover I was deeply changed. When that God-loving young girl died and my own daughter was spared and restored to me, I made up my mind to rededicate my life simply to being a better person. Up till then, there had been areas where I had fallen short, but ever since then I've tried very hard to be a better person, a decent person, a person less concerned with herself and more willing to reach out and help others. My daughter Lynne was changed too, from a take-it-all-for-granted, I'm-going-to-live-forever teen-ager to someone who knows how fragile and priceless and precious life really is.

So I've learned that God can bring something good out of any situation, even stark tragedy. To me, He's no longer a vague possibility; He's an absolute certainty. And this I know for sure: He is always with us, in life or in death.

God is our refuge and strength, a very present help in trouble. (Psalm 46:1)

"Trust the Lord, Corrie."

by CORRIE TEN BOOM

Some of my happiest days came when it was decided that I could work in the shop as an assistant to my kindly, bearded father. I loved being with him and I loved the shop itself. It had a very special atmosphere, and gradually I began to overcome my shyness and insecurity in meeting people, and I enjoyed selling the watches and clocks to our customers.

There were many ups and downs in the watchmaking business. Father loved his work, but he was not a money-maker, and times were often hard. Once I remember we were faced with a real financial crisis. A large bill had to be paid and there simply wasn't enough money. Then one day a well-dressed gentleman came into the shop and asked to see some very expensive watches. I stayed in the workshop and prayed, with one ear tuned to the conversation in the front room.

"Mmm . . . this is a fine watch, Mr. ten Boom," the customer said, turning a very costly timepiece over in his hands. "This is just what I've been looking for."

I held my breath as I saw the affluent customer reach into his inner pocket and pull out a thick wad of bills. Praise the Lord—cash! (I saw myself paying the overdue bill and being relieved of the burden of anxiety I had been carrying for the past few weeks.)

The customer looked at the watch admiringly and commented, "I had a good watchmaker here in Haarlem . . . his name was van Houten. Perhaps you knew him."

Father nodded his head. He knew almost everyone in Haarlem, especially other watchmakers.

"When van Houten died and his son took over the business, I kept on doing business with the young man. However, I bought a watch from him that didn't run at all. I sent it back three times, but he couldn't seem to fix it. That's why I decided to find another watchmaker."

"Will you show me that watch, please?" Father said.

The man took a large watch out of his vest and gave it to Father.

"Now, let me see," Father said, opening the back of the watch. He adjusted something and handed it back to the customer. "There, that was a very little mistake. It will be fine now. Sir, I trust the young watchmaker. Someday he will be just as good as his father. So if you ever have a problem with one of his watches, come to me. I'll help you out. Now I shall give you back your money and you return my watch."

I was horrified. I saw Father take back the watch and give the money to the customer. Then he opened the door for him and bowed deeply in his old-fashioned way.

My heart was where my feet should be as I emerged from the shelter of the workshop.

"Papa! How could you?"

Father looked at me patiently through his steel-rimmed glasses.

"Corrie," he said, "you know that I brought the Gospel at the burial of Mr. van Houten."

Of course I remembered. It was Father's job to speak at the burials of the watchmakers in Haarlem. He was greatly loved by his colleagues and was also a very good speaker; he always used the occasion to talk about the Lord Jesus.

"Corrie, what do you think that young man would have said when he heard that one of his good customers had gone to Mr. ten Boom? Do you think that the name of the Lord would be honored? As for the money, trust the Lord, Corrie. He owns the cattle on a thousand hills and He will take care of us."

I felt ashamed and I knew that Father was right. I wondered if I could ever have that kind of trust instead of blind determination to follow my own stubborn path. Could I really learn to trust God?

"Yes, Father," I answered quietly. Whom was I answering? My earthly father or my Father in Heaven?

How I Escaped From
<u>Me</u>

by DEAN JONES

In the early part of my acting career, I thought that if I could become a star, it would fill the emptiness I felt in my heart—but it did not.

There were other goals that I set for myself—money, security, cars and houses—but each time a goal was achieved, I would say, "There must be something more," and on to the next target.

More money changed nothing. Pretty, young actresses were momentary distractions. But nothing could ward off the depressions I fell into, sometimes for months at a time. A new picture or play would end the despondency and internal hostility for a short period, but the meaninglessness of life was the reality I lived in.

I would take my sports car up one of the canyon roads leading from the San Fernando Valley to the coast highway, not really caring if I lived or died. As that beautifully balanced machine screamed over the winding roads, my thoughts turned to negative possibilities.

I'm not going to try to end my life but . . . if I go past the point of my skill or the car's capacity to stay glued to the road, I won't care. It would be a relief to die.

I had begun to see life as a joke. I had stopped believing in God, but that didn't stop me from blaming Him for the dissatisfaction I felt.

I once took a motorcycle trip with two friends into Mexico's Baja Peninsula, miles from civilization. We stopped at a small shack where a family lived in incredible poverty. We gave our extra dungarees to the young boys, but it was the little girl who really touched my heart. Open sores covered her face, and there was, in the innocent eyes of one so young, a lifelessness that shook me. I was struck by the thought that she was only one of millions of hungry, diseased children on this planet.

I couldn't look any longer. I jumped on my bike and sped away. I opened the throttle wide—too wide for the rough terrain.

Shouting at the wind, I screamed, "What kind of God are You? Don't You see that little girl back there? How can You allow that pain and misery to exist?"

Tears blinded my eyes. The last thing I remember was a small gully ahead of me, triggering the thought, *Twist that throttle, Babe, and get that front wheel up.*

I didn't make it. The motorcycle's foot peg shot through my hip, shattering my pelvis in 13 places. A separated shoulder, a brain concussion and no memory also resulted. My friend, Gary, no more than three minutes behind, saved my life by putting his fist into the wound, stopping the blood.

How does a life of hostility, depression and defeat turn into a life of victory? It doesn't happen with our own strength and it cannot be at all, outside of God.

I began to discover this truth in 1972 when I was in Mexico City with my wife, Lory. We were visiting a Catholic shrine, Our Lady of Guadalupe, as tourists. Standing at the side altar, we were noticing the crutches and other paraphernalia left by those who had been healed, when a priest said, "If anyone has a physical problem, now is the time to pray."

Though Lory and I were still unbelievers, she caught my arm and said, "Why don't we pray that God will heal me?"

My wife had awakened that morning with her hands swollen and almost useless from arthritis. It had become a habit for me to massage them into a degree of flexibility. The doctor had prescribed a large dosage of aspirin as the only remedy for the pain. She was taking 30 to 40 a day.

So we prayed. I did not believe in faith healing, but I tried to suspend my skepticism for a moment while I whispered, "Lord God, heal Lory's arthritis."

You can imagine my surprise when, three days later, Lory said the pain in her hands had disappeared. Vanished. Her swollen knuckles were back to normal! She stopped taking aspirin and has not been bothered since.

One might suppose that a man who had seen his wife healed of an incurable disease would become a believer overnight. But I'm no brighter than those Jesus spoke of when He said, "Neither will they be persuaded, though one rose from the dead." (Luke 16:31)

It was eight months before I was born again spiritually.

I had just begun rehearsals for a play on the East Coast. Walking out on-stage, I was prepared to do everything in my power to exalt the name of Dean Jones. I was ready to discipline myself to the grueling schedule and willing to make any sacrifice to get good reviews and standing ovations. Maybe some night, I thought, by some magic, acting would somehow fill that emptiness in me. But, deep inside, something seemed to say, "This is never going to satisfy you."

I went back to the lodge near the playhouse that night and looked out over the sumptuous landscape. I should be happy! I had so much to live for—a beautiful wife who loved me, two wonderful and healthy children and my weekly salary was more than many men make in a year.

Looking back over my life, I suddenly realized how self-centered it had been. Everything I'd done had been with one person in mind—me. *Where does all this end*? I wondered. For some who worship fame, it concludes with suicide. That thought frightened me.

"Oh, God," I cried, "there must be something more!" I knelt by the bed and began to pour out my heart. I wept like a child.

During the next three days, whenever I was alone, I prayed, and each time I felt cleaner, more alive. Something extraordinary was happening to me, but I didn't know what.

Finally, the third night, I realized what I had to do. Give myself to God—end the separation that had existed between us. I said, "God, You probably don't even exist; maybe I'm just talking to the walls. But, if You're real, I'll give up myself into Your hands."

The moment I said those words, there came a flood of joy and peace into my heart that truly "passed all understanding." I had never known such a feeling of stillness and contentment. That empty spot, that "God-shaped vacuum" was filled!

I felt as if a weight was removed from my shoulders, a weight that I had not known was there until it was lifted. That was the burden of self.

"My yoke is easy and My burden light," Jesus said. (Matthew 11:30)

A moment before I had doubted God's existence, and now, I was sure of His reality. I had not reached an intellectual conclusion. I knew in my muscles and bones that God loved me. The joy and love and peace and hope and faith were the signs that I had asked for. And received—praise the Lord!

How hard it had been to let go of self and make a commitment to seek God's kingdom first. But what abundant life He gives in return.

"I am come that they might have life, and that they might have it more abundantly," said our Savior. (John 10:10)

On February 10, 1974, both Lory and I publicly confessed Jesus Christ as the Lord of our lives and we began to learn how meaningful and significant every moment of life can be when you're not empty any more, but filled and overflowing with the Holy Spirit of God.

We love Him, because He first loved us. (I John 4:19)

Two fliers were missing. No one could find
them. And then . . .

The Dream That
Wouldn't Go Away

by GEORGE HUNT

Back when I was a young livestock rancher north of
Roosevelt, Utah, the news, one cold November morning,
reported that a California doctor and his wife were missing on a
flight from Custer, South Dakota, to Salt Lake City. As a
student pilot, I had just completed my first cross-country flight
with an instructor, though I had only 20 solo hours.

Paying close attention to all radio reports on the search, I was
very disturbed two days later by a newscast saying that Dr.
Robert Dykes and his wife Margery, both in their late 20s and
parents of two young children, were not likely to be found until
spring—and maybe not even then. They had been missing four
days, and the temperature had been below zero every night.
There seemed little chance for their survival without food and
proper clothing.

That night before I retired I said a simple prayer for these
two people I didn't know. "Dear God, if they're alive, send
someone to them so they will be able to get back to their
family."

After a while I drifted off to sleep. In a dream I saw a red
plane on a snow-swept ridge and two people waving for help. I
awoke with a start. *Was it the Dykeses? What color was their
plane?* I didn't remember any of the news reports ever mentioning it.

I couldn't get back to sleep for some time. I kept reasoning
that because I'd been thinking of the couple before falling
asleep, it was natural for me to dream them. When I finally did

go to sleep, the dream came again! A red plane on a ridge—but now farther away. I could still see two people waving, and could now see some snow-covered mountain peaks in the background.

I got out of bed and spread out the only air chart I owned. It covered a remote area in Utah—the High Uintas region, along the Wyoming-Utah border. The Dykeses' flight plan presumably had to pass over this range. I was familiar with the rugged terrain, for I had fished and hunted it as a boy. My eyes scanned the names on the chart—Burro Peak, Painters Basin, Kings Peak, Gilbert Peak.

Again I went to bed. And again, incredibly, the dream returned! Now the plane was barely in sight. I could see a valley below. Then it came to me in a flash—Painters Basin and Gilbert Peak! I rose in a cold sweat. It was daylight.

Turning on the news, I found there had been no sign of the plane and the search had been called off. All that day, doing chores around the ranch, I could think of nothing but the Dykeses and my dream. I felt God had shown me where those people were and that they were alive. But who would believe me and what could I do about it? I knew I wasn't really qualified to search for them myself. I knew, too, that even trying to explain my dream to my flight instructor, a stern taskmaster named Joe Mower, would have me laughed out of the hangar.

I decided to go to our small rural airport anyway. When I arrived, a teen-aged boy who was watching the place told me Joe had gone to town for the mail.

The force that had been nudging me all morning seemed to say, "Go!" I had the boy help me push an Aeronca plane out. When he asked where I was going, I said, "To look for the Dykeses." I gave the plane the throttle and was on my way.

Trimming out, I began a steady climb and headed for Uinta Canyon. I knew what I was doing was unwise, even dangerous, but the danger seemed a small thing compared to what I felt in my heart.

As I turned east near Painters Basin, I was beginning to lose faith in my dream; there was no sign of the missing plane. The high winds, downdrafts and rough air were giving me trouble in the small 65-horsepower plane. Terribly disappointed as well as frightened, I was about to turn back when suddenly there it was! A red plane on Gilbert Peak, just as I had seen in my dream.

Coming closer, I could see two people waving. I was so happy I began to cry. "Thank You, God," I said over and over.

Opening the plane's window, I waved at the Dykeses and wigwagged my wings to let them know I saw them. Then I said a prayer to God to help me get back to the airport safely.

Thirty minutes later I was on the ground. When I taxied up and cut the motor, I gulped, for Joe Mower was there to greet me.

"You're grounded," he hollered. "You had no permission to take that plane up."

"Joe," I said quickly, "I know I did wrong, but listen, I found the Dykeses and they need help."

"You're crazy," Joe said, and he continued to yell at me. My finding that plane in an hour and a half when hundreds of planes had searched in vain for nearly a week was more than Joe could believe.

Finally I turned away from Joe, went straight for a telephone and did what I should have done in the first place. I called the CAP (Civil Air Patrol) in Salt Lake City. When they answered, I asked if there had been any word on the Dykeses' plane. They said there was no chance of their being alive now and that the search was ended.

"Well, I've found them," I said. "And they're both alive."

Behind me, Joe stopped chewing me out, his eyes wide and his mouth open.

"I'll round up food and supplies," I continued to the CAP, "and the people here will get it to them as soon as possible." The CAP gave me the go-ahead.

Everyone at the airport went into action. Within one hour we were on our way. A local expert pilot, Hal Crumbo, would fly in the supplies. I would lead the way in another plane. I wasn't grounded for long.

Back in the air, we headed for the high peaks. Hal's plane was bigger and faster than the Aeronca I was in. He was flying out ahead and above me. When I got to Painters Basin, at 11,000 feet, I met the severe downdrafts again. I could see Hal circling above me and knew he was in sight of the downed plane and ready to drop supplies. Since I couldn't go any higher, I turned around.

Back at the airport I joined a three-man ground rescue party, which would attempt to reach the couple by horseback.

Another rescue party had already left from the Wyoming side of the mountains. For the next 24 hours our party hiked through fierce winds and six-foot snowdrifts. At 12,000 feet, on a ridge near Gilbert Peak, we stopped. In the distance, some- one was yelling. Urging our frozen feet forward, we pressed on, tremendously excited. Suddenly, about 100 yards in front of us, the fuselage of a small red plane sat rammed into a snowbank. Nearby, two people flapped their arms wildly.

Charging ahead, we shouted with joy. At about the same time we reached the Dykeses, the other rescue party was coming over the opposite ridge.

After much hugging and thanking, I learned what a miracle the Dykeses' survival was. They had had nothing to eat but a candy bar, and their clothing was scant—Mrs. Dykes had a fur coat, but her husband had only a topcoat. The altitude made starting a fire impossible and at night they huddled together in their downed plane, too afraid to go asleep.

"We had all but given up, had even written notes as to who should look after the children,"Mrs. Dykes said. Then, turning to me, she said, "But when we saw your plane, it was the most wonderful thing . . . our prayers answered, a dream come true."

"Yes," I said, smiling, suddenly feeling as Solomon in the Bible must have felt after he received a visit from the Lord one night in a dream. (I Kings 3:5-14)

My dream, like Solomon's had occurred for a reason. In His own special way, God gave me that dream in order to help give life to two others. Even in the most mysterious of ways. He had shown me He is always there, always listening. He had heard my prayers and the Dykeses' prayers and had answered all of us in His own infallible way.

Dr. Raymond A. Moody Jr. gives a
fascinating, inspiring and reassuring account
of what he learned from his study of people
who have come back from the threshold of death.

Life After Life
and
Reflections on Life
After Life

by RAYMOND A. MOODY, M.D.

What is it like to die? This is a question that humanity has been asking itself ever since there have been humans. As a deeply interested physician, I have raised the question before a sizable number of audiences ranging from church organizations to professional societies of medicine, and I can safely say that this topic excites the most powerful feelings from people of many emotional types and walks of life.

During the past few years, I have encountered a large number of people who were involved in what I shall call "near-death experiences." I have met these persons in many ways. At first it was by coincidence. In 1965, when I was an undergraduate student studying philosophy at the University of Virginia, I met a man who was a clinical professor of psychiatry in the School of Medicine. I was struck from the beginning with his warmth, kindliness and humor. It came as a great surprise when I later learned that he had been pronounced dead—not just once but on two occasions—and that he had given a most fantastic account of what happened to him while he was "dead."

Some years later I was teaching in a university in eastern

North Carolina. After class one day a student stopped by to see me. He asked whether we might discuss the subject of immortality. He had an interest in the subject because his grandmother had "died" during an operation and had recounted a very amazing experience. I asked him to tell me about it, and much to my surprise, he related almost the same series of events which I had heard the psychiatry professor describe some years before.

What has amazed me since the beginning of my interest are the great similarities in the reports, despite the fact that they come from people of highly varied religious, social, and educational backgrounds. By the time I entered medical school in 1972, I had collected quite a few of these experiences. Now I know of at least 150.

The similarities among various reports are so great that one can easily pick out about 15 separate elements which recur again and again. On the basis of these points of likeness, let me construct a brief, theoretically "complete" experience which embodies all of the common elements, in the order in which it is typical for them to occur.

A man is dying and, as he reaches the point of greatest physical distress, he hears himself pronounced dead by his doctor. He begins to hear an uncomfortable noise, a loud ringing or buzzing, and at the same time feels himself moving very rapidly through a long dark tunnel. After this, he suddenly finds himself outside of his own physical body, but still in the immediate physical environment, and he sees his own body from a distance, as though he is a spectator. He watches the resuscitation attempt from this unusual vantage point and is in a state of emotional upheaval.

After a while, he collects himself and becomes more accustomed to his odd condition. He notices that he still has a "body," but one of a very different nature and with very different powers from the physical body he has left behind. Soon other things begin to happen. Others come to meet and to help him. He glimpses the spirits of relatives and friends who have already died, and a loving, warm spirit of a kind he has never encountered before—a being of light—appears before him. This being asks him a question, nonverbally, to make him evaluate his life, and helps him along by showing him a panoramic, instantaneous playback of the major events of his life. At some point he finds himself approaching some sort of barrier or border, apparently representing the limit between earthly life and the next life. Yet, he finds that he must go back to the earth, that the time for his death has not yet come. At this point he resists, for by now he is taken up with his experiences in the afterlife and does not want to return. He is overwhelmed by intense feelings of joy, love, and peace. Despite his attitude, though, he somehow reunites with his physical body and lives.

Later he tries to tell others, but he has trouble doing so. In the first place, he can find no human words adequate to describe these unearthly episodes. He also finds that others scoff, so he stops telling other people. Still, the experience affects his life profoundly, expecially his views about death and its relationship to life.

Many people describe extremely pleasant feelings and sensations during the early stages of their near-death experiences. A woman who was resuscitated after a heart attack remarks:

"I began to experience the most wonderful feelings. I couldn't feel a thing in the world except peace, comfort, ease—just quietness. I felt that all my troubles were gone. I thought to myself, 'Well, how quiet and peaceful, and I don't hurt at all.' "

Another woman who nearly died from internal bleeding says that at the moment she collapsed, "I began to hear music of some sort, a majestic, really beautiful sort of music."

Often people have the sensation of being pulled very rapidly through a dark space of some kind. A man who came very near death says:

"Suddenly, I was in a very dark, very deep valley. It was as though there was a pathway, almost a road, through the valley, and I was going down the path . . . Later, after I was well, the thought came to me, 'Well, now I know what the Bible means by "the valley of the shadow of death," because I've been there.' "

After this rapid passage through the dark, a dying person

often has an overwhelming surprise. For, at this point he may find himself looking upon his own physical body from a point outside of it. He many be out of his body for some time, desperately trying to sort out all the things that are happening to him and that are racing through his mind, before he realizes that he is dying, or even dead.

It is invariably reported that this spiritual body is weightless. Most first notice this when they find themselves floating right up to the ceiling of the room, or into the air. A person in the spiritual body is also in a privileged position in relation to the other persons around him. He can see and hear them, but they can't see or hear him.

Finally, almost everyone remarks upon the timelessness of this out-of-body state. Many say that although they must describe their interlude in the spiritual body in temporal terms (since human language is temporal), time was not really an element of their experience as it is in physical life.

Quite a few have told me that at some point while they were dying they became aware of the presence of other spiritual beings in their vicinity, beings who apparently were there to ease them through their transition into death.

Perhaps the most incredible common element in the accounts I have studied, and certainly the element which has the most profound effect upon the individual, is the encounter with a very bright light. At its first appearance this light is dim, but it rapidly gets brighter until it reaches an unearthly brilliance.

Not one person has expressed any doubt whatsoever that it was a being, a being of light, a personal being. The love and the warmth which emanate from this being to the dying person are utterly beyond words, and he feels completely surrounded by it and taken up in it, completely at ease and accepted in the presence of this being.

Most of those who are Christians in training or belief identify the light as Christ, and sometimes draw Biblical parallels in support of their interpretation.

Shortly after its appearance, the being begins to communicate with the person who is passing over.

Let us look at some firsthand accounts of this fantastic being:

"Everything was very black, except that, way off from me, I could see this light. It was a very, very brilliant light, but not too large at first. It grew larger as I came nearer and nearer to it."

"I was trying to get to that light at the end, because I felt that it was Christ, and I was trying to reach that point. It was not a frightening experience. It was more or less a pleasant thing. For immediately, being a Christian, I had connected the light with Christ Who said, 'I am the light of the world.' I said to myself, 'If this is it, if I am to die, then I know who waits for me at the end, there in the light.'"

"The thought came to my mind, 'Lovest thou me?' This was not exactly in the form of a question, but I guess the connotation of what the light said was, 'If you do love me, go back and complete what you began in your life.' And all during this time, I felt as though I were surrounded by an overwhelming love and compassion."

The initial appearance of the being of light and his probing, non-verbal questions are the prelude to a moment of startling intensity during which the being presents to the person a panoramic review of his life.

One person related:

"When the light appeared, the first thing he said to me was 'What, do you have to show me that you've done with your life?' And from then on, it was like I was walking from the time of my very early life, on through each year of my life, right up to the present."

Several people have told me that during their encounters with "death," they got brief glimpses of an entire separate realm of existence in which all knowledge—whether of past, present, or future—seemed to co-exist in a sort of timeless state. Alternately, this has been described as a moment of enlightenment in which the subject seemed to have complete knowledge. In trying to talk about this aspect of their experience, all have commented that this experience was ultimately inexpressible. Also, all agree that this feeling of complete knowledge did not persist after their return; that they did not bring back any sort of omniscience. They agree that this vision did not discourage them from trying to learn in this life, but, rather, encouraged them to do so.

> "I don't know how to explain it but I knew . . . As the Bible says, 'To you all things will be revealed.' For a minute, there was no question that didn't have an answer. How long I knew it, I couldn't say. It wasn't in earthly time, anyway."

In some instances, persons have described to me how during their near-death experience they seemed to be approaching what might be called a border or a limit of some kind. This has taken the form, in various accounts, of a body of water, a gray mist, a door, a fence across a field, or simply a line.

In several other cases, persons have told me that, though they were comfortable and secure in their new disembodied existence and were even enjoying it, they felt happy to be able to return to physical life since they had left some important task undone.

Others feel that they were in effect *allowed* to live by God, or by the being of light, either in response to their own request to be allowed to live (usually because the request was made unselfishly) or because God or the being apparently had some mission for them to fulfill.

As one man remembers:

> "I say God surely was good to me, because I was dead, and He let the doctors bring me back, for a purpose. The purpose was to help my wife, I think, because she had a drinking problem, and I know that she just couldn't have made it without me. She is better now, though, and I really think it had a lot to do with what I went through."

In some instances, persons have expressed the feeling that the love or prayers of others have in effect pulled them back from death regardless of their own wishes.

Considering the skepticism and lack of understanding that greet the attempt of a person to discuss his near-death experience, it is not surprising that almost everyone in this situation comes to feel that he is unique, that no one else has ever undergone what he has. For example, one man told me, "I have been somewhere nobody else has ever been."

Many have told me they felt that their lives were broadened and deepened by their experience. Because of it they became more reflective and more concerned with ultimate philosophical issues.

Others report a changed attitude or approach towards the physical life to which they have returned. One woman, for instance, says quite simply that "it made life much more precious to me."

No one that I interviewed has reported coming out of his experience feeling morally "purified" or perfected. No one with whom I have talked in any way evinces a "holier-than-thou" attitude. In fact, most have specifically brought up the point that they feel that they are still trying, still searching. Their vision left them with new goals, new moral principles, and a renewed determination to try to live in accordance with them, but with no feelings of instantaneous salvation or moral infallibility.

A few persons have drawn upon specific Biblical concepts when trying to elucidate or to explain to me what happened to them. Two persons mentioned Jesus' claim, "I am the light of the world." Apparently, it was at least partly on the basis of that phrase that both identified the light they met as Christ. One of them told me, "I didn't ever see a person in this light, but to me the light was a Christ—consciousness, a oneness with all things, a perfect love. I think that Jesus meant it literally when He said He was the light of the world." Another man said, most emphatically. "I *never* wanted to leave the presence of this being."

In addition, in my own reading I have come across a few seeming parallels which none of my subjects have mentioned.

The most interesting ones occur in the writings of the apostle Paul. He was a persecutor of Christians until he had his famous vision and conversion on the road to Damascus. He describes it thus:

"At midday, O king, I saw in the way a light from heaven, above the brightness of the sun, shining round about me and them which journeyed with me. And when we were all fallen to the earth, I heard a voice speaking unto me, and saying in the Hebrew tongue, 'Saul, Saul, why perse-cutest thou me? It is hard for thee to kick against the pricks.'

"And I said, 'Who art thou, Lord?' And He said, 'I am Jesus, Whom thou persecutest. But rise, and stand upon thy feet: for I have appeared unto thee for this purpose, to make thee a minister and a witness, both of these things which thou hast seen, and of those things in which I will appear unto thee . . . ' " (Acts 26:13-16)

This episode obviously bears some resemblance to the en-counter with the being of light in near-death experiences. First of all, the being is endowed with personality, though no physi-cal form is seen, and a "voice" which asks a question and issues instructions emanates from it. When Paul tries to tell others, he is mocked and labeled as "insane." Nonetheless, the vision changed the course of his life: He henceforth became the leading proponent of Christianity as a way of life entailing love of others.

"There was differences, too, of course. Paul did not come near death in the course of his vision. Also, interestingly enough, Paul reports that he was blinded by the light, and was unable to see for three days afterward. This runs contrary to the reports of those who say that though the light was indescribably brilliant, it in no way blinded them.

I have talked with numerous individuals who tell with re-markable consistency of catching glimpses of other realms of being which might well be termed "heavenly." It is interesting to me that in several of these accounts a single phrase—"a city of light"—occurs. In this and several other respects the imag-ery in which these scenes are described seems to be reminis-cent of what is found in the Bible.

One middle-aged man who had a cardiac arrest related:

"All of a sudden I was just somewhere else. There was a gold-looking light everywhere. Beautiful. I couldn't find a source anywhere. It was just all around, coming from everywhere. There was music. And I seemed to be in a countryside with streams, grass and trees, mountains. But when I looked around—if you want to put it that way—

they were not trees and things like we know them to be. The strangest thing to me about it was that there were people there. Not in any kind of form or body as we know it; they were just there.

There was a sense of perfect peace and contentment; love. It was like I was part of it. That experience could have lasted the whole night or just a second . . . I don't know."

Several people have reported to me that at some point they glimpsed other beings who seemed to be "trapped" in an apparently most unfortunate state of existence. Those who described seeing these confused beings are in agreement on several points. First, they state that these beings seemed to be, in effect, unable to surrender their attachments to the physical world. One man recounted that the spirits he saw apparently "couldn't progress on the other side because their god is still living here." That is, they seemed bound to some particular object, person or habit. Secondly, all have remarked that these beings appeared " dulled," that their consciousness seemed somehow limited in contrast with that of others. Thirdly, they say it appeared that these "dulled spirits" were to be there only until they solved whatever problem or difficulty was keeping them in the perplexed state.

In several accounts I have collected, persons say that they had near-death experiences through which they were saved from physical death by the interposition of some spirtual agent or being. In each case, the person involved found himself (knowingly or unknowingly) in a potentially fatal accident or set of circumstances from which it was beyond his own powers to escape. He may even have given up and prepared himself to die. However, at this point a voice or a light manifested itself and rescued him from the brink of death. Persons undergoing this relate that afterward their lives were changed, that they came to feel they were saved from death for a purpose. They have all reported that their religious beliefs were strengthened. One man reported:

"This was during World War II . . . and I was serving in the infantry in Europe. I had an experience I won't ever forget . . . I saw an enemy plane diving toward the building we were in, and it had opened fire on us . . . The dust from the bullets was headed in a path right toward us. I was very scared and thought we would all be killed. I didn't see a thing, but I felt a wonderful, comforting presence there with me, and a kind, gentle voice said, 'I'm here with you, Reid. Your time has not come yet.' I was so relaxed and comfortable in that presence . . . Since that day, I have not been one bit afraid of death."

Given the fact that some people who have been revived from very close encounters with death have reported spiritual experiences, some have asked how these reports bear on the issue of suicide. The first thing that one must point out is that consideration of near-death experiences does not give us final answers to the many different kinds of puzzles we have about suicide. All we can do is address ourselves to two questions. First: Do persons who have had near-death experiences from causes other than suicidal attempts come back with any particular attitude toward suicide? And second: Do reported near-death experiences which resulted from suicidal attempts differ in any way from those which had other causes?

All of these people agree on one point: They felt their suicidal attempts solved nothing. They found that they were involved in exactly the same problems from which they had been trying to extricate themselves by suicide. Whatever difficulty they had been trying to get away from was still there on the other side, unresolved.

All mentioned that after their experiences, they would never consider trying suicide again. Their common attitude is that they had made a mistake, and that they were very glad they had not succeeded in their attempts.

When asked about such matters, a psychiatrist friend of mine, who had an "other-world" experience during an apparent clinical death from an infection, gave an interesting answer. He expressed the belief that God is much more forgiving, understanding and just, than we as humans are able to comprehend, and that God will take care of these things in accordance with His love and wisdom. What a suicidal person needs from us as fellow humans is not judgment, but love and understanding.

I find that even after I have asserted that I am not trying to prove that there is life after death and have made all of my usual qualifying remarks, some people with whom I talk are still not satisfied. They want to know what I, Raymond Moody, *feel*. I believe this is a legitimate question, as long as it is understood that this is a psychological matter and not a matter of logical conclusion that I am trying to force on anyone else. My own feeling is that, *within the context of science alone*, there may never be a proof of life after death.

I have come to accept as a matter of religious faith that there is a life after death, and I believe that the phenomenon we have been examining is a manifestation of that life.

TO THE ONE I LOVE

. . . I do not need some tremendous
               miracle
To give me faith in God:
A violet would do,
Or a spire of goldenrod,
Or a daisy or two.
But if I had to have
A magic and a wonder
To rend my doubts asunder,
To prove God true—
That would be you!
                 Archibald Rutledge

A great tennis champion tells how the
spiritual emptiness inside her was filled.

Winning Is Not Enough

by MARGARET COURT
Three-Time Wimbledon Winner

For many years as a tournament tennis player I thought my
life had all the ingredients for happiness. I had a fine
marriage, two lovely children, great success in my tennis career, financial security, everything. It all should have been very
satisfying, and for years it was.

But the time finally came when it was not.

I remember the very first tennis racket that came my way,
back when I was a youngster growing up in Australia. My
mother had a visitor one day who noticed some of us kids
playing in the street in front of our home in Albury. We were
having a hit at an old tennis ball we'd found. I was using a piece
of wood—Mum couldn't afford to buy me a proper racket.
When our visitor saw this, she told Mum, "I've got an old racket
at home that Marg can have."

On her next visit, the woman brought along a big, old-
fashioned racket with a square head and broken strings. But I
was thrilled. Eventually, I won my first tournament with it.

As a teen-age student at St. Augustine's School I had been
playing tennis steadily for six or seven years, but I was debating
whether or not to give it up. I had done well in the sport locally,
but some people whose opinion I respected didn't approve of
women taking part in athletics. It just wasn't ladylike, they
said.

One day the principal of the school stopped me on the path
and asked why I wasn't on my way to tennis practice. I told her
that I had almost decided to give it up.

"Now Margaret," she said, suddenly becoming stern, "you're wrong about that. I've seen you play. With you, tennis is a gift. A gift from God. It would be ungrateful for you to throw it away."

Tennis a gift? I had never thought of it that way before. Some people, I knew, had the gift of making a speech or painting a picture. There were gifted musicians too. But never until then had I realized that God has a way of giving each person something special to use. . .and that He had given me tennis.

After that I dedicated myself wholeheartedly to the game. My gift became my life. During the next 17 years, I played tennis all over the world. And the dedication paid off. I won championships at Wimbledon and Forest Hills several times, and other tournaments as well.

But year after year, as I kept on playing, even returning to competition after having two children, I began to feel a kind of emptiness somewhere deep inside me. I still considered my tennis ability a gift from God. I still attended Mass when I could. But the emptiness kept growing, sometimes making me impatient and irritable with my husband Barry and the children, and jittery on the tennis court as well.

After we had our second baby in 1974, tennis was still so much a part of my life that I returned to play some more. In September, 1975, after touring Japan, I went home to Australia to rest. One day in Perth, I ran into an old friend, Ann Brinkworth. Ann was looking radiant, better than I'd ever seen her look.

"What's your secret, Ann?" I asked half-joking, half-serious.

"Come with me tonight and I'll show you," she said. "I'm going to a prayer meeting."

Somehow hesitantly, I told her I'd come along. Later, I wondered why I had agreed. Ever since my days at St. Augustine's, I'd always refused when someone invited me to a church function. If anyone gave me a religious book to read, I'd usually toss it out later on. I knew God had provided me with a rare talent—but I didn't want to look beyond that.

So something in me resisted the idea of going with Ann, but something also seemed to be urging me to go. And when I did go, something unforeseen and almost indescribable happened. The room seemed to come alive with a warmth I'd never experienced before. When Ann and the others began praying and talking with Jesus Christ, it was as if He were right there with them, sitting with them as a friend.

As the evening wore on, I began to feel His presence, too. What's more, as the hours passed, He seemed to be knocking on the door of my mind and my heart—asking to be let in. I left the prayer meeting confused, yet filled with a kind of mounting excitement.

The meeting was only the beginning of that excitement. Later the next night I got up out of bed and went into our daughter Marika's bedroom to check on her. As I entered Marika's room, I shivered in my robe; a light breeze was coming through an open window. Bending down, I kissed Marika. Then, looking up, I saw something that made my heart give a violent leap. Above the door a beautiful woman seemed to be looking down at me, and I knew instantly that it was Our Lady, the mother of Jesus. One moment she was there, as real as I was. The next moment she was gone.

I went back to bed with my mind in a whirl. Were my eyes playing tricks on me? Could it have just been moonlight and shadows and the wind playing tricks with the lace curtains? No, I knew it was more than that.

The next night I had another vision. This time I seemed to see a gate, again on Marika's wall. The gate kept opening and closing before me. Now, deeply moved, I prayed for an explanation.

The third night still another vision came, this time on my bedroom wall I saw a window, and in the distance, a cross on a hill surrounded by glowing colors, by pinks and blues. I stared at the cross for a long time, wondering. What did these manifestations mean?

Though I wanted to tell Barry everything, I needed spiritual reassurance first, and so I went to our local priest. Father Miller urged me to read the Bible, something I had long neglected. He said understanding would come to me. And slowly, as I read His word, I began to grasp what was happening. The visions, I realized, were confirming what I had felt so strongly in that prayer meeting: that Jesus Christ *was* real, that He *was* a Friend and Savior Who could help me and give me strength when I needed it. All I had to do was come to Him— come through His always open gate and believe in Him by keeping my eye upon the Cross. After years of being half-dead spiritually, I was being reborn into the Christian life.

The change in my life was profound and, oh, so beneficial. Knowing the Lord as I now did in a personal way had a calming effect on me. On the tennis court my nervousness and tension were gone. At home, where once I had been plagued by impatience with Barry and the children, the Lord replaced all that with understanding and tolerance. Where once I found it difficult to reach out to people—sometimes even in my own family—He gave me a deep and loving concern.

He gave me a calm acceptance of His will for me, too. When I learned I was pregnant with a third child, Barry and I, over-joyed, began to plan for our new little Court. But the pregnancy did not seem right from the beginning, and eventually, I lost the baby. If that had happened to the old Margaret Court, she would have been crushed, embittered. But now, even though I was terribly disappointed, I was able to say, "Thy will be done"—and accept it.

What does all this mean? To me it means that it's not enough merely to receive God's gifts or take them for granted. He wants and expects more from us than that. He wants us to know Him and love Him, because He knows that when we truly love Him we will be able to love ourselves and our neighbors.

I wish I had learned all this years ago. But, thanks to Him, I know it now. And, best of all, I've just begun to learn.

My Escape From Doubt

by JIM BISHOP

At the age of four, I knew that God was everywhere. I spoke to Him, on my knees, and He heard me. Sometimes He listened with sympathy. I was astounded that He did indeed send a bicycle with a coaster brake. When I reasoned in my boy's mind that the world was at war and that millions of soldiers of many nations were praying to be spared, it was beyond credence that He had had the time and inclination to send that bike.

That was an unforgettable memory in boyhood. As I grew toward manhood, the more I learned, the less I believed in God. I told myself that He had been invented by ancients who feared the eternal darkness of death. Their egos were bruised. They could not concede that at some point in life there would be a final breach, a last sigh. Even worse, they fashioned Him unto their likenesses. He was a fierce, bearded man glaring down at us from a cloud.

When I was 21, my superior intellect told me that God was a fake. There was nothing out there in space. Heaven could not be up and hell down, because in the slow spinning of this planet there was no up or down. Then, too, I knew that everything in creation dies, including the smallest insect and the biggest star.

In following years, there were times of industry and some small success, but they were not happy years. There was a bedtime carousel of the mind in which the horses of doubt swung in slow circles to tinny music. They carried empty

325

saddles and they pranced with a fury of faithlessness in God, in myself, in my work, in my wife, in mankind, even my mother and father. Now and then my parents asked if I attended church services, and I responded with asperity, "No . . . thank . . . you. . . ."

The harder I studied to learn, the less I knew. I disputed facts. I reached a point where nothing was as it seemed to be.

Then one day I felt a new experience. I saw the miracle of birth, and it turned my wandering mind around. I had seen babies before, of course, in bassinets, had cooed at them, chucked them under the chin, observed their gummy grins and hoped they would not cry. I had romped with children until exhausted.

But this miracle was Virginia Lee. A child of my own had been born. She was just another infant (a very beautiful one, to be sure), but so close to me that, this time, I questioned birth and life.

Why, I wondered for the first time, did we take birth so for granted? How could an infant, unconscious of life and the struggle for existence, fashion the correct number of limbs and toes and fingers and eyes and ears?

If it was a matter of genes, who invented them? Did they fashion themselves? Maybe they evolved over millions of years. From what? I began to doubt my doubts.

For days I could forget my wonderment at the miracle of birth. Then it would return unbidden. My thoughts tumbled like a mountain freshet over stones. It became a lonely, losing fight with logic. A young Japanese scientist discovered a dying red star two billion light-years away. It required two billion years for the light from that ancient sun to reach his eyes He reasoned that the star had died long ago and was now a blackened mass of gas far, far away. If this was so, then the red rays he saw had started across the vastness of space millions of years ago, even though the star from which they had emanated long since winked out.

Such wonder led me to try to understand space. No matter how vast, space must end, too. Emptiness could not go on to infinity because everything is finite. Where, then, were the walls? At what point did the millions of universes stop? How did they arrange their orderly rotations so that they are more predictable than the finest chronometer? Who keeps the billions of huge bodies from colliding?

Gradually I lost faith in my so-called superior intellect. Intellect alone could not supply the needed answers. I could not see air, but without it I would die. Thus it is, I decided, with the spirit of man. I needed Something to breathe life into a soul that had been crushed by the dominance of the human mind.

In a span of nine weeks I saw my mind proved a helpless instrument. My mother and my wife were both taken. They went off quietly, rich in faith, strong in the knowledge of where they were going. The sumptuous caskets framing their waxen bodies did nothing to encourage faith for me. I wanted to cry out. "Why me, Lord?" But it seemed to border on idiocy. If I had been God, I would have taken me in death and spared them.

The weeks dragged. The months appeared to be in a freeze frame. Sometimes, lost in a labyrinth of complexities, I was forced to return to the beginning. Over and over again I argued the possibilities: (1)That there is no God; (2)That there is. I began to see that nothing is accidental. All the good and bad events are part of a divine scheme in balance.

I was a slow learner. But somehow, somewhere, as I groped my painful way, I found my soul. Overnight, I knew it was there. It was present and alive—wounded, bleeding perhaps, but alive.

If one concedes there is a soul, there must be a God. Science cannot measure a soul. Call it conscience, call it reasoning between right and wrong, call it a spiritual being—it is there because He willed it.

I began to pray. I found that I could murmur a quick prayer at any time —while driving, while watching a commercial on television, while shaving, while thinking of Him and His Almighty Presence. I began to ask for things. Not small things. I asked for world peace. I asked for faith for the faithless. I asked that the poor be fed and clothed and housed. I asked for health for the sick, the old, the lonely. As faith returned to me, I feared that it might dissolve again. So I prayed for continuing faith, too.

Faith does not come as quickly as these words. It starts. It stops. It floods and recedes. Sometimes, when I was certain that I had it, my mind said: "The whole thing is preposterous. There is no God. There is no hereafter. We are nothing." Then I would remember Dr. Richard Hoffman's atheistic words: "I don't believe in Him, but I sure hope He believes in me."

For a time I felt that I was wooing faith. Cultivating it as one might a friend one never met. Grasping. Clawing. Reaching. When at last my frenzy died, calmness came. When I gave up, I could feel His presence. There were no apparitions, no wraiths on the wall. He was there and I knew it.

The less I sought the more I got. What I wanted was proof. He wanted me to believe without revealing Himself. I was here as part of an enormous test. He had given me custody of my soul; some day He would beckon and ask me to account for my stewardship.

I had spent half of my life kicking and punching that soul into a state of unconsciousness. He would not be fooled by any device of mine to get back in His grace. So I murmured, "Forgive me. Make me more pleasing to Thee." I timed the prayer. Exactly four seconds. It was murmured over and over again. And I also said, "Dear God, I was a little boy once who prayed, not even knowing what faith was, and You gave me a bike I didn't deserve. Please remember me."

Finally, like the bicycle, light came. For the first time I comprehended that it would not be in God's interest to reveal Himself to us. If He did, none of us would require faith. We would believe because we saw Him. There would be no point in struggling to keep alive if we were so easily assured that eternal life in paradise is waiting on the far side of this life.

No, it was a far better test of our devotion if He remained mystical and obscure, just beyond the range of our senses. Much better.

I had wanted proof, something for my eyes or ears or hands. He wanted me to believe without it. Faith was what He required of me. And He never rested till I found it.

The Secret Behind My Success

by CAROL BURNETT

My career—TV, stage, movies, all of it—was founded on a strange event that was to be a deep mystery to me for years. Only after my life had changed drastically did I begin to solve the puzzle I was confronted with one long-ago June evening in California.

In those days I was one of a group of stage-struck drama-school students at UCLA, living on hopes and dreams and not much else. As school ended, one of our professors was leaving for a vacation in Europe. He had a house near San Diego, and a *bon voyage* party was planned. It was suggested that some of us drama students might drive down and entertain his supper guests with scenes from musical comedies.

Nine of us agreed to go. One of the boys and I had rehearsed a scene from *Annie Get Your Gun*, I remember, and that was our part of the program.

Everything went well. The guests seemed to enjoy our singing, and we enjoyed it, too.

After our performance, supper was announced. I was standing at the buffet when a man I had never seen before spoke to me pleasantly. He said he had admired our performance. Then he asked me what I intended to do with my life.

I told him that I hoped to go to New York some day and make a career for myself on the stage. When he asked what was stopping me, I told him truthfully that I barely had enough money to get back to Los Angeles, let alone New York. I might have added, but didn't, that at times my grandmother, my mother, my sister and I had been on welfare. The man smiled and said that he would be happy to lend me the money to go to

New York. A thousand dollars, he added, should be enough to get me started.

Well, in those days I was pretty innocent, but not *that* innocent. So I refused his offer politely. He went away, but in a few moments he was back with a pleasant-faced lady whom he introduced as his wife. Then he made his offer all over again. He was quite serious, he said. There were only three conditions. First, if I did meet with success, I was to repay the loan without interest in five years. Next, I was never to reveal his identity to anyone. Finally, if I accepted his offer, I was eventually to pass the kindness along, to help some other person in similar circumstances when I was able to do so.

He told me to think it over and telephone him when I got back to Los Angeles. He added that he was prepared to make a similar offer to my partner in the scene from *Annie Get Your Gun*, and he gave me his telephone number.

The next day, half convinced I had dreamed the whole thing, I called the number. I was told that if I had decided to accept the conditions, I could drive down on Monday morning and pick up my check. Still unbelieving, I told my mother and grandmother. Their reaction, not surprisingly, was to urge me strongly not to have anything to do with my mysterious benefactor. But somehow I was convinced that the man was sincere, and I believed, furthermore, that the good Lord was giving me, Carol Burnett, a strong and unmistakable push. I was *supposed* to accept the offer. I was being *guided*. And if I didn't go, I would regret it for the rest of my life.

At sun-up on Monday morning my partner and I were on the road. We drove for three hours. At nine o'clock, we were at the man's office. We had to wait perhaps half an hour—and believe me, that was the longest half hour of my life! But finally we were ushered in. Our friend was crisp, serious, business-like. He reminded us of the conditions, especially the one about not revealing his identity. Then he had his secretary bring in the checks. I watched as he signed them. I had never seen so many beautiful zeros in my life.

We tried to thank him, but he just smiled and ushered us out. When we came to the car, still dazed, we realized we didn't have enough gasoline to get back to Los Angeles—and not enough cash to buy any. We had to go to a bank, present one of the $1000 checks, then wait while the astonished bank officials telephoned our friend's office to make sure that we weren't a pair of international forgers. But finally they did cash it for us.

Back in Los Angeles, I wasted no time. I spent a little of the money on a visit to the dentist where I had two teeth filled and one extracted—I hadn't been able to afford a dentist for years. Then, with my family's anxious admonitions ringing in my ears, I headed for New York.

In all of that vast city I knew just one soul, a girl named Eleanore Ebe. I called her up and found that she was staying at the Rehearsal Club, where in those days young theatrical hopefuls could find room and board for $18 a week. So I moved in with Ellie, and settled down to the long grind of finding work on the New York stage.

It was the old story. No experience? Then no work. But how can you get experience if you can't get work? My funds got lower and lower. I went to work as a hat check girl in a restaurant. Unfortunately, it catered mostly to ladies who had no desire or reason to check their hats. Still, I managed to make about $30 a week from tips—enough to get by.

My grandmother wrote me sternly that if I hadn't found a job on the stage by Christmas I had better come home. So I redoubled my visits to theatrical agencies. Finally one agent said wearily, "Why don't you put on your own show? Maybe then you'd stop bothering us!"

That sparked an idea. Back at the Rehearsal Club I talked to all my jobless friends. If we were really bursting with talent, as we were sure we were, why not hire a hall, send out invitations to all the agents and critics in town, and put on our own revue?

Everyone agreed that it was a great idea. We started chipping in 50 cents apiece each night for a fund to hire the hall. Talented youngsters took on the task of creating scenery, writing music and lyrics, doing the choreography. When our first act was ready, we performed it for the board of directors of the Club who then gave us some additional help. When the "Rehearsal Club Revue" finally opened and ran for three nights, it seemed to us that everyone in New York show business was in the audience. The day after it closed, three agents called me with offers of jobs. From that point on, the magic doors swung open and I was on my way.

I reported all my progress to my benefactor back on the West Coast, but I heard very little from him. He continued to insist upon his anonymity. He showed no desire to share any spotlights, take any credit.

Five years to the day after I accepted his loan, I paid him back, and since then I've kept my pledge never to reveal his identity. He never told me his reasons for helping me in the manner he did, but as the years have gone by I've been able to unravel the mystery of this man, at least to my own satisfaction, and in the process I've discovered a powerful spiritual principle to use in my own life.

I stumbled upon the key clue one day when I was glancing through a copy of the recently-published Living Bible. I had turned to the sixth chapter of Matthew because I wanted to see how the Lord's Prayer had been translated. Suddenly, some verses seemed to leap out of the page: "When you give a gift to a beggar, don't shout about it as the hypocrites do . . . When you do a kindness to someone, do it secretly . . . And your Father Who knows all secrets will reward you . . . " (Matthew 6:2-4)

Do it secretly, the passage read, and at once I thought of my secretive friend. From that moment, what he had done and how he had done it began to make sense.

I began to see that when he made his offer to me, my benefactor had employed the spiritual principle of giving-in-secret-without-seeking-credit. He had done it partly to be kind, of course, but also because he knew that great dividends flow back to anyone who is wise enough to practice this kind of giving.

I believe that, as the Bible says, there is a great liberating force in not trying to take credit for one's good deeds. It tames the ego. It moves us away from petty vanity—and I'm convinced that the further we move away from ourselves, the closer we come to God.

So that's the story of how my career began. I shall always be grateful to my anonymous friend. With pride I repaid his loan.

and with pride I have kept his name secret. As for his stipulation about passing the kindness along to others—well, that's *my* secret!

A Fragile Moment of Love

When we moved from California to a small Illinois town, I was anxious to enroll my six-year-old daughter Dixie in her new school right away. But I stopped short in the doorway of the first-grade room when I glanced in and saw the valentine box on the teacher's desk.

"I think I'd better bring Dixie back tomorrow," I said, as my shy little daughter's fingers curled tightly in mine. "I forgot it was Valentine's Day." *Starting in a new school is difficult enough*, I thought, *without being left out the very first day*. All the other children would surely be exchanging valentines that day.

"Come in, come in," the teacher insisted. "I'm Mrs. Elmer. We're going to have a party and that's a good way for Dixie to get acquainted. Sit there, Dixie," she said, pointing to a desk up near the front of the room.

Feeling like a traitor, I tried to smile as my daughter sat down. Poor Dixie! I thought. Why couldn't that teacher have been more understanding? I wondered. Dixie was so vulnerable. I wanted to protect her from being hurt.

At home all day I watched the clock. Finally the back door slammed. "Mommy!" Dixie yelled. "I got three valentines!" Skipping into the kitchen, she shoved three hearts into my hands. I took them and turned them over. "To Dixie with love." "To my new friend." "To Dixie."

When Dixie wasn't looking, I held them up to the light. Faint lines dented the shiny surfaces, as if something had been erased. I had to squint to make out:

"To my teacher." "To Mrs. Elmer." And a few letters, "For m- t-ac--r."

Dixie danced toward me. She grabbed the valentines and hugged them to her. "I have three friends," she bubbled. "And a nice teacher."

"Yes, you do," I said, smiling.

Fanny-Maude Evans

There are times when God seems to reveal Himself to us by a show of power that defies explanation. Here is a case in point.

The Picture in Aunt Lana's Mind

by ROBERT J. FOSS

Pacific Beach, Washington, where Grandma and Aunt Lana lived for many years, is a very small town in a very bleak part of the world. Forlorn, one could call it. Not many people want to live there, or go there, for it rains incessantly, the people are poor, and the Pacific's waves are much too rough for surfing or swimming. Still, I loved my visits there, and never more that during the summer of '73, when Aunt Lana included me in one of her spiritual "adventures." It was an adventure in blind trust.

Aunt Lana and Grandma went to live in Pacific Beach because that's the only place where Aunt Lana could find employment. She's a teacher. She is also handicapped. In 1949, she was struck down by polio, and this robust, six-foot-two woman has been in a wheelchair ever since. Aunt Lana is a triumphant woman, however, with a hard, practical hold on life and a bold grip on the life of the spirit. I think she's especially attuned to spiritual things *because* she's handicapped, and not running around wastefully the way most of us are.

On the last day of my summer visit in '73, when I was 14, I realized that something was troubling Aunt Lana. The sun was dancing across the surf when I went down to the kitchen that lovely morning. But as we breakfasted on apricots, toast and hard-boiled eggs, Aunt Lana was silent. Not so Grandma. "The sun always shines once a day in Pacific Beach," she said cheerily. "But for the rest of the day you'd better keep your coat on."

We cleared the table, and just as I was about to go back upstairs, I saw Aunt Lana sitting in her room, just staring.

"Anything I can do?" I said, concerned. She shook her head. Then, as I was about to leave, she changed her mind.

"Well, maybe there *is* something you can do. I'm stymied."

She told me a strange story about a picture that had come into her mind a few days before. She hadn't paid much attention to it at first, for it was simply a scene that had flashed into her consciousness—some sand and some rocks and a body of water, that's all. But the scene kept coming back, persistently intruding on her prayers and thoughts.

"I have a feeling that the picture comes from the Lord, that He's trying to tell me something," Aunt Lana said. "But what?"

To me, this was pretty deep spiritual stuff. I felt a little timid about presuming to advise Aunt Lana in this special area of hers, but I was soon deeply involved—and fascinated. We talked for a while, and then, remembering that Aunt Lana loved stories, I said, "What do you think one of your detectives would do?" That started Aunt Lana taking the picture apart, piece by piece, as though each held a clue.

"All right," she said, closing her eyes and summoning the picture into view. "The sun is shining. There's water on the left, sand on the right, a bluff of rock hovering over that—so that must be north. And if that's so, then this is very likely a beach on the West Coast."

"Maybe one here in Washington?"

"Yes, it looks like our shoreline," Aunt Lana replied, "but there's nothing to distinguish it, no man-made sign." She was silent now, here eyes still closed. "But the water," she said so suddenly that I jumped, "look at the water! It's smooth, no ripples. That could mean a cove of some sort." Then, a little sadly, "But not on this wild coast of ours."

Aunt Lana and I wrestled with these meager facts for a little while, and then we had to admit that we could make nothing of them. Still, Aunt Lana couldn't shake the conviction that the picture had some special meaning for her.

At noon we were just getting ready to dry the luncheon dishes and Aunt Lana was reaching for the dish towel when her hand stopped in mid-air. "Bobby," she said, "there's some quiet water up north of here, up in the Indian reservation. I feel sure I've seen some."

"Let's try to find it," I said, and with a flurry of excitement we made plans to make the search. We were about ready to leave when Grandma suggested that so long as we were heading up near the Quinault reservation, we might drop off some old clothes she'd been saving to give away. Aunt Lana thought that a good idea. One of her students lived up in Taholah with an aged grandmother. Maybe they'd have some use for them.

With Aunt Lana at the wheel of her white Impala—with the hand brake she'd designed herself and had someone weld—we headed north. The road paralleled the ocean, winding over hills and through creek canyons. We passed storm-sculptured rocks where sea birds took shelter from the turbulent breakers. Bizarre pillars of stone dotted the beaches like human forms in windblown garments. "The Indians say that those pillars are women waiting for the men to return from the sea," Aunt Lana said, filling me with wonderful facts about the Quinault Indians who once had earned their livelihood from whaling.

We traveled on. The road narrowed and threatened to become gravel, though it never quite did. Soon we crossed into the Quinault reservation. About a mile or so deeper in, she stopped the car. "Point Grenville!" she shouted. "Quick, Bob, over there! Run to the beach. See what's there." I was out of the car lickety-split, and in a few minutes came panting back.

"It's there!" I called. I described the cove with the ocean on the left and the beach with the looming rocks on the right, and the sun's rays glistening on the water's quiet ripples.

Aunt Lana threw up her arms in a wild expression of joy. She reached over and hugged me and kissed me on the forehead. Then she became serious. "Now tell me what else you saw."

"I didn't see anything else, Aunt Lana."

"Nobody was there?"

"Nobody."

"You didn't see anything odd?" I shook my head. Aunt Lana's face darkened. She put her head down on the steering wheel; I knew she was praying.

"Well," she said finally, "I don't know what it means. Stymied again."

It seemed a shame to give up now. We discussed the possibility of our just staying there and waiting for something to happen, and for a while that's what we did. As time passed, I guess we both felt disillusioned. At one point I looked into the back seat and saw the boxes of clothes Grandma had given us; I suggested that we bring them to the Indian family.

"What clothes?" Aunt Lana said. She'd forgotten about them. My idea prevailed, however, and we started up again and drove toward the little town huddled in a small valley by a river. In Taholah, Aunt Lana drove up to the fish cannery and sent me in with instructions to buy a fish for dinner. I bought a small salmon, wrapped it in three layers of the *Aberdeen World*, and put it in the trunk. Fishing meant jobs, and the noble salmon provided for the needs of many of the town's families, most of whom were desperately poor.

After that we drove to Second Street and turned down it. The houses we passed were blank-walled—the Indians thought that a house facing the street would be haunted and bring bad luck. We drove to the house on the corner, the only one that was painted, and that one a bright canary yellow with a blue stripe around the middle. Aunt Lana honked the horn and presently a small child toddled out, squinted at us, and ran back inside.

"The grandmother is very old," Aunt Lana explained to me. "I am told that she has eighteen children of her own, and who knows how many grandchildren."

Soon the old grandmother appeared. By the time she shuffled up to Aunt Lana's door I was out of the car and waiting with a box of clothes. The old Indian reached out to touch Aunt Lana's outstretched hand. "You've come," she said. "I've been expecting you."

Aunt Lana and I looked at each other. Then we both looked at the grandmother. Perhaps we hadn't heard her correctly.

"You were expecting us?"

"Yes, yes," she said, and gradually, in stops and starts, fumbling for words, she told us about the trouble in the family, the people out of work, someone in jail, the hunger, the lack of warm clothing, the ever-pervasive need. Then one day, she continued, when her feeling of helplessness was at its worst, she had wandered down to the beach.

As the old woman mentioned the word "beach," I saw a glimmer come into Aunt Lana's eyes. "And then?" Aunt Lana said.

"I walk along the edge of the water. A long time." As she talked I pictured her moving aimlessly among the rocks while the great waves thundered and splashed. "Then I come to a place where the ocean is more quiet and the wind is very kind . . ."

A cove, I wanted to say. *You came to a cove.*

" . . . and there I talk to God. 'Please, God,' I say, 'tell someone to bring help. Not for me, God—for the little ones.' "

It was almost unnecessary to ask her when she had prayed in the quiet cove. I knew, Aunt Lana knew, that the old woman had been talking to her God three days before, the very day, the very hour, when the picture first came into Aunt Lana's mind. And so it proved to be.

I carried the boxes of clothes into the house while Aunt Lana sat in the car making arrangements for help. Then we left. The old grandmother, surrounded now by a crowd of children, waved good-bye. "God is taking care," I heard her say. "God is taking care."

At the end of the day, just before leaving Aunt Lana's home for my own, I took a last walk on the beach. I wore a coat to shield me from the windblown rain. The beginning of a storm brought waves from the southwest that washed my rubber boots. It had been a day like no other, a day in which Aunt Lana had helped me learn what she had known for a long time: that God has countless ways of letting us know that He is there, taking care.

Why I Believe in Life After Death

by NORMAN VINCENT PEALE

Not long ago, at a luncheon in London, I found myself sitting beside a well-known British publisher. Near the end of the meal, he turned to me suddenly and asked point-blank, "Doctor Peale, do you really believe in a life after death?"

"Yes, I really do," I told him. "I believe because the Bible tells us that God's creation—man—is a spiritual being, and things of the spirit are eternal."

"I want to believe that," he said a bit wistfully, "but intellectually I find it difficult. I wish we had time to discuss it further."

Later, when I sat down to write him a note explaining in more detail my convictions about an afterlife, something I'd written many years earlier came into my mind. *The Blessed Assurance*. I thought it might be helpful, so I sent it to my friend. Still later, because they thought it might also be helpful to our readers, the editors of Guideposts asked me to present it again.

Here, then, is that message, just as I wrote it many Easters ago:

All members of the human race have two things in common: Each of us was born, and each of us must die. Most of us are not too concerned with the circumstances of our birth—we don't remember it; it lies far behind us. But the thought of dying is another matter. The knowledge that our days on this earth will come to an end is an inescapable part of our existence—somber, mysterious and sometimes frightening.

Quite often people come to me and confess that they are

haunted by a fear of death that they try to conceal from other people, and even from themselves. These people are not necessarily old or ill. Often they are in the prime of life, with many useful years ahead of them. But sometimes, it seems, the more they love life, the more they dread death.

What I usually do with such people is admit that I, too, have moments when I flinch from the thought of dying. I suggest that this is perfectly natural, that in my opinion the good Lord planted a certain amount of this fear in all of us so that we would not be tempted to relinquish the trials and responsibilities of this life too easily. But, I add, I'm sure the Lord didn't intend us to be panicky about it. Finally I try to reassure these troubled souls by outlining the thoughts that have helped me rise above the fear of death—or at least keep it under control.

Take, for example, the inevitability of dying. This seems to appall some people, but it always struck me as a merciful thing. Suppose there were loopholes in this universal law; suppose that somehow there was a one per cent chance of avoiding death. Consider how frantically we'd search for that loophole, how wretched we'd be not to find it.

But consider how wretched we'd be if we did find it! No one would be happy trying to live forever. It's a little like being at a wonderful play. During the performance, one hopes it will go on and on, but one wouldn't really like to stay in the theater all night or until boredom set in.

Another thing I tell the worried ones is this: You may be frightened in advance, but it is almost certain that when the time comes you will not fear death at all. I have talked to doctors and nurses who have seen hundreds of people die, and they all tell me that at the end, unless they are tormented by a guilty conscience, people go peacefully and thankfully. The truth is, death has been miscast as a grim reaper. To almost everyone, when it finally comes, it comes as a friend.

"That may be true," say some of the fearful ones. "The moment of death may be less terrifying than we thought. But then what? Is there a life after death? Is there any proof?"

To these I reply, "It depends on what you mean by proof. To me the evidence is overwhelming, whether you consult your reason or your instincts. Look at the vast universe that surrounds us, the laws that govern the spinning solar systems and the whirling electrons, the balance and economy of a stupendous Reality that uses everything and wastes nothing. Does it seem reasonable that the Intelligence behind such a Reality would create a being as complex and sensitive as man just to snuff him out forever like the flame of a candle? Of course it doesn't!"

What is death, then? Obviously it is a change into some new form of existence. We are not permitted to know exactly what this new existence is like, but I believe that sometimes we are given glimpses. Time and again it has been reported of people on the brink of death that they seem to become aware of a great radiance or hear beautiful music or see the faces of departed loved ones who are apparently waiting for them across the line. Are these just hallucinations? I don't think so. Several such episodes have happened within my own family.

My father, who died at 85 after a distinguished career as both a physician and a minister, struggled against a very real fear of death. But not long after he died, my stepmother dreamed that he came to her and told her that his fears had been groundless.

"Don't ever worry about dying," he said to her. "There's nothing to it!" The dream was so vivid that she woke up, astounded. And I believe that my father did come to reassure her because that is precisely the phrase I had heard him use a thousand times to dismiss something as unimportant or trivial.

In 1939, when news reached me that my mother had died unexpectedly in another town, I was alone in my office, numb with grief and loss. There was a Bible on my desk, and I put my hand on it, staring blindly out of the window. As I did so, I felt a pair of hands touch my head, gently, lovingly, unmistakably. The pressure lasted only an instant; then it was gone. An illusion? A hallucination caused by grief? I don't think so. I think my mother was permitted to reach across the gulf of death to touch and reassure me.

One year when I was preaching at a Methodist gathering in Georgia, I had the most startling experience of all. At the end of the final session, the presiding bishop asked all the ministers in the audience to come forward, form a choir and sing an old, familiar hymn.

I was sitting on the speakers' platform, watching them come down the aisles. And suddenly, among them, I saw my father. I saw him as plainly as I ever saw him when he was alive. He seemed about 40, vital and handsome. He was singing with the others. When he smiled at me and put up his hand in an old familiar gesture, for several unforgettable seconds it was as if my father and I were alone in that big auditorium. Then he was gone, but in my heart the certainty of his presence was indisputable. He was *there*, and I know that some day, somewhere, I'll meet him again.

We don't try to prove immortality so that we can believe in it; we try to prove it because we cannot help believing in it. Instinct whispers to us that death is not the end, reason supports it; psychic phenomena uphold it. Even science, in its own way, now insists that the universe is more spiritual than material. Einstein's great equation indicates that matter and energy are interchangeable. Where does that leave us, if not in an immaterial universe? The great psychologist William James said, "Apparently there is one great universal mind, and since man enters into this universal mind, he is a fragment of it."

This intangible in all of us, this fragment of the universal mind, is what religion calls the soul, and it is indestructible because—as James said—it is at one with God. The Founder of Christianity said specifically that there is a life beyond the grave. Not only that, Jesus proved it by rising from the dead Himself. If you believe that it happened, death should hold little terror for you. If you don't believe it, you are really not a completely fulfilled Christian.

The Easter message is one of such hope and joy that even unbelievers are thrilled by it. A reporter I know covered the sunrise service that is held each Easter on the rim of the Grand Canyon. It was cold—below freezing, actually—and he had not worn an overcoat. Not a particularly religious man, he stood there shivering dolefully and wishing himself back in bed.

"But then," he told me, "when the sun cleared the canyon rim, and light poured into that stupendous chasm, I forgot all about being cold. One moment everything was gray, formless. Then came torrents of light plunging down the canyon walls, making them blaze with color, dissolving the blackness into purple shadows that eddied like smoke. Standing there, I had a most indescribable feeling, a conviction that the darkness that had filled the great gorge was an illusion, that only the light was real, and that we silent watchers on the canyon rim were somehow a part of the light. . . ."

Strange words, coming from a hardboiled reporter, but close to a profound truth. Darkness *is* powerless before the onslaught of light. And so it is with death. We have allowed ourselves to think of it as a dark door, when actually it is a rainbow bridge spanning the gulf between two worlds. That is the Easter message.

Yet there are people, even good Christians, who accept it with their minds, but really never feel it in their hearts. I know this from personal experience—the message never got through fully to me until I went to the Holy Land and saw with my own eyes the hills and fields and roads where Jesus actually walked.

One day we visited the beatuiful little village of Bethany. This was the home of Mary and Martha and Lazarus. And there is still a tomb there, said to be the tomb of Lazarus. We went into the tomb, down 22 steps and saw the place where the body of Lazarus is presumed to have lain until the voice of Jesus wakened him from the dead. I was so deeply moved that when we came up out of the tomb I turned to my wife and said, "We are standing where the greatest statement ever uttered was made: 'I am the resurrection and the life, he that believeth in Me, though he were dead, yet shall he live.' " (John 11:25)

At that moment, for the first time in my life, Easter really happened to me, and I shall never be the same again. For the rest of my days I shall preach, out of a conviction so deep that it can never be shaken, that if people will accept Jesus Christ they will have eternal life.

Once I was at Mount Holyoke College in New England, visiting my daughter Elizabeth, who was a student there, walking around the campus, we came upon a sundial with an inscription: *"To larger sight, the rim of shadow is the line of light."*

There you have it in just 12 words. Believe me, death is only a momentary rim of shadow. Beyond it, waiting for all of us who believe is the radiance of eternal life.

The Greatest of These Is Love

by SAINT PAUL

THOUGH I speak with the tongues of men and of angels, and have not love, I am become *as* sounding brass, or a tinkling cymbal.

And though I have *the gift of* prophecy, and understand all mysteries, and all knowledge; and though I have all faith, so that I could remove mountains, and have not love, I am nothing.

And though I bestow all my goods to feed *the poor*, and though I give my body to be burnèd, and have not love, it profiteth me nothing.

Love suffereth long, *and* is kind; love envieth not; love vaunteth not itself, is not puffed up,

Doth not behave itself unseemly, seeketh not her own, is not easily provoked, thinketh no evil;

Rejoiceth not in iniquity, but rejoiceth in the truth;

Beareth all things, believeth all things, hopeth all things, endureth all things.

Love never faileth: but whether *there be* prophecies, they shall fail; whether *there be* tongues, they shall cease; whether *there be* knowledge, it shall vanish away.

For we know in part, and we prophesy in part.

But when that which is perfect is come, then that which is in part shall be done away.

When I was a child, I spake as a child, I understood as a child, I thought as a child: but when I became a man, I put away childish things.

For now we see through a glass, darkly; but then face to face: now I know in part; but then shall I know even as also I am known.

And now abideth faith, hope, love, these three; but the greatest of these *is* love.

(I Corinthians 13:1-13)